GAY MONARCH

Books by Virginia Cowles

LOOKING FOR TROUBLE

NO CAUSE FOR ALARM

WINSTON CHURCHILL
The Era and the Man

GAY MONARCH
The Life and Pleasures of Edward VII

GAY MONARCH

THE LIFE AND PLEASURES OF EDWARD VII

by

Virginia Cowles

ILLUSTRATED

HARPER & BROTHERS, PUBLISHERS

New York

GAY MONARCH: The Life and Pleasures of Edward VII

Printed in the United States of America

This book is published in England under the title of
EDWARD VII AND HIS CIRCLE

Library of Congress catalog card number: 56-8748

FOR
AIDAN

ACKNOWLEDGMENTS

I would like to thank the following publishers for the use of quotations from books published by them:

Appleton-Century-Crofts: *The Life of His Royal Highness, the Prince Consort,* Theodore Martin; *The Edwardian Era,* André Maurois (referred to in footnotes by British title, *King Edward VII and His Times); Things Past,* the Duchess of Sermoneta; *The Private Life of Edward VII* (by a member of the Royal Household)

Ernest Benn, Ltd.: *Charles Bradlaugh,* Hypatia Bradlaugh Bonner

Cassell & Co.: *Afterthoughts,* Frances, Countess of Warwick

Doubleday and Co.: *The Autobiography of Margot Asquith; The Days I Knew,* Lillie Langtry; *King George the Fifth,* Sir Harold Nicolson; *The Greville Diary,* Philip Whitwell Wilson (ed.)

E. P. Dutton & Co.: *Better Left Unsaid,* Daisy, Princess of Pless (referred to in footnotes by British title, *What I Left Unsaid); Recollections of Three Reigns,* Sir Frederick Ponsonby

Robert Hale, Ltd.: *The Magnificent Rothschilds,* Cecil Roth

Harper & Brothers: *German Diplomatic Documents,* E. T. S. Dugdale (trans.)

Hodder & Stoughton, Ltd.: *Recollections,* Sir John Fisher; *The Life of the Rt. Hon. Sir Henry Campbell-Bannerman,* J. A. Spender

Henry Holt & Co.: *The Remarkable Mr. Jerome,* Anita Leslie (referred to in footnotes by British title, *The Fabulous Mr. Jerome)*

Houghton Mifflin Co.: *Portrait of a Diplomatist,* Sir Harold Nicolson

Hutchinson & Co.: *Memoirs,* Sir Almeric Fitzroy; *In My Tower* and *The Private Life of Queen Alexandra,* Hans Madol; *King Edward VII at Marienbad,* Sigmund Münz; *Embassies of Other Days,* Walpurga Paget

William Kimber & Co., Ltd.: *Royal Chef,* Gabriel Tschumi

Little, Brown & Co.: *A Century of Fashion,* J. P. Worth

Longmans, Green & Co.: *Memoirs of Baron Stockmar,* Ernest von Stockmar

The Macmillan Co.: *King Edward VII,* Sir Sidney Lee

Macmillan & Co., Ltd.: *Lord Lansdowne,* Lord Newton; *Henry Ponsonby; His Life from His Letters,* Arthur Ponsonby

Methuen & Co.: *At the Court of the Last Czar,* A. A. Mossolov

John Murray, Ltd.: *King Edward VII and His Court,* Sir Lionel Cust; *The Life of Sir Charles Dilke,* Gwynne and Tuckwell; *The Diaries of Frederick Weymouth Gibbs; Letters of Sarah, Lady Lyttleton; The Letters of Queen Victoria*

Nicholson, Ivor and Watson, Ltd.: *The Influence of King Edward,* Lord Esher

Odhams Press, Ltd.: *Lord Randolph Churchill,* Sir Winston Churchill

Putnam & Co., Ltd.: *Memoirs,* Prince von Bülow

G. P. Putnam's Sons: *Edwardian Hey-days,* George Cornwallis-West; *A King's Story,* H.R.H. The Duke of Windsor

The Right Book Club: *Memoirs,* Prince Christopher of Greece

Charles Scribner's Sons: *A Roving Commission,* Sir Winston Churchill (referred to in footnotes by British title, *My Early Life*); *The Journals and Letters of Lord Esher*

Scribner & Welford: *The Memoirs of an Ex-Minister,* Lord Malmesbury

H.M. Stationery Office: *British Documents on the Origin of the War,* Gooch and Temperley (ed.)

Allan Wingate, Ltd.: *Fashion in London,* Barbara Worsley-Gough

VIRGINIA COWLES

CONTENTS

PART I

AS PRINCE OF WALES

PART II

AS KING

ILLUSTRATIONS

The following are grouped in a separate section after page 96:

PART ONE

AS PRINCE OF WALES

CHAPTER ONE

THE QUEEN, THE PRINCE AND THE BARON

WHEN Queen Victoria gave birth to her eldest son, on November 11, 1841, cannons roared, flags fluttered, and many a loyal subject went to bed tipsy. There was more excitement than usual, for the Prince was the first male heir to be born to a reigning sovereign for seventy-nine years. *Punch*, a satirical magazine only five months old, gave vent to the national sentiment in a long poem that began:

> *Huzza! we've a little Prince at last,*
> *A roaring Royal boy;*
> *And all day long the booming bells*
> *Have rung their peals of joy.*

The Queen was delighted with her son. 'Our little boy,' she wrote to her Uncle Leopold, King of the Belgians, 'is a wonderfully strong and large child, with very large dark blue eyes, a finely formed but somewhat large nose, and a pretty little mouth. . . .' But her delight sprang not so much from the child himself, as in the delectable prospect that he might grow up to resemble the husband with whom she was so madly in love. 'You will understand *how* fervent my prayers and I am [sure] *everybody's* must be, to see him resemble his angelic dearest father in *every*, *every* respect, both in body and mind. Oh! my dearest Uncle, I am sure if you knew *how* happy, how blessed I feel, and how *proud* I feel in possessing *such* a perfect being as my husband, as he is, and if you think that you have been instrumental in bringing about this union, it must gladden your heart! How happy I should be to see our child grow up *just* like him!'

The Queen expressed the same sentiments to her Prime Minister, Lord Melbourne, and informed him that she was planning to name the child 'Albert Edward'. The wise old statesman replied with his usual tact. 'Your Majesty,' he wrote, 'cannot offer up for the young Prince a more safe and judicious prayer than that he may resemble his father.' But as far as the names were concerned he pointed out that '*Edward* is a good English appellation, and has a certain degree of popularity attached to it from ancient recollections. Albert is also an old Anglo-Saxon name—the same, Lord Melbourne believes, as Ethelred—but it has not been so common nor so much in use since the Conquest. However, your Majesty's feelings, which Lord Melbourne perfectly understands, must determine this point.'[1]

The Queen did not take Lord Melbourne's hint. The child was named Albert Edward, and was christened in great splendour at St. George's Chapel at the end of January. Over £200,000 was spent on festivities surrounding the ceremony. King Frederick William IV of Prussia was the chief godfather, and after the ceremony a banquet was given in the State dining room at Windsor Castle. An enormous punch bowl designed by George IV was filled with thirty dozen bottles of mulled claret and toasts were drunk to the infant Prince and the royal visitors. Later in the evening the Queen held a reception in the Waterloo Chamber where a christening cake that measured over eight feet round was cut up and distributed.

Among the guests at the reception was an obscure little German doctor whom few people outside the Queen's circle knew either by sight or by name. This was

[1] *The Letters of Queen Victoria.*

the Baron Stockmar. His presence amidst the wealth and glamour and rejoicing was like the appearance of the bad fairy, for he was destined to darken and distort the childhood of the Prince of Wales.

THOSE who moved in the inner conclave were well aware that Baron Stockmar was the most powerful man at Court. He was private counsellor to the royal couple, and did not hesitate to give his advice on subjects ranging from domestic problems to matters of state. This advice was invariably taken, for in the eyes of the Queen and the Prince, Stockmar could do no wrong. He was allowed unheard-of liberties. He was his own master. He came and went as he pleased. Even the rigid etiquette that surrounded court life had no inconveniences for him. Because of his rheumatism he was the only person permitted to wear long wool trousers instead of the prescribed stockings and knee-breeches. And at the stiff restrained dinner parties that Greville described as 'so dull it is a marvel how anyone can like such a life', he astonished English guests by quitting the Queen's drawing-room, soon after dinner, without so much as a 'by your leave'. 'When the Queen had risen from the table,' wrote the Baron's son, 'and after holding a circle had sat down again to tea, Stockmar would generally be seen walking straight through the drawing room and returning to his apartment, there to study his own comfort. That he should sacrifice the latter to etiquette was not expected of him. . . .'[1] On these occasions his excuse was dyspepsia.

How had this shrewd, dominating little foreigner acquired such an impregnable position at the Court of

[1] *Memoirs of Baron Stockmar:* Ernest von Stockmar.

St. James's? He had begun his climb to power, twenty-five years previously, when he had made friends with an illustrious countryman, Prince Leopold of Coburg. Leopold had been struck by the doctor's personality and his forceful, long-sighted views. When he became engaged to the Princess Charlotte, the only daughter and heiress of George IV, he decided that Stockmar would make a valuable counsellor, and invited him to England. But during the first year of his marriage, the Prince seemed to forget about the little German who waited patiently in the shadows of the palace. However, when the Princess Charlotte died in child-birth, robbing Leopold not only of a wife but of the enviable prospect of being the husband of the Queen of England, he flung himself into Stockmar's arms and cried, 'Never leave me.'

Stockmar served the Prince well. After much manœuvring he secured him the vacant Belgian throne, and was given a barony for his labours. The Belgian crown was better than nothing; nevertheless it was small beer compared to the prestige of the English monarchy. The two men looked disconsolately at the European stage on which they had hoped to play a leading role. Then the prospect brightened. It was becoming increasingly likely, through want of a male heir, that Leopold's niece, the Princess Victoria, one day would become the English queen. She was the daughter of his widowed sister, the Duchess of Kent. And since she had no father, Leopold began to fill his place. Not a week passed without his writing her a long, high-minded, affectionate letter, carefully vetted by Stockmar. He noticed with satisfaction that she replied in warm and grateful terms.

Uncle Leopold was the most respected influence in Victoria's life when she ascended the throne. Stockmar was despatched to her side post-haste to make sure that she did not fall prey to any undesirable pressures, and to report to Leopold what was going on. Stockmar could always be relied upon to cast his spell over those he wished to control, and a short while after his arrival the Queen was writing her uncle enthusiastically, 'Let me tell you how happy and thankful I am to have Stockmar here; he has *been*, and *is* of the *greatest* possible use, and be assured, dearest Uncle, that he possesses *my entire confidence*!'[1]

Stockmar was not so generous in his praise of the eighteen-year-old Queen. He did not form a very high opinion of her mental capacities. He regarded her as headstrong, impulsive and often foolish. She was not pretty. Her blue eyes protruded slightly, her chin fell away too suddenly, and she spoke in a high, thin voice. But she had the bloom and vitality of youth, and with her high position it would not be difficult to find her a husband.

The following year Uncle Leopold decided that she must start to think of marriage. He had always hoped she would settle upon his nephew (and her first cousin), Prince Albert of Coburg. Before pushing the match, however, he felt it would be wise for Stockmar to take the young man on a long trip, study him, and report whether he still believed he would make a suitable husband.

The nineteen-year-old Prince was exceedingly handsome. Stockmar noticed with satisfaction, however, that he had no frivolous tendencies of any kind. He seemed completely indifferent to the company of women, and preferred to spend his evenings talking to learned men. He was artistic, intellectual and deeply concerned with philosophic subjects. He showed little interest in politics, but Stockmar was confident that a feeling for power could be implanted in him. Needless to say, the Baron exercised his magic on his youthful charge, and soon had Albert worshipping at his feet. The Prince's regard for Stockmar lasted all his life. Of course the Baron reported

[1] *The Letters of Queen Victoria.*

favourably on the youth. He brought him to England at the end of the trip and Victoria fell madly in love with him; the wedding took place in February 1840.

STOCKMAR's first task was to strengthen the monarchy. He believed that the Crown had been dangerously weakened by the shocking behaviour of Victoria's dissipated uncles who lived in a colony of mistresses and illegitimate children. The Baron was genuinely high-minded, but his nobler qualities were often in danger of being swamped by his rigid, Germanic outlook, his intolerance and inflexibility. He was fanatical on the subject of duty and morality, and lectured the Queen and the Prince almost daily on the necessity of presenting a faultless example to the nation. Court life must be absolutely spotless. No one with a breath of scandal attached to their names should be allowed access to the palace. Duty and morality. They heard it over and over again. In Albert it aroused emotions which grew into a dedicated purpose, and in Victoria it struck the more prosaic chord of royal obligation.

Stockmar even went so far as to lecture the Queen's Prime Minister, Lord Melbourne, on the subject of morality until the latter ejaculated wearily, 'This damn'd morality will ruin everything.' The Baron was furious at this cynical outlook. Years later it still made him angry to think about and he declared passionately, 'Let men like the late Lord Melbourne explain as they please "that damn'd morality is sure to ruin everything"; I, on the other hand can testify before God, that the English machine works smoothly and well only when the Sovereign is upright and truthful and that when he has been insincere, mendacious and wicked, it has creaked and fouled and jolted within an ace of coming to a deadlock.'[1]

Stockmar doubtless decided that if the time ever came when he could destroy Lord Melbourne's influence he would do so. In the meantime, he concentrated on strengthening Albert's position. He did not have to worry so far as the Queen was concerned. She was so much in love with her husband that his domination increased with the passing of each day. Her imperious nature was now almost completely subservient to his will. No longer did she crave company and wish to dance until daybreak. She was perfectly happy spending her evenings quietly at home, cross-stitching, while Albert improved her mind by reading aloud Hallam's *Constitutional History of England.*

But Stockmar was not content that the Queen should speak with Albert's voice. Albert must acquire prestige of his own. He must work hard, he must master every detail of policy both at home and abroad. 'Never relax' was Stockmar's advice, and Albert took his words so seriously, that his eyes began to show a harassed, almost feverish look. 'The weight of business which by degrees the Prince took upon himself,' wrote his librarian, Herr Meyer, 'was so great, that he had got into the habit in all his movements, even when passing along the corridors, of going at double quick time.'[2]

Not a day passed without the Prince consulting Stockmar. Wherever the royal couple moved, Stockmar moved with them. Whether it was Buckingham Palace, Windsor or, later, Osborne, rooms were set aside known as 'the Baron's study'. 'Commonly toward evening,' wrote Meyer, 'when he (the Prince) had returned from a drive or business, he came running to the Baron's rooms, his arms full of papers and despatch boxes, with

[1] *Life of the Prince Consort:* Theodore Martin.
[2] *A Memoir of Baron Stockmar:* Friedrich Carl Meyer.

the impetuosity peculiar to him, and, telling his own news and asking for ours, flung himself down to rest on the sofa, while his old friend, first listening observantly, and anon breaking into talk, walked up and down, and poured forth a sparkling store of mixed experiences, maxims, anecdotes, and illustrations for the most part from his own life.'[1]

Prince Albert became so dependent on Stockmar that he could scarcely bear to be parted from him. However, the Baron had private obligations of his own. He had a long-suffering wife and children in Coburg, with whom he felt he must spend at least four months of the year. 'He hated taking leave,' his son explained, 'and his room would one fine morning be found empty.' Then a wail of anguish would arise from Victoria and Albert. 'Alas,' wrote the Queen to Uncle Leopold, 'the inestimable good, dear Stockmar has gone without a word! My poor Albert!' And Albert himself yearned after the absent figure. 'I will send after you only one word of the dismay occasioned by your sudden disappearance. There was an outcry throughout the house from great and small, young and old! The Baron is gone!'[2] On another occasion the Prince wrote even more despairingly begging the doctor to return. 'Come, as you love me, as you love Victoria, as you love *your German Fatherland.*'[2]

It almost seemed as though Albert could not live without the stern voice of duty the Baron had come to represent. However, the little man always reappeared. Two months before the Prince of Wales was born Lord Melbourne's Government fell, and he drew a breath of relief that at last the Queen would be rid of the statesman's worldly outlook. He was surprised to learn, however, that Melbourne continued to write to the Queen almost daily. Surely it could not be constitutional for

[1] *A Memoir of Baron Stockmar:* Friedrich Carl Meyer.
[2] *The Life of the Prince Consort:* Theodore Martin.

the leader of the Opposition to acquaint the Sovereign with his views on personalities and matters of state. He sent several messages to Melbourne pointing out his objections, but the old man refused to take heed. 'God Eternal, damn it,' he ejaculated. 'Flesh and blood cannot stand this.' But Stockmar returned to the attack repeatedly. Lord Melbourne knew that fundamentally his opponent was right, and in the end he was forced to bow to Stockmar's insistence. The correspondence ceased.

Stockmar was elated at his victory, for he genuinely believed Lord Melbourne's influence to be harmful. Not long before his triumph the Queen had written to the old man confiding in him the responsibility she felt for the upbringing of her newly born son and heir. 'Be not over solicitous about education,' replied Melbourne. 'It may be able to do much, but it does not do so much as is expected from it. It may mould and direct the character, but it rarely alters it.' 'The character,' he pointed out, 'depends much upon the race, and on both sides he has a good chance.'[1]

This remark aroused Stockmar's ire. How dare the frivolous Melbourne flatter the royal couple and attempt to deceive them? As far as race was concerned the royal children had a very poor chance indeed. Aside from Victoria's uncles, the disreputable sons of George III, there were Albert's promiscuous parents; his mother was known to have had an affair with a Jewish court chamberlain and some even went so far as to say that Albert was the outcome. No; one could only hope that the bad blood might be watered down. Stockmar took the exactly opposite view from Melbourne. Education and education alone could counteract hereditary weaknesses.

He promptly sat down and wrote a memorandum

[1] *The Letters of Queen Victoria.*

running into thousands of words giving his views on the subject. 'Good education,' he declared, 'cannot begin too soon. "To neglect beginnings", says Locke, "is the fundamental error into which most parents fall." ' Stockmar went on to point out that although the private life of George III was exemplary, 'he did not properly understand his duties as a parent or he neglected them.' The errors of his sons, he goes on to say, 'were of the most glaring kind, and we can find their explanation only in the supposition that their tutors were either incapable of engrafting on their minds during their youth the principles of truth and morality, or that they most culpably neglected their duties, or were not supported in them by the royal parents'.[1]

The gist of Stockmar's conclusions were that, first, the education of the children 'ought to be from its earliest beginning *a truly moral and a truly English one*'; second, that the children should only be surrounded by 'those who are good and pure, who will teach not only by precept but by living example'; and third, that the royal parents should give the governess and tutors their 'full and implicit confidence'.

BUT the royal children were not yet to feel the impact of the Baron's relentless German reasoning. Albert Edward, who was the particular target, was too young to be anything more than a subject for theorising. After much deliberation the Queen decided that a lady of high rank must be placed in charge of the nursery and with Stockmar's approval selected her Lady-of-the-Bedchamber, the fifty-five-year-old Lady Lyttelton, a daughter of Earl Spencer.

[1] *Memoirs of Baron Stockmar:* Ernest von Stockmar.

The children flourished under the kindly and intelligent supervision of this devoted and excellent lady. Albert Edward shared the nursery with his year-old sister, the Princess Royal, known to her family as 'Puss' or 'Vicky'; and during the next ten years five more children joined them; Alice, Alfred, Helena, Louise, and Arthur.[1]

At the time of Albert Edward's birth, the Queen still enjoyed the novelty of being a mother. The two infants often found themselves whirled into carriages and trains, with an army of nursemaids carrying shawls and rusks and bibs and tuckers, to accompany their royal parents on tours and visits to various parts of England. When the baby Prince, now known as 'Bertie', was a year old, he and his two-year-old sister were taken off by their parents to stay with the aged Duke of Wellington at Walmer Castle. 'The children will grow up under the strangest delusions as to what travelling means,' wrote Lady Lyttelton, 'and the usual condition of the people in England! They must suppose one always finds them shouting and grinning and squeezing, surrounded by banners and garlands. "Where's the Prince? Show him! Turn him this way! Bless his little face! What a pretty boy! How like his father!" was screamed at us incessantly; and once, as I was overheard to say to Mrs. Sly, "Hold up the Prince of Wales," I was complimented with, "Well done! That's right, old girl!" At one place, where we had got out and were returning to the carriage through a thick avenue of the principal people of the place (I believe Rochester), a great fat lady, very smartly dressed, caught hold of the Prince of Wales, and, almost dragging him out of Sly's arms, gave him the loudest kiss. "Well done! I give you credit for that," said an amiable gentleman of the company. Mrs. Sly has not

[1] Queen Victoria had nine children in all, Prince Leopold and Princess Beatrice being born in 1853 and 1857.

yet cooled down, her rage was such at being taken by surprise.'[1]

THE first seven years of Bertie's life were untrammelled. The months passed with continuous movement; to Buckingham Palace, back to Windsor, to the Isle of Wight in the summer; perhaps to Scotland, perhaps to Ireland, sometimes on cruises in the *Victoria and Albert*. Young Albert Edward dressed in a sailor suit met with a storm of approval from the Queen's loyal subjects in Wales and Scotland. His portrait, done by Winterhalter, was reproduced in cheap prints which adorned most of the pubs of England; and *Punch* ran a picture sentimentally entitled: 'Every Inch a Sailor.'

From Lady Lyttelton's letters we catch fleeting glimpses of the boy; at six months old we read of his 'noble countenance and calm manner', and how he 'looks through his large clear blue eyes full at one'; at three how 'he bows and offers his hand beautifully, besides saluting *à la militaire*—all unbidden'; at five how he asked the Queen, 'Pray, Mama, is not a pink the female of a carnation?'; at six, how brave he was when his pony, Arthur, ran away with him; how enchanted he was with Astley's circus; how thrilled he was when his mother invited General Tom Thumb, the American dwarf, to Buckingham Palace. We read of him sketching, playing the piano, working at carpentry in a Swiss cottage his father set up for him in the gardens at Osborne; we hear of him sitting through interminable performances of Shakespeare and taking part in amateur productions of Schiller and Racine. The only interference by Baron Stockmar seems to be a stiff letter instructing

[1] *Lady Lyttelton's Correspondence.*

him 'that one in his position should write a firm, large and legible hand'; also to appoint governesses to teach the children French and German as well as English. Apparently German was stressed the most, for Baron Bunsen, the German Ambassador, was surprised to find that the children 'all spoke German like their native tongue, even to one another'.[1] The result was that Bertie never completely mastered the English accent, retaining the guttural 'r' all his life.

The eminent men and women who met the boy were usually favourably impressed. The future Archbishop of Canterbury, Edward Benson, describes him as 'a rather fair little lad of rather a slender make with an intelligent expression'; and Lady Lyttelton testifies to a warm and sympathetic nature: 'The Prince of Wales continues most promising for kindness and nobleness of mind. His sister (the Princess Royal) has been lately often in disgrace, and though she is not "Alee" [Princess Alice, his greatest favourite] his little attentions on the sad occasions have been very nice. Never losing sight of her through a longish imprisonment in her own room, and stealing to the door to give a kind message or tell a morsel of pleasant news, his own toys quite neglected, and his lovely face quite pale till the disgrace was over. And such truth! He inherits all his mother's.'[2]

Yet something was wrong. In the Queen's wide correspondence, one can glean no sign of affection for the eldest son. Vicky, the Princess Royal, was Albert's favourite and remained so all his life. This made her doubly dear to her mother, and soon after Bertie's birth we find Victoria writing almost defensively, 'Pussy (Vicky) dear child, is still *the* great pet amongst us all, and is getting so fat and strong again.'[3]

[1] *Memoirs:* Baron Bunsen.
[2] *Lady Lyttelton's Correspondence.*
[3] *The Letters of Queen Victoria.*

Allusions to the daughter appear with increasing delight and frequency. 'She is such an amusement to us that I can't bear to move without her'; 'We find Pussy amazingly advanced in intellect'; 'You have no idea *what* a knowing . . . little rogue she is'; 'It is quite extraordinary how popular she is in Society.'[1] Yet in all the published letters which range over the Prince's childhood, there is not one word of praise for his character, not a single endearing anecdote, not a trace of pride or pleasure in his personality; only perfunctory references.

Instead we have Greville repeating gossip heard from Lady Beauvais, a sister-in-law of Lord Melbourne. 'The Princess Royal is very clever, strong in body and in mind; the Prince of Wales weaker and more timid, and the Queen says he is a stupid boy, but the hereditary and unfailing antipathy of our Sovereigns to their Heirs Apparent seems thus early to be taking root, and the Queen does not much like the child.' Despite the fact that Lady Lyttelton often remarked on Bertie's truthfulness, Greville goes on to report: 'He seems too to have an incipient propensity to that sort of romancing which distinguished his uncle, George IV. The child told Lady Beauvais that during their cruise he was very nearly thrown overboard, and was proceeding to tell her how, when the Queen overheard him, sent him off with a flea in his ear, and told her it was totally untrue.'[2]

[1] *The Letters of Queen Victoria.*

[2] *The Greville Diaries:* edited by Philip Whitwell Wilson.

CHAPTER TWO

HIS UPBRINGING

WHEN the Prince of Wales was seven and a half Baron Stockmar decided that the time had come to take his education firmly in hand. The boy feared and disliked the stern unbending doctor who regarded childish faults with unforgiving disapproval. And the child's instinct was right, for Stockmar never lost an opportunity to prejudice the Queen and the Prince against their eldest son. Perhaps he took a genuinely poor view of Bertie's capacities. Certainly the child's nature was completely opposite to his own. The German pedant could find nothing to praise in Bertie's sociability; he could only deplore the fact that, unlike his elder sister, Bertie found his lessons a frightful bore.

Perhaps the Baron was also irritated by the knowledge that if the Queen died, the worthy father would be left without position while the boy would mount the throne. And perhaps Albert shared in this jealousy, and the Queen in her infatuation, felt a touch of it too. Whatever the reason, Stockmar supplied the royal parents with a constant flow of deprecating reports and succeeded in permanently establishing the idea that the heir to the throne was made of very poor clay.

This idea in itself, of course, increased Stockmar's authority. In anxiety the parents turned to the learned doctor for guidance concerning every detail of Bertie's education. After much deliberation Mr. Henry Birch, the rector of Prestwich, who had taken high honours at Cambridge, and spent four years as an assistant master at Eton, was selected as tutor. 'It is an important step,' wrote the Prince Consort, 'and God's blessing be upon it, for upon the good education of princes, and especially of those who are destined to govern, the welfare of the world in these days greatly depends.'[1]

The cornerstone of Stockmar's philosophy was mental discipline. If Bertie did not like study, study must be doubled. Games and recreation were a waste of time, and youthful companionship was positively harmful. He still believed what he had written in his memorandum, that children must be surrounded 'only by those who are good and pure', and naturally it would not do at all to allow the Prince to come into contact with the mischievous ways of schoolboys.

A long and arduous schedule was drawn up in which every minute of the day was accounted for. Sometimes riding and rowing on the lake were permitted, but for the most part recreation consisted of afternoon walks, amateur theatricals, and recitations. However, the full impact of this desperately monotonous life was spared the Prince for another two years for the simple reason that Mr. Birch was an immensely human man. Bertie loved him and Birch returned the affection. The afternoon walks were transformed into exciting games, discipline was used in moderation, and as far as studies were concerned Bertie did not even strike his tutor as backward. Although Stockmar gave Birch instructions that he was to write the frankest memoranda on the boy's conduct and work, Birch found very little to criticise. This at once made Stockmar suspicious, and he soon began to tell the parents that Birch was not the right man for Bertie. At the end of two years the tutor was dismissed by Prince Albert on the pretext that he attached undue importance to the Church catechism.

Bertie's misery at the parting was described by Lady

[1] *The Life of the Prince Consort:* Theodore Martin.

Canning, one of the Queen's ladies-in-waiting. 'It has been a trouble and a sorrow to the Prince of Wales, who has done no end of touching things since he heard that he was to lose him three weeks ago. He is such an affectionate dear little fellow; his notes and presents which Mr. Birch used to find on his pillow were really too moving.'[1]

Even the new tutor, a humourless, dour barrister by the name of Frederick Gibbs, could not escape the pang of sorrow his advent was bringing. 'I came here on the 15th of January,' he wrote in his diary, 'and began my work on the following Wednesday. I spent the intervening days chiefly with the Princes and Mr. Birch, observing the former, and learning from the latter the general rules and arrangements of the day—the wishes of the Queen on a number of small points—and generally the host of nothings which became important only when neglected. He was very ready to give me assistance, and I found it more agreeable to learn from him than to discover for myself. He was out of spirits, for the boys and he were very much attached to each other, and both parties felt the separation. "Poor Mr. Birch was quite overcome at parting," said the Queen.

'The Prince of Wales . . . thought it necessary to make a sort of apology in his walk for his sorrow, "You can't wonder if we are rather dull today, we are very sorry Mr. Birch is gone. It is very natural, is it not? He has been with us so long." The Prince is conscious of owing a great deal to Mr. Birch, and really loves and respects him. He takes pleasure in writing him accounts of what goes on, and looks forward to receiving letters from him and seeing him again with sincere affection. . . .'[2]

Mr. Gibbs was much more to Stockmar's liking. He

[1] *Lady Lyttelton's Correspondence.*

[2] From *The Diaries of Frederick Weymouth Gibbs*, published in the *Cornhill Magazine*, Spring, 1951.

was strict and unsmiling and shared the Baron's horror of childish faults. He had not been in the Palace a fortnight before Stockmar was elaborating on the defects of Bertie's character. 'You must do anything you think right and you will be supported,' he told him. 'It is a very difficult case, and requires the exercise of intellectual labour and thought.'[1]

Mr. Gibbs had charge of both nine-year-old Bertie and his six-year-old brother, Alfred. He listened with deep respect to the Baron's pronouncements and won the latter's goodwill by keeping him supplied with daily details of Bertie's shortcomings. 'We must make experiments,' Stockmar told him, 'and we shall see what will answer. I have talked to the Prince and the Queen, and have told them that they must be able to answer to their consciences for having done everything that could be suggested—and you will have no difficulty with them. You shall have all my influence to help you, as long as I live. . . . Then the Queen is young and we may hope that she will live some time.'[1]

The Queen herself was anxious that none of Bertie's idiosyncrasies should escape Gibbs' eye, and soon after the tutor arrived, bade him walk with her in the garden. 'She spoke a good deal about the Prince,' wrote Gibbs, 'and made me notice two peculiarities in the Prince of Wales. First, at times he hangs his head, and looks at his feet, and invariably within a day or two, has one of his fits of nervous, unmanageable temper. Secondly, riding hard, or after he has become fatigued, has been often followed by outbursts of temper. The Queen said this had been noticed by Miss Hillyard (a former governess) and wished me to observe it carefully. She told me he had been injured by being with the Princess Royal, who was very clever, and a child far above her age; she put him down by a look—or a word—and their natural affection

[1] *The Diaries of Frederick Weymouth Gibbs.*

had been, she feared, impaired by this state of things.'[1]

Mr. Gibbs was quick to catch the flavour of royal disapproval that surrounded Bertie, and his diary faithfully reflects the atmosphere. No detail of the children's misbehaviour was too trivial to be recorded and the grim pages poignantly reveal the wretchedness of the little victims.

Jan. 27

'The P. of W. was still in an excited state. In the morning it was difficult to fix his attention on his arithmetic. . . . The music with Mrs. Anderson was not a good lesson. In the afternoon he quarrelled with Prince Alfred in the Conservatory. In the evening I read the story of Robert Bruce to him. I was astonished by the eager interest he took in it. . . .

Jan. 28

'Began better—we finished the sums left unfinished yesterday—but walking, he was excited and disobedient —trying to make Prince Alfred disobedient also—going where I wished not to go—threatening to go even when he did not go—and breaking and plucking the trees in the Copse.

I played with them, but it only partially succeeded. On the Terrace he quarrelled with, and struck, P. Alfred, and I had to hasten home. We met the Queen while this was occurring. . . .

Jan. 29

'Mr. Leitch the drawing Master came. P. of W. very angry with P. Alfred, and pulled his hair, brandishing a paper-knife. I forbade the lesson—he was at first very angry, remained so some time, but cooled.[1]

[1] *The Diaries of Frederick Weymouth Gibbs.*

Out walking I joined their play. The amusement is to act a play—fighting, brigands, knights, etc., form the chief personages—generally the chief part taken by himself. Subordinate given to P. Alfred. I noticed the influence of the plays he saw in the characters, names and incidents. . . .

Feb. 28

'Last Thursday afternoon the two sons of Mr. Van de Meyer came to play with the Princes. They were eager and excited.

Afterwards I had to do some arithmetic with the P. of W. Immediately he became passionate, the pencil was flung to the end of the room, the stool was kicked away, and he was hardly able to apply at all. That night he woke twice. Next day he became very passionate because I told him he must not take out a walking stick, and in consequence of something crossing him when dressing. Later in the day he became violently angry because I wanted some Latin done. He flung things about—made grimaces—called me names, and would not do anything for a long time. . . .

March 8. Osborne

'A very bad day. The P. of W. has been like a person half silly. I could not gain his attention. He was very rude, particularly in the afternoon, throwing stones in my face.

During his lesson in the morning, he was running first in one place, then in another. He made faces, and spat. Dr. Becher complained of his great naughtiness. There was a great deal of bad words.'[1]

Although Stockmar congratulated Gibbs warmly on his reports, and flattered him by emphasising the

[1] *The Diaries of Frederick Weymouth Gibbs.*

Queen's high regard for him, Gibbs began to get worried by his pupil's reactions. The royal family moved *en masse* to Balmoral and Gibbs noted anxiously: 'During the last few days the P. of W. has not been in a good state. He gave me the idea of a person who has had too strong a tonic . . . I advised that he should be taken out deer-stalking as much as possible, and but little work exacted.'

Alas, these indulgences were all too infrequent.

For the next eight years Gibbs continued in his post as tutor, and Bertie was subjected to his prison-like existence. Concentration, the Baron proclaimed, was to be developed by the unremitting study of literature, science, archæology, history and art. Story books of all kinds were banned, and even Sir Walter Scott's novels were prohibited as being too frivolous.

The Prince of Wales fretted and stamped and protested but to no avail; the awful, exacting, deadly-dull curriculum was carried out day after day, and year after year. As a special treat Prince Albert took his son to speech days at Eton and Harrow where he heard the sixth form boys reciting Demosthenes, Aeschylus and Cicero. 'I can see his poor bored little face now,' wrote Lord Redesdale. 'It was pitiful.'[1] Prince Albert also allowed his son occasionally to have a few especially selected Eton boys to tea. The group consisted of the son of the great Gladstone, and the future earls Derby, Halifax, Sandwich and Cadogan. Prince Albert felt it his duty to supervise the tea party, which was soon regarded as a dreaded ordeal.

Despite the fact that Stockmar's instructions were

[1] *King Edward VII:* Lord Redesdale.

carried out to the letter, Prince Albert remained dissatisfied with his son's progress. Even Gibbs began to wonder whether it was a good idea to deprive him of youthful companionship. Finally Lord Granville, a close friend of the royal couple, spoke out bluntly and told Albert that the visits of Eton boys to the Castle for a few hours were useless; Bertie should be sent off with a few companions on a walking tour.

Albert finally agreed to this great adventure, and under Gibbs' supervision young Henry Gladstone, George Cadogan, Frederick Stanley and Charles Wood accompanied Bertie on a walking trip through the Lake District. Their only excitement was one brief moment when Cadogan and the Prince chased a flock of sheep and were reproved by the irate female owner. Prince Albert frowned at the report of this unseemly conduct; nevertheless the following year he allowed the Prince and the same group of companions to take a trip to Bonn and Königsberg 'to study German literature'. This trip, too, was fairly grim. Noses were kept to the grindstone and recreation consisted of intensive sightseeing. The Prince was allowed to meet the aged Prince Metternich who wrote of him: 'Il avait l'air embarrassé et très triste.'[1]

Probably the only exciting event of the Prince's youth was just before his fourteenth birthday when Queen Victoria took him to France to pay a state visit to the gay imperial court of Napoleon III and the beautiful Empress Eugénie. The French crowds went mad about the boy in Highland dress, and he was thrilled with the easy luxury of St. Cloud and the wonderful amiability of his hosts. Paris was beautiful with the sun shining on the chestnuts, flags flying, the Zouaves in brilliant uniforms; but above all he revelled in the gaiety of the waltz music, the flashing smiles and high spirits of all

[1] *Memoirs:* Prince Metternich.

around him. The night before his departure he went to the lovely Empress and begged her to let him stay a little longer. She told him kindly that his mother couldn't spare him. 'Don't you believe it,' Bertie replied. 'There are six more of us at home, and Mamma won't miss me at all.'[1]

The little Prince was obliged to return to the stiffness of Windsor, but he was to see a great deal more of Paris in the years to come.

Baron Stockmar sighed wearily: 'The nursery gives me more trouble than the government of a Kingdom would do.'[2] Yet he was not prepared to forgo his authority in any way, and he remained the final arbiter of every important decision in the Prince's life.

HOWEVER, the troubles of the nursery did not prevent Stockmar from taking a hand in government. He was no lover of power merely for a sense of exhilaration; power was the tool by which he could force his own determined ideas into being. And Baron Stockmar's ideas were almost a religion. All his life he had been consumed by one great passion: to see the small, scattered states of Germany united into one powerful nation under the leadership of Prussia. After his death his son wrote, 'A yearning after the unity, power, and greatness of the Fatherland filled . . . the soul of the youth, as it afterwards inspired the man to his latest breath.'[2]

Stockmar worked unceasingly to see his ends fulfilled. He had, of course, imbued his pupil with his ideas and Prince Albert spoke out strongly whenever he found occasion. Lord Aberdeen, the Prime Minister, told Greville that 'the Prince's views were generally sound

[1] *King Edward and His Times:* André Maurois.

[2] *Memoirs of Baron Stockmar:* Ernest von Stockmar.

and wise, with one exception which was his violent and incorrigible German Unionism and his abetting of German dangers. He . . . insists on a new German Empire with Prussia at its head.'[1]

The indoctrination of the Prince and the Queen was only one step. The second step was to persuade Victoria to use the royal prerogative more forcefully. In a memorandum to Albert in 1850 he urged that Victoria should lose no opportunity of '*asserting the power of the throne*'. A year later, in another letter he claimed that 'the Monarch is the Permanent Premier, the Permanent President of the Council', and went on to emphasise 'that Foreign Affairs should really not be subject to the control of Parliament, but "the special concerns of Royal and Imperial minds".'[2]

His reasoning is not difficult to follow. If only his royal masters would exert enough power and authority, they could give Prussia the necessary encouragement to create a united Germany; and with a strong Germany and a strong England marching hand in hand the problems of Europe would be solved.

Both Victoria and Albert were much taken with Stockmar's arguments. At a public dinner Albert made the surprising statement that William III, who had presided over his own council, 'was the greatest monarch the country had to boast of'.[2] And Victoria asserted her sovereignty with increasing insistence. But her ministers were difficult to manage. Lord Palmerston, her Foreign Secretary, and later her Prime Minister, seemed to regard foreign affairs as his own exclusive pigeon. The Queen wrote dictatorial minutes, she stormed, threatened and protested. But the Government carried on the business of the day with imperturbable indifference.

[1] *Greville Diaries:* edited by Philip Whitwell Wilson.
[2] *Life of the Prince Consort:* Theodore Martin.

Nevertheless there were certain practical steps that could be taken, quite outside the province of statesmen, to ensure that the dream of an Anglo-German alliance might one day become a reality. Stockmar decided that it was important to marry the Princess Royal to the young man who would one day become King of Prussia. He prepared the ground carefully with Albert and Victoria and persuaded them to invite the 23-year-old Prince Frederick William to Balmoral. Vicky was only fourteen years old, but Stockmar was not going to run any risks of her hand being won by another. So the school-girl Princess who had never even been for a walk without a chaperone, suddenly found herself alone on the moors with a suitor. According to the gossip of the day, as told to Greville, 'the young Prince went to Balmoral resolved to see what the Princess was like, and if he did not find her attractive to retire without making any sign, and never more to return to England. But after a week passed in her society, he fell head and ears in love with her, and one day, walking on the hills, he asked her whether she could like him enough to leave her country and family and become his wife. The sentiment was mutual, and she at once replied in the affirmative; she was only fourteen and a mere child. When she got home she was terrified at what she had done, and went in great agitation and in floods of tears to confess to her parents what she had done, which she seemed to think would be considered a great crime. She found herself forgiven, and from that time the engagement was concluded, but the Queen and the Prince regretted that they had suffered her to be exposed to such temptation, and to become contracted in marriage before she was out of the nursery. . . .'[1]

Because of Vicky's extreme youth it was decided not to make the engagement public for another two years.

[1] *Greville Diaries:* edited by Philip Whitwell Wilson.

It was announced in April 1857, and the marriage took place the following January.

But the poor Princess was doomed to unhappiness. Although her marriage was successful, she was never popular in Germany. Bertie's social gifts, so despised by his parents, were not shared by the intellectual Vicky, and she invariably succeeded in antagonising those around her.

Bertie felt the parting with his sister acutely; but he was to see much of her in the years to come; and also of her disturbing son, the future German Emperor.

As Bertie neared his seventeenth birthday several important changes took place. First of all Baron Stockmar retired to Germany. The doctor was old and ill. Besides, his work was done. Prince Albert would faithfully carry out the ideas he had implanted in him, and he longed to spend his last years in the Fatherland. His departure did not mean that Bertie's life immediately became more agreeable. Albert kept up a steady correspondence with the old man, and still accepted his advice on his son's education. Nevertheless, it meant that Bertie was relieved of paying dutiful calls on a man whom many years later he was still to look back upon with bitter resentment.

With Stockmar's departure, Prince Albert decided the time had come for Bertie to have an establishment of his own. The White Lodge in Richmond Park was selected, and under Gibbs' authority three elderly equerries were appointed. These gentlemen were the height of respectability, but since nothing was to be left to chance, the Queen and the Prince Consort sent them a rigid code of disciplinary rules. They were not to indulge in 'lounging ways, such a lolling in armchairs or sofas'; they were not to permit themselves 'a slouching gait with hands in the pocket'. Their task was to prepare the Prince to be 'the first gentleman in the country'. His clothes were to be well made and not 'slang'; he was not to be taught the 'frivolity and foolish vanity of dandyism'; he was not to indulge in 'satirical or bantering expressions'; and '*a practical joke* was never to be permitted'. It was suggested that the Prince spend some of his leisure moments in elevating his mind by 'looking over drawings or engravings'.[1] Learned or distinguished men might occasionally be invited to dinner, but the Prince Consort still frowned on any companions of Bertie's own age.

On his birthday morning other changes took place. He was gazetted as an honorary colonel and made a Knight of the Garter. But he also learned that Gibbs was to leave, and Colonel Bruce, a sour, dour martinet was to become his 'governor'. On his breakfast table was a long memorandum from the Queen and the Prince which contained the following lines: 'You are placed under the supervision and guidance of a governor selected from among the members of the aristocracy and the superior officers of the army. . . . The Equerries will take and receive their orders from the Governor. You will never leave the house without reporting yourself, and he will settle who is to accompany you, and will give general directions as to the disposition of the day.'

The Prince of Wales wept when he read the long dictum, which went on to tell him that 'life is composed of duties' and 'you will have to be taught what to do and what not to do'.[1]

Although at this period Bertie's cousin, the Duke of Cambridge, wrote that he was 'really a charming and unaffected lad' and Disraeli described him as 'intelli-

[1] *The Influence of King Edward:* Lord Esher.

gent, informed and with a singularly sweet manner', the Queen and the Prince Consort still regarded him with great disfavour. Colonel Bruce pleased them by the mean, petty judgments which flowed almost unceasingly from his pen. He wrote to them that Bertie was 'prone to frivolous disputes'; that he had 'little respect for learning'; that he tended 'to exaggerate the importance of dress and etiquette'. The Queen read his complaints with high approval. 'He seems,' she wrote, 'to judge his charge's character so truly and to do always the right things. All this is a great comfort to us.'[1]

THE next few years have a nightmarish quality about them. Under the icy stare of Colonel Bruce and his equally cold wife, the Prince was even more restricted than before. Although for many months he had pleaded with his father to allow him to go into the army, Bruce defeated the proposition by elaborating on the 'temptation and unprofitable companionship of military life'.

Several trips were arranged for Bertie, but Colonel Bruce and the Prince Consort always contrived to make them as uncongenial as possible. One was to Berlin to visit his sister Vicky; but Albert wrote asking the Prince Regent only to show his son 'such slender courtesies as are suitable to a member, and a very young one, of the family'. He also bade Vicky to 'read aloud improving books'.

Another trip was to Rome, where Bruce insisted on his carrying out a rigid time-table. 'He learns by heart', wrote Bruce to the Prince Consort, 'in the morning before breakfast, and prepares for his Italian master who comes from 10 to 11 a.m. He reads with Mr. Tarver from 11 to 12, and translates French from 5 to 6 p.m.

[1] *King Edward VII:* Sir Sidney Lee.

and has the next hour in the evening for private reading or music. He has a piano in his room.'[1] In the afternoon he studied ancient monuments and works of art.

This sort of schedule delighted Prince Albert, and after an 'educational conference' with several eminent people, he decided that since Bertie belonged to the nation he must go to as many universities as possible. First he was sent to Edinburgh to study applied sciences under a phalanx of professors. Then to Oxford, and finally to Cambridge. At none of these universities was he allowed to mix with the undergraduates. In Edinburgh he lived drearily in Holyrood Palace under Bruce's chaperonage. And at Oxford, in spite of Dean Liddell's protestations, he was not allowed to belong to a college but given a residence, Frewin Hall, off Cornmarket Street. Liddell tried to point out that the Prince would miss the full benefits of university life by his seclusion, but Albert insisted that 'the only use of Oxford is that it is a place of *study*'.

Even the public was growing alarmed at the harshness of Bertie's upbringing. On September 20, 1859, *Punch* came out with a poem which began:

Thou dear little Wales, sure the saddest of tales,
Is the tale of the studies with which they are cramming thee
In the tucker and bibs handed over to Gibbs
Who for eight years with solid instruction was ramming thee.

The jingle went on to speculate mischievously:

Where next the boy may go to swell the farrago
We haven't yet heard, but the Palace they're plotting in;
To Berlin, Jena, Bonn, he'll no doubt be passed on,
And drop in for a finishing touch, p'raps at Gottingen.

The sallies of *Punch* made no impression on Bertie's formidable parents, and Albert's educational plan moved

[1] *King Edward VII:* Sir Sidney Lee.

ponderously forward. As far as Bertie's misery was concerned, Queen Victoria played a strangely passive part. The truth was that her attitude to her offspring was abnormally egotistical. As very young children they offered her amusement and release from her daily routine; but as soon as she had to begin to reckon with them as adults she was bored and ill at ease. In a letter written to the Queen of Prussia when Bertie was approaching his fifteenth birthday, and the affianced Vicky, once her mother's little darling, was sixteen, she said, 'I see the children much less & even here, where Albert is often away all day long, I find no especial pleasure or compensation in the company of the elder children. You will remember that I told you this at Osborne. Usually they go out with me in the afternoon (Vicky mostly, & the others also sometimes), or occasionally in the mornings when I drive or walk or ride, accompanied by my lady-in-waiting, & only very occasionally do I find the rather intimate intercourse with them either agreeable or easy. You will not understand this, but it is caused by various factors. Firstly, I only feel properly *à mon aise* and quite happy when Albert is with me; secondly, I am used to carrying on my many affairs quite alone; & then I have grown up all alone, accustomed to the society of adult (& never with younger) people. . . .'[1]

This illuminating letter, revealing Queen Victoria's indifference towards her growing-up children, explains why she was always ready to accept blindly Albert's appraisal of Bertie's capacity. Yet it is more difficult to reconcile the fact that while she talked incessantly of working for Bertie's good, she managed, in fact, to do him inestimable harm. No maternal loyalty prevented her from informing members of her household that he was stupid and inconsequential. Major Elphinstone, who

[1] *Henry Ponsonby : His Life from His Letters:* Arthur Ponsonby.

was engaged to supervise Prince Alfred, was surprised at her openness. He had been at the palace less than a month when he was writing in his diary, 'I had an interview with the Queen. She said, "With the Prince of Wales . . . one had to contend with an unhappy temper, incapacity of concentrating his mind and defective mental qualities". '[1] These observations, made so freely, soon became common gossip.

They were ridiculously exaggerated. The Heir Apparent was not a clever boy, yet he had keen perception, and when his imagination was stirred was capable of lively interest. Before Dr. Leonard Schmitz coached him in Greek and Roman history at Oxford he had been warned by Victoria's physician that he would 'find the Prince very backward for his age' and that it would be difficult 'to keep up his attention even for a short time'. The professor soon reported with asperity that his 'powers of application' were greatly underrated.[2] And Charles Kingsley, author of *Westward Ho!* and Professor of Modern History at Cambridge, became so fond of the young man that when he died his daughter wrote to Bertie saying: 'Next to his own children I can truly say there was no human being my father loved as he did you.'

However, unlike *Punch*, *The Times* under the editorship of Delane accepted the prevailing wind of deprecation and in a leading article stated patronisingly: 'It is the happiness of a King of England that we expect of him no brilliant military achievements, no extraordinary diplomatic legerdemain, no startling effects, no scenic pomps, no histrionic dexterity. He may be great without the possession of extraordinary talents and famous without dazzling exploits.'[3]

[1] *The Queen Thanks Sir Howard:* Mary Howard McClintock.
[2] *King Edward VII:* Sir Sidney Lee.
[3] *The Times:* November 9, 1859.

THE four dismal years between the Prince's seventeenth and twenty-first birthday were alleviated by only a few agreeable interludes, the chief of which was a trip to Canada and the United States.

To Bertie the visit to the New World was magic. Overnight the badgered, harassed, eighteen-year-old undergraduate found himself the object of frenzied admiration. Although he was accompanied by the Duke of Newcastle (Secretary of State for the Colonies), and, of course, General Bruce, there was no time for tutors and lessons. By comparison the endless procession of addresses, levées, parades and official banquets seemed sheer bliss. For the first time the Prince's social talents were given full play; at Newfoundland he answered fourteen addresses with originality and aplomb, and the Duke wrote to the Queen how surprisingly well he was handling himself. Even General Bruce[1] was obliged to report favourably, although he could not resist a back-handed cut in his sentence: 'H.R.H. acquitted himself admirably and seems pleased with everything, himself included.'[2]

The trip through Canada was 'official', with the Prince opening the new railway bridge across the St. Lawrence at Montreal, and laying the corner stone for the Parliament House. But when the royal party crossed into the United States in order to pay a visit to President Buchanan, Bertie suddenly became 'Baron Renfrew'. This did not dampen the enthusiasm of the crowds, who were not only passionately determined to catch a glimpse of the great-grandson of George III but prepared to give him a boisterous cheer as well. The climax of the American welcome came in New York. The Duke of Newcastle wrote the Queen that 'he certainly never ventured to hope for anything approaching such a scene

[1] Bruce had just been promoted Major-General.

[2] *King Edward VII:* Sir Sidney Lee.

as probably was never witnessed before—the enthusiasm of much more than half a million people worked up almost to madness and yet self-restrained within the bounds of the most perfect courtesy. . . .'[1]

The perfect courtesy, however, did not last for long. A ball was arranged for the Prince at the Academy of Music on East Fourteenth Street. Three thousand people were invited and five thousand turned up, whereupon the floor promptly caved in. It was not, as the Duke put it, 'well managed'. But American ingenuity came to the rescue. Carpenters were sent for on the spot, and the dancers waited while they nailed back the boards. Half-hourly bulletins were sent to the *New York Herald*. At midnight the dancing began but there was such a crush it was difficult to move. Pretty girls crowded around Bertie, and the Duke reported critically that 'the Prince was somewhat persecuted by attentions not in strict accordance with good breeding'. However, there is nothing to indicate that Bertie found this disagreeable.

Certainly he was astonished and delighted to discover what a celebrity he was. The Americans were energetic souvenir hunters, and an enterprising army sergeant, who had access to the dining room after a military review and luncheon in the Prince's honour, made nearly $50 selling duck bones which he claimed had been left by the Prince. The first buyer got the original article, but the unsuspecting ones who came after had the bones off the guests' plates, carefully wrapped in neat parcels.

The English papers reported every detail of the Heir Apparent's successes, and *Punch* was quick to see that now that the young man had tasted the delights of adulation his father might not find him so malleable in the future. The editor ran a cartoon showing the Prince sitting in an armchair, a top hat tipped over his brow, his feet on the fender, an empty glass beside him and a cigar

[1] *King Edward VII:* Sir Sidney Lee.

in the corner of his mouth, saying to a shocked Albert: 'Now, Sir-ree, if you'll sit down and liquor up I'll tell you all about my travels.'

The royal parents thanked Bertie for performing his duties well, but let him understand that the success of the tour, and even the success of Bertie's behaviour, was mainly due to General Bruce. To make this quite clear the Queen wrote Lord Palmerston and asked him to decorate Bruce on the grounds that her son's personal triumphs were largely gained because of his control. Perhaps the Prime Minister was shocked by this ungenerous attitude; at any rate he replied bluntly that Bruce's services 'were of a private character which it would be inappropriate to recognise with a public distinction'.[1] The Queen countered sharply that the Order of the Bath was instituted to reward 'services to the Crown'. But Lord Palmerston stood firm; and although the Queen fumed, General Bruce did not receive his ribbon.

DESPITE the fact that Bertie had been fêted and applauded and for the first time tasted the pleasure of both freedom and approval, his father insisted that he resume his studies at Oxford; and resume them in the same, prison-like atmosphere, with General Bruce regulating all his movements. This was almost more than the young man could bear. He stormed and protested but his father was adamant. The only games his parents approved of were tennis and racquets; they objected to hunting for fear it would bring him into too close contact with the frivolous members of the aristocracy of whom they strongly disapproved.

But occasionally Bertie persuaded General Bruce to relent and on a few occasions he was allowed to hunt

[1] *King Edward VII:* Sir Sidney Lee.

with the South Oxfordshire pack. Here he met two young rips, Henry (later Viscount) Chaplin and Sir Frederick Johnstone, members of the Oxford Bullingdon Club, who were to remain lifelong friends. And if the Queen had discovered that these young men had introduced her son to the awful habit of tobacco she would have been more convinced than ever of the wickedness of the aristocracy.

Cambridge was even duller than Oxford, and now the Prince of Wales' outbursts of temper were more frequent than ever. Once he defied General Bruce, skipped out of the house and caught a train to London. However, one of the equerries telegraphed ahead; and when poor Bertie arrived at the station he found a royal carriage waiting for him. The cowed young man climbed in and was promptly driven to Buckingham Palace. The Prince Consort shook his head wearily over his son's behaviour. There was only one hope left. Bertie must marry.

CHAPTER THREE

HIS MARRIAGE

THE Prince Consort decided to confide in his favourite daughter, Vicky, now the Princess Frederick, and ask her to help him in selecting a wife for her brother. But he would have to wait a bit, for Vicky was expecting her first baby. The Queen was worried about her, for ever since she had quitted the shores of England with her German husband, she had found life trying and difficult. Leaving her parents was bad enough.

'The poor child,' wrote Queen Victoria, 'was *quite* heart-broken at parting from her dearest beloved papa, whom she idolizes'.[1] Then there had been the disagreeable trip to Germany in bitterly cold February weather. The conventions which governed Prussian royalty were elaborate and antiquated. As the bridal train approached Berlin, the royal party was obliged to change into full evening dress; the windows of the coaches were opened and Princess Frederick had to sit in the freezing atmosphere, her arms and shoulders bare, smiling and bowing to the populace. She drove with her Prince through the streets of the great, frowning city in a glass coach which had little more warmth to offer. The Queen of Prussia, who hated England, greeted the poor bride with a haughty smile. 'Are you not frozen?' she asked. 'All except my heart which is warm,' replied the Princess quickly.[2]

This is one of the few instances in which Vicky displayed tact. She was clever, high-spirited and affection-

[1] *The Letters of Queen Victoria.*

[2] *Embassies of Other Days:* Walburga, Lady Paget.

ate, but she lacked the diplomatic instinct which was second nature to her brother Bertie. She had been brought up to say what she thought, and she saw no reason to change her ways. Besides there was plenty to criticize. She found that she was expected to live in a huge medieval schloss with wide stone passages, dark draughty rooms and creaking floors. It was believed to be haunted and scarcely a week passed without someone, from a sentry to a lady-in-waiting, declaring that he or she had seen the 'White Lady' glide by. Even worse was the fact that there was no plumbing. The stoves were so far from the bedrooms that by the time tubs of hot water were brought upstairs they were invariably cold.

Vicky complained loudly but she discovered that no changes could be made without the approval of old King Frederick William IV, who was fast becoming permanently insane. After some months she was given another residence, the Palace of Unter den Linden. But as far as the plumbing was concerned this left just as much to be desired as the first. She bombarded the senile King with requests to be allowed to make alterations and one day he gave his consent and the next withdrew it. It was not until Vicky's father-in-law was appointed Prince Regent that she was able to settle down in any comfort.

The long illness of the old King curtailed festivities and threw a pall over the Court, which in ordinary times was stiff enough. Vicky developed a passionate hatred of Prussian boots and silver plate, and complained that the eating habits were positively barbaric. Dinner was always between two and five in the afternoon. Everyone had to be attired in evening dress and sometimes the long, heavy meals in the full glare of daylight reduced her ladies-in-waiting to a half-fainting condition. This was the main meal of the day. At night there was 'supper' which consisted of tea and bread and cheese. However, Princess Frederick's choice of food was scarcely more orthodox. For breakfast she insisted on oysters and port wine. And once, when she was travelling and felt like something more substantial, she consumed seven hard-boiled eggs.

Nevertheless, the Princess was fortunate in two things: the devotion of her affable husband, whom she completely dominated, and the companionship of her eighteen-year-old maid of honour, Countess von Hohenthal, generally known as 'Wally'. This young lady had visited England before the Princess' marriage, had been greatly admired for her beauty and spirit, and consequently was a passionate Anglophile.

Queen Victoria had instructed Wally to write to her regularly, giving detailed news of Vicky. This was not easy, for the Queen used the information in order to proffer advice. When it was announced that Vicky was 'in an interesting condition' the Queen's zest seemed to double. Stockmar went to Berlin to visit Vicky, then in his usual interfering way announced to Lord Clarendon who was also in the city, that the Queen was 'behaving abominably' to her daughter. 'The Queen wishes to exercise the same authority and control over her that she did before her marriage and she writes her constant letters full of anger and reproaches, desiring all sorts of things to be done that it is neither right nor desirable that she should do and complaining of her remissness in writing to her sisters or to Miss Hillyard, and of her forgetting what is due to her own family and country, till the poor child [as Stockmar called her] is made seriously ill, and put in a state dangerous to her in her actual condition.'[1]

Some weeks later Princess Frederick gave birth to a son, an heir to the Prussian throne and Queen Victoria's first grandchild. The birth was difficult, and, incredibly enough, no one discovered for three days that the baby's

[1] *Greville Diaries*: edited by Philip Whitwell Wilson.

shoulder had been pulled from the socket during the delivery. The doctors then said it was too late to repair it. The child was named Wilhelm, and was destined to become known to the world as 'The Kaiser'.

Vicky was deeply distressed by her baby's handicap, but wrote her mother that she was 'very proud of him and very proud of being a Mama'. She told Queen Victoria: 'Your grandson is exceedingly lively and when awake will not be satisfied unless kept dancing about continually. He scratches his face and tears his caps and makes every sort of extraordinary little noise. I am so thankful, so happy, he is a boy. I longed for one more than I can describe, my whole heart was set upon a boy, therefore I did not expect one. I cannot say I think him like anyone at present, although now and then he reminds me of Bertie and Leopold, which I fear you won't like. . . .'[1]

Six months after the birth of her son, Princess Frederick went to England to visit her mother and father, accompanied by Wally. The two girls spent several months at Osborne. Once they went to Oxford to visit Bertie, but General Bruce's formidable wife eyed the beautiful Countess with deep suspicions, and let the Queen know that she disapproved of such frivolous interruptions. A few days later the young lady was informed that the Queen did not like Bertie to receive social calls when he was supposed to be attending to his work.

It was on this visit to England that Prince Albert took the Princess and Wally into his confidence, and told them that he would like to find a wife for his eldest son. The year before, when Bertie was only seventeen, Uncle

[1] *Letters of the Empress Frederick.*

Leopold, aided by Stockmar, had drawn up a list of eligible Princesses. Most of the young ladies were German. Somewhere near the bottom of the list came the name of Princess Alexandra of Denmark. Although Prince Albert had been told that this young girl was remarkably attractive he regarded her name with little interest. Politically it would be most unsound for the heir to the British throne to forge any links with Denmark. For more than ten years Prussia and Denmark had been engaged in a bitter dispute over the Baltic provinces of Schleswig and Holstein. Apart from the intricacy of the claims and counter-claims, it was obvious that Prussia was determined to extend her Baltic sea-board, and that the Duchies were the most inflammable spot in Europe. And since Prince Albert was wedded to his vision of a strong Germany united to Britain, he did not want his son arousing sympathies for the wrong cause by marrying a Danish princess. He put Alexandra's name out of his head, and asked Vicky to look over the eligible princesses residing in Germany, and report to him.

Princess Frederick was delighted at the notion of finding a wife for her brother. She decided that the inspecting should be done without delay. 'In vain,' wrote Countess von Hohenthal in her memoirs, 'I represented that he (the Prince of Wales) was too young, not only in age but also in disposition, but the Queen and Prince Consort thought it would keep him out of mischief. I alone was to accompany the Princess, who was to be sent in search of the lady, on this expedition, everyone else returning to Berlin. I was so wrapt up in Tennyson's *Idylls of the King*, which had just then appeared, that I remembered nothing of the journey until we arrived at Düsseldorf, where there was a huge supper party at the Duke of Hohenzollern's with every available young German Princess. The only one, however, who in later life became remarkable was Carmen Sylva, Queen of Roumania, at that time the Princess Elizabeth of Wied. This young lady was in her nineteenth year and looked insignificant then. She was hardly pretty—beauty in my own mind I had settled on as a *sine qua non* for the Prince of Wales's wife. We therefore returned to Berlin having mercifully done nothing.'[1]

The Prince Consort persisted with the search, however, and during the next two years Bertie was introduced to several of Uncle Leopold's eligible young ladies; but they made no impression on him. Then fortune intervened. Countess von Hohenthal married Mr. Augustus Paget, a British diplomat stationed in Copenhagen. On a honeymoon visit to England she sat next to the Prince Consort at dinner. 'I told him,' she wrote, 'that Mr. Paget had often seen Princess Alix [of Denmark] and thought her the most charming, pretty and delightful young princess it was possible to imagine. The Prince repeated all this to the Queen, who was sitting on his other side, and after dinner Her Majesty asked me to send her the photograph of the young princess and to write about her to Princess Alice and to get all the information I could.'[1]

When a few months later Mrs. Paget herself met the seventeen-year-old Alexandra she was so struck by her charm and beauty that she was determined not to let matters drop, and wrote to Princess Frederick that she was convinced it would be impossible to find anyone better suited to the Prince of Wales. She hinted that the Czar of Russia was looking towards Copenhagen for a wife for his son, and there was no time to lose.

Princess Frederick sprang into action. She asked her old friend the Grand Duchess of Mecklenburg-Strelitz to invite herself and the Danish Princess for a two-day visit, which was promptly done. And this visit sealed the fate

[1] *Embassies of Other Days:* Walburga, Lady Paget.

of Bertie. Vicky wrote to Wally Paget ecstatically, 'Quite enchanted I returned from Strelitz and you are the first to whom I hasten to impart my impressions. Princess Alix is the most fascinating creature in the world. You did not say nearly enough. For a long time I have seen nobody who pleased me so much as this lovely and charming girl, not to speak of a Princess. . . . Princess Alix and I got to know each other very soon and in those few days I have got to love her very deeply, she is simply charming.'[1]

Princess Frederick did not let matters stand here, but hurried to England to persuade her father and mother to allow Bertie and Alix to meet. The Prince Consort was now desperate—for Bertie was nearly twenty-one—and finally gave his permission. A meeting was arranged between the young couple 'as if by accident' at the Cathedral of Speier in Germany. And another meeting was fixed at Heidelberg for the next day. The young couple exchanged a few words while the masses of relatives looked discreetly in the other direction, and a few days later the Prince Consort wrote to his daughter. 'We hear nothing but good of Princess Alexandra. The young couple seem to have taken a warm liking to one another.'

After much agitated reflection, the Prince Consort decided that if Victoria made it quite plain from the very start that Bertie was taking the Princess but *not* her family, there was no reason for Britain to get involved in the Danish-Prussian dispute. Yet ever since the young couple had met, there had been angry rumblings from Germany. The Prince Consort found it necessary to rebuke his brother, Duke Ernest of Coburg, who had taken matters into his own hands and gone so far as to tell Bertie that the only princess in Europe he must not marry was Alexandra of Denmark. 'We took care not to

[1] *Embassies of Other Days:* Walburga, Lady Paget.

let Bertie know about the existence of Princess Alexandra,' he wrote to the Duke, 'but told him of all the other possibilities. We find it rather strange that you should tell him about this one princess and warn him not to marry her nor to allow himself to be induced to marry her.

'I will not waste any words about the fact that we as his parents might expect to be told that you wanted to warn him: it was wrong to do so behind our backs. Now he has heard from all sides about the beauty of the Princess, and he has seen photos of her in the rooms of the Duchess of Cambridge at Kew, and they have confirmed what he heard. We explained the political differences such a marriage would bring with it as well as we could. He understood as far as a young man of his age and his capacities is able to understand them. But as we practically have the public opinion against us, and as we should have our Ministers, people, and the Press against us, we were anxious to find another lady suitable for Bertie. (It is his wish to marry soon, and it is in his interest morally, socially, and politically.) But we find there is really no other lady he could marry. The Princess of Meiningen and the daughter of Prince Albrecht of Prussia, whom he had an opportunity of seeing in Berlin, did not please him. Vicky [the Princess Royal] has racked her brain, too, to help us to find someone, but in vain. The daughter of Prince Frederick of the Netherlands (Mary) is too ugly. There are positively no other princesses, except the sister of Louis [of Hesse]. This would connect us for a second time with Darmstadt. All that made it clear to us that Princess Alexandra is the only one to be chosen.

'But now we must see that this marriage is not looked upon as a triumph of Denmark over us and Prussia: that it came about without the Danes knowing about it, without the knowledge of our Ministers and the Cambridges, but quite alone through the mediation of our Prussian children. In this manner alone we can avoid getting into trouble with Prussia . . .'[1]

THEN, in December, 1861, came the Prince Consort's death. The Queen's grief was so terrible, the people around her feared her mind would become unbalanced. During her husband's illness she never once admitted the possibility of tragedy. The Prince had gone to Cambridge to remonstrate with the rebellious Bertie about his disappointing progress. On the way home he had caught a cold which developed into typhoid fever. At the end of three weeks there was no improvement, but Victoria refused to take anything but an optimistic view, and wrote to her Uncle Leopold: 'I can again report favourably on our *most* precious invalid.' Two days later he was dead.

The Queen in her wild sorrow poured out her heart to all those about her. To Uncle Leopold she wrote in tones bordering on hysteria 'My *life* as a *happy* one is *ended*! the world is gone for *me*! If I *must live* on (and I will do nothing to make me worse than I am), it is henceforth for our poor fatherless children—for my unhappy country, which has lost *all* in losing him—and in *only* doing what I know and *feel* he would wish, for he *is* near me—his spirit will guide and inspire me! But oh! to be cut off in the prime of life—to see our pure, happy, quiet, domestic life, which *alone* enabled me to bear my *much* disliked position, CUT OFF at forty-two—when I *had* hoped with such instinctive certainty that God never *would* part us and would let us grow old together (though he always talked of the shortness of life)—is *too awful*, too cruel! . . .'[2]

[1] *The Private Life of Queen Alexandra:* Hans Roger Madol.
[2] *The Letters of Queen Victoria.*

But in a few days Victoria had recovered from the initial, blinding shock and was writing to Uncle Leopold in a more purposeful vein, 'My spirit rises when I think *any* wish or plan of his is to be touched or changed . . .' She told her uncle that she was anxious to make one thing clear; and that 'is *my firm* resolve, my *irrevocable decision*, viz. that *his* wishes—*his* plans about everything, *his* views about *every*thing are to be *my law*! And *no human power* will make me swerve from *what he* decided and wished—and I look to *you* to *support* and *help* me in this. I apply this particularly as regards our children—Bertie, etc.—for whose future he had traced everything so carefully. I am *also determined* that *no one* person, may *he* be ever so good, ever so devoted among my servants—is to lead or guide or dictate *to me*. I know *how he* would disapprove it . . .'[1]

There was another person, whose grief was almost as deep as Victoria's. This was the aged Stockmar who saw in Albert's death the ruin of years of careful work. 'I feel right well,' he wrote, 'that I cannot judge this matter as one in full possession of his senses; for the thought of the malignity of my personal fate, which has allowed me to live so long that I should endure this cruel blow, drives me at times half mad. An edifice which, for a great and noble purpose had been reared, with a devout sense of duty, by twenty-three years of laborious toil, has been shattered to its very foundations.'[2]

When he saw Victoria a few months later he wept with her and lamented, 'My dear good Prince! How happy I shall be to see him again! and it will not be long.'[3] As usual Stockmar was right. The following year he, too, was dead.

[1] *The Letters of Queen Victoria.*
[2] *Memoirs of Baron Stockmar:* Ernest von Stockmar.
[3] *Early Years of Prince Consort:* Grey.

In the meantime what about Princess Alexandra? When Uncle Leopold first sent her name to Queen Victoria she was barely fourteen years old. Her father, Prince Christian of Schleswig - Holstein - Sonderburg - Glucksburg, was an impoverished officer in the Guards who tried to support his family on ten pounds a month. Although the Prince improved his social position by marrying Louisa, the daughter of the wealthy Landgrave of Hesse, who could claim descent from George II, he added nothing to his purse, for the old Landgrave was provincial and miserly. He allowed Prince Christian's family to live in a large, ramshackle building in his own grounds, known as the 'Yellow Palace', but the fact that they were hard pressed for pocket money left him unmoved. The Landgrave was not noted for his imagination; his impressive residence contained a large library and he formed the inflexible habit of reading through his books in the order in which they had been bought. It was considered ironical that he only reached Knigge's famous treatise, *The Art of Human Intercourse*, on the day he died.

Prince Christian's family struggled along as best it could. The Prince gave his five children a course of gymnastics every morning, and the Princess taught them English, French and German. For the girls the high-light of the day was dressing up for an afternoon walk with their governess. But as soon as they returned Mama saw that their finery was removed, for fear of it being spoilt.

Alexandra shared an attic bedroom with her sister, Dagmar. Both girls made their own clothes, and on the infrequent occasions when the family had guests to meals, Alexandra and Dagmar waited on the table, while their brothers, Freddie and Willy, saw that the glasses were filled. Little did these visitors think that the soup was being passed by the future Queen of England and

Empress of Russia, and the beer being poured by the future Kings of Denmark and Greece.

Except for the fun which the children managed to drum up on their own, life in Denmark was dull and narrow. Prince Christian's family had little to do with court circles which were extremely bourgeois yet at the same time considered 'not quite nice' for young people. The monarch, Frederick VII, was an enormously fat man who, despite three marriages, had never been able to produce a son. Once, when a rumour spread that one of his wives was expecting a baby, Louis-Philippe, King of France, exclaimed: 'God bless the father whoever it is!' But the gossip proved unfounded.

King Frederick, however, was extremely happy with his third and morganatic wife, whom he created Countess Danner. But Copenhagen society was shocked, first because she had been a milliner and a dancer, and second because she was almost as fat as he was. Nevertheless the masses loved the king because he had given them a Constitution, and the royal couple lived a happy, parochial life dining at five o'clock on pea soup and bacon, and drinking quantities of beer and corn whisky.

Princess Christian, a solid, virtuous woman, became tight-lipped whenever the Court was mentioned and refused to let any intimacy develop between the two families. This did not endear her to the King; and although in 1852 it was decided that Prince Christian, by dint of his wife's connections, must succeed to the throne, the old monarch did not bother to create the family 'Royal Highnesses' until six years later.

Princess Alexandra was not told that she was being considered as a wife for the Prince of Wales until she was seventeen. She was thrilled by the prospect of such a brilliant life and when she met Bertie and found him agreeable and attractive her cup was overflowing. Then came the news of the Prince Consort's death. Panic gripped the family. Would this mean the end of the delicate negotiations that had been begun?

There was no need for anxiety. Albert had decided that Bertie must marry Alexandra, and the Queen was determined that his wishes should be fulfilled. Six months after Albert's death Victoria wrote and formally requested the Princess's hand for her son. But Bertie was told that he could not propose himself until the Queen had met the young lady, and this meeting took place under Uncle Leopold's auspices in September. Alexandra was warned to dress very simply and not to smile, for the Queen could not bear to see anyone looking happy. She made a good impression on Victoria, although the Queen was mainly immersed in her own tragedy. The beautiful 'Wally' who had played such a large part in arranging the match was present, and the Queen wept and put her head on the latter's shoulder saying: 'You, dear Wally, will quite understand what I feel at this moment, you have a husband you love and you know what I have lost.'[1]

At last the stage was set for Bertie. He announced gaily to Wally: 'Now I will take a walk with Princess Alix in the garden and in three-quarters of an hour I will take her into the Grotto and there I will propose, and I hope it will be to everyone's satisfaction.'[1]

It was certainly to Bertie's satisfaction. At last he could escape from continuous surveillance, and what luck to have found such a pretty princess! The fact that he was eager and attentive gave the proceedings an air of real romance, and Uncle Leopold was able to write to Victoria that 'the match is quite a love-match. Bertie is extremely happy and in admiration of his very lovely bride. All the arguments that one forced him to marry a young lady that he had never seen fall most completely to the ground. All this is important, particu-

[1] *Embassies of Other Days:* Walburga, Lady Paget.

larly for England, where it will please people very much that the Prince of Wales, like his parents, should marry from affection.'[1]

But Queen Victoria was not yet satisfied. There was one more duty she must perform during the six months before the wedding took place. She must have a heart to heart talk with Alexandra and make it clear what Albert had so often said; that Bertie was marrying Alexandra and *not* her family. The Queen told her son that Alexandra must spend several weeks with her at Osborne and Windsor—alone. Bertie protested and pointed out that it was an ordeal for so young a girl, but Victoria was adamant. First she packed Bertie off on a Mediterranean trip with his sister Vicky and her husband Prince Frederick. Then she received Alexandra.

The atmosphere was painfully solemn. Smiles were still considered bad taste, and in the sad, sombre setting the Queen told the Princess very firmly that although she was right to love her country she must avoid the danger of 'using her influence to make the Prince a partisan in any political question at home or abroad'.[2] After several talks in this vein, Alexandra was sent back to Denmark, and the Queen pronounced herself well satisfied with the way 'dear sweet Alix' had accepted her advice.

THE wedding was fixed for March 10, 1863, and most people believed it would be held in St. Paul's or Westminster Abbey. But a London wedding would mean a State procession, and the Queen would have to show herself to her people. This she abso-

[1] *The Letters of Queen Victoria.*
[2] *Embassies of Other Days:* Walburga, Lady Paget.

lutely refused to do. Psychologically she collapsed at the thought of facing crowds without Albert at her side, and she was determined not to abandon her heavy mourning, not even for a day. She decided that the ceremony must take place in St. George's Chapel at Windsor Castle. It held only 900 people and she would be able to enter quietly and take an obscure place concealed from prying eyes.

There was much criticism of Victoria's decision. *Punch* observed acidly that as the wedding was to be 'in an obscure Berkshire village, noted only for an old castle with no sanitary arrangements,' the greatest secrecy should be preserved in the announcements. It went on to suggest that the only notice should be inserted in the marriage columns of *The Times*, and worded: "On the 10th inst., at Windsor, by Dr. Longley, assisted by Dr. Thomson, Albert Edward England K.G. to Alexandra Denmark. No cards." '

Criticism continued, for the public was in a holiday mood, and looking forward to a spectacular celebration. Not only were the wedding plans a disappointment but there were many protests about the shabby arrangements for Alexandra's welcome. Lord Malmesbury, a former Foreign Secretary, reflected the general feeling when he wrote:

'It was the coldest day we have had for a long time; no sun, with occasional showers, and we were half frozen standing on the balconies. The Duke of Cambridge rode by two or three times with his staff and was greatly cheered. Lord Ranelagh passed at the head of his Brigade of Volunteers. Then appeared the Royal carriages, and I was never more surprised and disappointed. The first five contained the suite and brothers and sisters of the Princess. The carriages looked old and shabby, and the horses very poor, with no trappings, not even rosettes, and no outriders. In short the shabbiness of the whole cortège was beyond anything one could imagine, everybody asking: Who is the Master of the Horse?

'The Princess kept bowing right and left very gracefully. The moment the procession had passed the crowds dispersed, but there were universal remarks and compliments on the Princess's beauty—I heard that on the arrival of the Prince and Princess at Slough the horses of the first carriage jibbed and the leaders of the second turned right around upon the wheelers, the harness got entangled, and the confusion was very great. Altogether everything done by the Court authorities was bad and the management of the City not less so. The streets were quite blocked up, and if it had not been for the good temper of the people some dreadful catastrophe must have occurred.'[1]

As if to make up for the half-hearted arrangements, a gushing, burbling river of praise flowed forth from the pens of journalists and poets in praise of the beautiful bride and the handsome groom. The ceremony in St. George's was a brilliant spectacle. 'The most moving sight I ever saw,' said Bishop Wilberforce. 'A fine affair, a thing to remember,' said Disraeli. 'The bride's face,' said Charles Dickens, 'was very pale, and full of a sort of awe and wonder, but the face of no ordinary bride, not simply a timid shrinking girl, but with character distinctive of her own, prepared to act a part greatly. . . .' The Poet-Laureate, Tennyson, outdid himself with a eulogy which apparently fitted the sentiments of the day but now verges on the comical:

'Sea-kings' daughter as happy as fair,
Blissful bride of a blissful heir,
Bride of the heir of the king of the sea—
Oh joy to the people and joy to the throne,
Come to us, love us and make us your own:

[1] *The Memoirs of an Ex-Minister:* Lord Malmesbury.

For Saxon or Dane or Norman we,
Teuton or Celt, or whatever we be,
We are each all Dane in our welcome to thee, Alexandra!'

The only friction that occurred during the solemn service sprang from the activity of Bertie's four-year-old nephew, the son of Princess Frederick, one day to become William II. The child was seated between two young uncles, Prince Alfred and Prince Leopold. All three were wearing the kilt and when little Willie conceived the idea of taking his skian dhu and throwing it across the choir the two princes were forced to restrain him; Willie showed his displeasure by biting them hard on the legs.

This lively scene escaped the attention of Queen Victoria who sat half-hidden in a gallery above the chancel. She refused to discard her mourning, but consented to wear the star and the blue sash of the Garter. For her it was anything but a festive occasion. 'Ah, dear brother,' she wrote to the King of Prussia. 'What a sad, dismal ceremony it was! How very different to that unforgettably beautiful one [the marriage of the Princess Royal] on January 25, 1858! Ah, but then my mother and my angel of a husband were with me and there was nothing to mar my happiness! My present numbed existence is not a real life at all, and it is difficult to watch his children starting off on their own lives when one feels so utterly dead oneself! And yet how happy and wonderful all that might have been! However, I wish to say nothing more about myself! My dear Albert's longfelt desire has been fulfilled and may God bless the young couple and guide them along their path of duty, which alone leads to true happiness!'[1]

The Eton boys did not share the Queen's gloom. They were given a holiday, and flung themselves into the

[1] *The Private Life of Queen Alexandra:* Hans Roger Madol.

celebrations with relentless energy. One of the boys wrote to his father describing the great moment when the bride and bridegroom departed for their honeymoon. 'We all rushed upon the carriage. (I was right in front of the charge; it was a second Balaclava.) Nothing stood before us; the policemen charged in a body, but they were knocked down. There was a chain put across the road, but we broke that; several old *genteel* ladies tried to stop me, but I snapped my fingers in their face and cried "Hurrah!" and "What larks!" I frightened some of them horribly. There was a wooden palisade put up at the station [it was the Great Western], but we broke it down; and there, to my unspeakable grief, I was bereaved of a portion of my clothing, viz. my hat. Somebody knocked it off. I could not stop to pick it up. I shrieked out a convulsive "Oh, my hat!" and was then borne on. I got right down to the door of the carriage where the Prince of Wales was, wildly shouting "Hurrah!" He bowed to me, I am perfectly certain; but I shrieked louder. I am sure, if the Princess did not possess very strong nerves, she would have been frightened; but all she did was to smile blandly. At last the train moved off. . . .'[1]

The author of this graphic chronicle was Winston Churchill's father, the fourteen-year-old Lord Randolph.

[1] *Lord Randolph Churchill:* Winston S. Churchill.

CHAPTER FOUR

THE GAY SIXTIES

At last Bertie was free; and considering that even tight-lipped Victorians had regarded his upbringing as unduly strict, it is small wonder that freedom went to his head. Until his wedding day he was treated like a schoolboy, then suddenly the tutors and governors vanished and he found himself with the most beautiful princess in Europe as a wife; with Marlborough House and Sandringham, and, later, Abergeldie Castle in Scotland; and most important of all, with £100,000 a year to maintain his royal pleasure.

It was an intoxicating reversal for a repressed young man of twenty-two. There was scarcely a cloud on the horizon, for parental authority was now being exercised by remote control. The Queen was still in the deepest mourning. The robes of state were repellent to her, and she refused to show herself to the public on grounds of ill health. She rarely came to London, but remained buried in Windsor Castle, or at inaccessible Osborne, or remote Balmoral. Later on she disappeared twice a year to an even deeper retreat—a cottage which she bought in the Scottish mountains where, literally, there was no communication with the outside world at all.

She bombarded Bertie with letters and instructions, but a good many of them he could ignore, for it was not at all the same thing as being confronted by her formidable personality in the flesh. Albert's death had not drawn her any closer to her eldest son; on the contrary, in view of the sad contrast between the characters of father and son, she seemed more determined than ever to shut him out from her confidence.

She did not want him to step into his father's shoes in any way; she scarcely liked the idea of his stepping into his own. Reluctantly she allowed 'dear sweet Alix' and himself to preside at drawing rooms and levées, because somebody had to be there; and even more reluctantly she allowed Bertie to receive foreign royalties when they came to England, for the public, with its unreasonable notions, seemed to expect hospitality to be shown to any stray Prince 'who chose to set foot on these shores'. And of course she could not prevent him from laying foundation stones, and attending dinners and garden parties as the Heir Apparent.

Young Bertie was only too ready to do his duty, since at last duty and pleasure were scarcely distinguishable. He was expected to play a leading role in society; and both he and society were delighted. For twenty years the Prince Consort's dislike of 'the Higher Classes' had cut off many aristocratic families from any intimacy with the blood royal. Now the great ladies of England eagerly prostrated themselves before the royal pair and hailed them as their leaders. They praised Alexandra's beauty and copied her curls; they expressed themselves enchanted with Bertie's affability and went so far as to describe him as 'exceedingly handsome'.

This last was not strictly accurate. Those with steadier equilibrium found Bertie too short for masculine beauty. He spoke with a guttural r, his eyes were slightly bulging and, like his mother, his chin dropped away too abruptly. However, a luxurious beard hid this last defect, and the elegance of his clothes did the rest.

There was no doubt that he was immensely agreeable, for he was immensely happy. In the sixties pleasure was taken seriously, and nowhere in the world was it better organised or more varied than in England. Within a few months of his marriage Bertie's life had taken shape in the smart, restless routine it was to follow for many years. In August he went to Cowes for the yacht races; in September he went abroad, usually to the fashionable resorts in Germany; in October he went to Scotland for the deer stalking; during the winter he hunted and shot and paid visits to his friends, using Sandringham as his base; in the early spring he went to the Riviera; and at the beginning of May he came to London for 'the Season', which lasted three months. Besides all this, there were several visits to Paris each year *en garçon*, and, of course, he rarely missed a race meeting at Goodwood or Ascot, while the Derby and the Grand National always found him in the royal box.

This routine was not in the least original. Almost all the gay young noblemen of the day followed the same pattern with minor deviations. Society in those days was composed exclusively of the landed aristocracy who only came to London for the three months when the hunting and shooting had ended and the yachting and deer stalking had not yet begun.

The London season was splendid and expensive. It consisted of a hectic round of parades and drives in the park, luncheon parties (for men only; ladies did not lunch out), dinners, operas, and a choice of four or five balls a night. The ladies often changed their clothes four times a day and the only garments a gentleman could be seen in were riding-clothes; a frock coat; or tails. At the end of July the lords and ladies departed with their children, their head servants, and the family silver. Their London houses were draped in dust sheets and remained idle and forlorn until the following May.

The only people of any consequence who returned to the metropolis in the autumn were the wives of Members of Parliament. Although in those days Parliament only sat six months a year, the poor ladies found the off-season very trying. One of them, the wife of Sir William Senlac-Hastings, M.P., wrote to her mother: 'It seems *mad* and *odd* to be in London in November, and the poor house seems so dismal with half the rooms in their holland covers, even the *tongs* and the *fender* in holland bags, and smelling sadly of camphor, but William says the dining-room and library and my boudoir must suffice, I am *not* to open the drawing room as there is *no one* in London to receive there, and we go home to dear Forbury at Christmas.'[1]

ALTHOUGH the Victorian creed of duty and respectability had already impressed itself firmly on the middle classes, it had made little headway with the two extremes of society, 'the swells' and 'the roughs'. Perhaps a faint echo of it could be caught in the insistence of the *grandes dames* that they were taking part in the season not to enjoy themselves but to 'help trade'; but here it seemed to end.

The rich and pleasure-loving aristocrats of the sixties led almost the same wild and extravagant lives as their Regency grandfathers. They raced and gambled and sought the company of low women. Their wives regarded it as a natural course of events. It was an accepted fact that the pleasures of men were gross; indeed it was a sign of masculine virility. So the ladies turned a blind eye to the amusements of their husbands, and their husbands led a brilliantly organised double life.

It is not surprising that the Prince of Wales was attracted to the *bons vivants*. It was a natural reaction from the middle-aged pedants with whom he had always been surrounded. The enjoyment of life was a philosophy from which he had been carefully guarded and he

[1] *Fashions in London:* Barbara Worsley-Gough.

now found it intoxicating. During the first few years of his marriage he collected around him a group of high-spirited aristocrats who provided London with half its gossip. Among his circle was Henry Chaplin, a son-in-law of the Duke of Sutherland; Sir Frederick Johnstone, a connoisseur of horses and women; Lord Royston, the heir of the Earl of Hardwicke and an artist in the matter of dress; the Marquis of Waterford, a gay, young Irish peer who startled society by eloping with his best friend's wife; Valentine Baker, the colonel of the fashionable 10th Hussars; Lord Hartington, who managed to keep several mistresses at once and still remain a pillar of society; and the wild young Marquis of Hastings who lost a fortune and died of consumption at the age of twenty-six.

Bertie accepted his new friends on a fairly equal footing. Not completely, of course, but almost. Once when he was playing billiards and missed a shot, a young companion said jovially, 'Pull yourself together, Wales.' Whether from pique at the turn of the game or offended dignity, we do not know, but the Prince immediately informed the offender that his carriage was at the door.

So one could not go too far with Bertie; on the other hand Bertie was desperately anxious to be one of the boys. This did not spring from any democratic instinct. Bertie adored being royal, and he loved all the splash and colour and ceremony that went with it. But he also adored having fun, and it was plain that some fun could only be had without the royal trappings. Early on, the Prince of Wales developed the habit of sending the royal coachman home, and hiring public cabs.

In this way it was possible for him to move about London, paying calls from *cinq à sept*, and even to visit the night haunts of the less respectable world, without being recognised. In the sixties photography was in its infancy and the daily papers had not yet learnt the technicalities of reproducing pictures. Only the cartoonists could make a man's physiognomy famous. Indeed, just before his marriage the Prince had travelled in an ordinary coach from Windsor to London and only one lady had spotted him. She reported that the unsuspecting porter asked the Prince to 'show his ticket'. She was amazed when His Royal Highness hopped off at one of the stations to buy a copy of *Punch* and actually paid for it! He must be 'of no mind at all' she reported.

A great many people were shocked by the Prince's unconventional habits and felt he should not forget his royal role for a single moment. When he became a member of White's, in 1867, *The Star* criticised the informal manner in which his friends greeted him, pointing out that they did not even bow when he entered the club. *The Tomahawk*, a satirical magazine that made a speciality of pricking bubbles, immediately countered with the following suggestion:

'On his arrival at the top of St. James's Street, H.R.H. will be received by the members of White's dressed in the Windsor uniform, the committee appearing in full Court costume. An address will then be presented to the Prince to which H.R.H. will return gracious answers. H.R.H. will then be conducted to the reading room by the chairman walking backwards and carrying a candlestick in each hand. H.R.H. will then peruse for a few minutes a copy of *The Times* printed on silk. This done, he will be escorted to the smoking room by the Committee—club boys strewing flowers before them—and conducted to a throne under a canopy erected in that department. A jewelled meerschaum will be presented to him . . . which he will smoke for five minutes . . . then H.R.H. will drive away in his state coach to Marlborough House, accompanied by his military escort, amid the shouts of the people and the boom of artillery.'[1]

[1] *The Tomahawk*, June 22, 1867.

The Prince ignored this mild flutter over the conventions and pursued his private life with vigour. As an unsophisticated youth he eagerly followed the example of his knowing friends, and one of the first to show him the excitements of London's hidden world was the Marquis of Hastings. Hastings was the leader of most of the devilry that took place among the young bloods. Dark, handsome, wildly improvident and wildly rich, he had his own racing stable at the age of twenty-two. He staggered the dealers by paying the unheard of sum of £13,500 for a thoroughbred which turned out to be a screw, and he would gamble, literally, on anything. Once he wagered a huge sum on drops of rain running down a window pane; another time on which lump of sugar a fly would settle upon.

The Marquis was always bored by conventional society and almost every night set out with friends for the more disreputable parts of the metropolis. These were not far afield. Leicester Square was a refuse heap, and the streets behind it, running across Shaftesbury Avenue and the Charing Cross Road, abounded with 'night-houses' of every description. These establishments remained open all night and many of them were crowded with card-sharpers, pick-pockets, pugilists, money-lenders, tradesmen (known as 'shop-boys') and prostitutes. A dance band blared, and food and drinks were plentiful. Scarcely a night passed without a fight breaking out, usually over someone smashing someone else's top hat.

But Hastings and his friends often ventured further abroad. Sometimes they attended the public hangings in front of Newgate Prison, which were as much of an 'occasion' as a Test Match is today; sometimes they went down to the Docks where opium dens and drunken sailors with knives in their belts provided real danger. Although cock-fighting was illegal, it still existed and the Marquis frequently led a group to Faultless' pit in Endell Street, where he matched his birds against the Duke of Hamilton's. Another favourite sport was betting on how many sewer rats a terrier could kill in an hour. When Hastings arrived for one of these 'ratting matches' the gentleman in charge of the ring would announce in a loud voice: 'the Markis is in the chair.' And the Marquis invariably obliged by ordering six cases of champagne.

The most famous haunts were 'Mott's' and the 'Cremorne'. Almost every night these houses were packed with 'swells' ranging from royalty to subalterns. Champagne flowed freely, and high gambling took place. One evening Hastings upset the usual routine by arriving with 200 sewer rats concealed in large sacks. At a given signal, a friend cut off the gaslights, the sacks were cut open, and the Marquis fled shutting the door firmly behind him. This action was regarded as a particularly humorous joke by those fortunate enough not to have been there.

However, the chief attraction of Mott's and the Cremorne were the pretty girls they employed, who were always ready to make themselves agreeable. In the curious jargon of the day these ladies were known as 'soiled doves' or 'houris'. Many of them became famous. There was Cora Pearl who made a name and fortune as a demi-mondaine in Paris but finally died as a beggar-woman; there was Nellie Fowler, who was alleged to have a natural perfume so delicate that love-sick swains begged her to sleep with their handkerchiefs under her pillow; there was Polly Ash, who was admired for many years by the Maharajah Dhuleep Singh; there was Nellie Clifton, Baby Jordan, and, most spectacular of all, 'Skittles'.

Skittles became almost an institution. Her real name was Catherine Walters. She was reputed to be the daughter of a sea captain from Liverpool. She earned her sobriquet when she picked a drunken quarrel with a group of Guards officers and informed then she would knock them down like 'a row of bloody skittles'. Apparently she was a dream of beauty. She had dozens of rich admirers, chief among them Lord Hartington who set her up in splendid style and for many years was thought to be married to her.

At the fashionable hour Skittles was seen in the park every afternoon driving a wonderfully smart victoria with a pair of high-stepping ponies. Crowds gathered to watch her, and there were many complaints that she was blocking the traffic on its way from the South Kensington Exhibition. As a joke, a young journalist on *The Times* wrote a letter to his paper, pretending to be an innocent spectator, eager to solve the traffic tangle. 'Sir: Early in the season of 1861 a young lady whom I must call Anonyma, for I have never been able to learn her name, made her appearance in Hyde Park. She was a charming creature, beautifully dressed, and she drove with ease and spirit two of the handsomest brown ponies eye ever beheld . . . A good many young gentlemen seemed to be acquainted with her . . . Last year she avoided crowds and affected unfrequented roads . . . but as the fame of her beauty and equipage spread this privacy became impossible to her. The fashionable world eagerly migrated in search of her from the Ladies' Mile to the Kensington Road. . . . Could you not, sir, whose business it is to know everything and everyone, and who possibly, therefore, may know Anonyma herself, prevail on her to drive in some other portion of the Park as long as the Exhibition lasts?'[1]

The *Daily Telegraph* found out that young Matthew Higgins had written the letter, and in a pungent leader that makes present-day invective look tepid gave both Skittles and *The Times* a scorching indictment:

[1] *The Times*, July 3, 1862.

'The plain truth of the matter is that Hyde Park, like every other place of public resort, has been for a lengthened period infested by a number of lewd women, who, being well paid by wealthy profligates for selling their miserable bodies for the purpose of debauchery, are enabled to dress splendidly, and drive handsome equipages. Many of these shameful creatures are the daughters of stablemen and rough riders in the country and elsewhere; and are dexterous enough in using the whips, which, in the old Bridewell days, would have been laid about their own shoulders . . . Their principal pre-occupation is to interchange salutes with Lord Dundreary, and to stare modest women out of countenance. This is "Anonyma". She has neither wit nor sense, nor manners nor morals; but she has plenty of fine clothes and sparkling jewels, and a pretty body which she sells to the highest bidder . . . This is the ingenious creature whom *The Times* is endeavouring, under a preposterous alias, to convert into a heroine. Is *The Times* newspaper powerful enough to persuade its readers that any good can accrue from petting and patting on the back, and simpering over the splendid shame of these impudent wenches? We think not . . . For "Anonyma" in her pony carriage we have not one grain of pity or sympathy. She is a worthless and shameful jade, and it is a scandal to have to mention her.'[1]

THERE was scarcely an important demi-mondaine who did not claim an acquaintance with the Prince of Wales. Tales of Bertie's frivolities reached Queen Victoria, and she put them down to the bad example set by his aristocratic friends. As early as 1864 she was writing him

[1] *Daily Telegraph:* July 4, 1862.

stinging letters comparing the Higher Classes to the French aristocracy on the eve of the Revolution. Bertie answered her solemnly, 'With regard to what you say concerning the Aristocracy or "upper Ten Thousand", I quite agree that in many instances amusement and self-indulgence, etc., predominate, but it is hard to say that all are so. I know of so many instances where those of the highest rank are excellent country gentlemen—are Chairmen of Quarter Sessions, Magistrates, etc., and the ladies attend to their duties also. In every country a great proportion of the Aristocracy will be idle and fond of amusement and have always been so, but I think in no country more than ours do the Higher Classes occupy themselves, which is certainly not much the case in other countries. We have always been an Aristocratic Country, and I hope we shall always remain so, as they are the mainstay of this country, unless we become so Americanised that they are swept away, and then the state of things will be quite according to Mr. Bright's views, who wishes only for the Sovereign and the People, and no class between.'[1]

In spite of the Prince's arguments, there was much to be said on Queen Victoria's side. Her dislike of the pleasure-loving aristocracy was not entirely due to priggishness. The sixties abounded in scandals, and many of them involved litigation which brought them into the courts. As a result they were printed in all the newspapers. The majority concerned some combination of nobleman and prostitute. Making allowances for the fact that it was considered right and proper for a young aristocrat to patronise the demi-monde until he had acquired the necessary sophistication to make a good husband, there seems to have been an epidemic of *nostalgie de la boue*. If you turn the pages of *The Times*

[1] *King Edward VII:* Sir Sidney Lee.

during the sixties, you learn that the nephew and heir of the Earl of Wicklow died in a brothel, and that his notorious wife tried to pass off an adopted child as his next of kin; that Lord Willoughby d'Eresby, Joint Hereditary Grand Chamberlain of England, fleeced his French mistress of thousands of pounds, then ran off with her maid; that Lord Euston, the son and heir of the Duke of Grafton, made a disastrous marriage with a woman of low repute, then thought he was free when he discovered she was a bigamist, but sadly learned he was legally married when he found that her first husband had also been a bigamist.

These lurid tangles were relieved by the more orthodox scandals of eldest sons who dissipated or gambled away their fortunes. One of the greatest sensations involved two of the Prince's closest friends, the Marquis of Hastings and Mr. Henry Chaplin, who later became Viscount Chaplin. Chaplin was one of the most popular young men of the day, and stood out, even in those luxury-loving times, as an arbiter of the comfortable life. He had met the Prince of Wales at Oxford, on the rare occasions when the latter was allowed to hunt with the South Oxfordshire pack. While still an undergraduate, Chaplin had inherited a large estate, Blankney, and a fortune to go with it.

But unlike his ancestors, who played their parts as conscientious squires, Harry was attracted by the more sophisticated pleasures of Mayfair and the Turf. Everything he did was done on a grand scale. He was known as a 'magnifico'. He adored food and whenever a dish particularly pleased him, he put a gold sovereign on the plate for the cook. He entertained enormous parties at Blankney. He had his own coach and four, and he thoughtfully kept two packs of hounds so that his friends could hunt six days a week. He casually purchased a deer forest in Scotland for occasional sport, and, like the

Marquis of Hastings, started a racing stud and paid unheard-of prices for horses. He bought two three-year-olds for eleven thousand guineas. 'He never dreamed of stinting himself of any pleasure which money could procure,' wrote E. F. Benson, 'and his purse was equally wide-mouthed for the entertainment of those with similar tastes.'[1]

When Chaplin was twenty-four he became engaged to Lord Anglesey's daughter, Lady Florence Paget, who was known as 'the Pocket Venus' of the day. The date for the wedding was fixed, presents were flowing in, and Blankney was waiting for the arrival of the bride.

But Lady Florence was not reliable. One day Chaplin took her to Marshall and Snelgrove's to do a little shopping. She disappeared out of the back entrance, where Lord Hastings was waiting for her with a marriage licence, and eloped with him.

This was dramatic enough, but the climax of the story was even more sensational. Chaplin and Hastings both had racing stables, and were in keen competition. Although Chaplin recovered from his chagrin, and with remarkable generosity refused to bear ill-will to either Hastings or Lady Florence, the wild young Marquis seemed determined to triumph over Harry on the track as well as at the altar. Chaplin had entered his horse Hermit for the Derby of 1867. A fortnight before the race was to be run Hermit was given 'a Derby trial' at Newmarket and developed a hæmorrhage that was thought to come from the lungs. No one believed he would be able to run, but Chaplin refused to scratch him. A week later, it became apparent that the hæmorrhage was from a blood vessel, and there was nothing seriously wrong with the horse after all. Nevertheless the news of his mishap had become widely known and when Hermit lined up at Epsom the odds against him were

[1] *As We Were:* E. F. Benson.

66 to 1. Chaplin backed him heavily, while Lord Hastings, on a strange, almost psychopathic impulse, staked a fortune against him.

The Prince of Wales was entertaining a great many friends in the royal box, of whom Chaplin was one. It was a bitterly cold day with snow and sleet. Onlookers wrapped themselves in furs and blankets. Hermit's coat had not been cut and he caused a good deal of derision as people watched him in the paddock. However, in one of the most exciting races on record, Hermit won by a neck and brought Harry Chaplin £140,000. £80,000 of this huge sum was due from Hastings, who altogether lost £120,000 on the race, and was finally a ruined man.

He died bankrupt the following year. *The Times* wrote a stinging obituary pointing out that 'when a Peer of high rank drags his dignity in the dirt, he stains not only his own honour but that of his Order. . . .'[1] Chaplin lived till well over seventy and served for many years as a Member of Parliament. He married the Duke of Sutherland's daughter and was extremely happy. But he, too, squandered his fortune. Finally he was obliged to sell Blankney; and although he remained a connoisseur of food and wine, and the Sutherlands put more than one roof over his head, he was no longer able to parade as a magnifico.

Queen Victoria read these shocking stories in *The Times*, and they confirmed her own horror of gambling which she had communicated so often to her son. She was anxious about the amount of time he was spending on the Turf and she disapproved of his fast, racing friends. 'DEAREST BERTIE,' she wrote him. 'Now that the Ascot Races are approaching, I wish to *repeat earnestly and seriously*, and with reference to my letters this spring, that I trust you will . . . as my Uncle William IV and Aunt, and we ourselves did, *confine* your *visits* to the

[1] *The Times*, November 11, 1868.

Races, to the *two* days *Tuesday* and *Thursday* and not go on *Wednesday* and *Friday*, to which William IV never went, nor did we . . . Your example can do *much* for good and can do a great deal for evil . . . I hear every true and attached friend of ours expressing *such anxiety* that you should gather round you the really good, steady, and distinguished people . . .'[1]

The Prince must have had a sudden burst of self-confidence, for on this rare occasion he discarded the over-polite tone he usually adopted to his mother, and wrote a rather tart reply. 'I fear, dear Mama, that no year goes round without your giving me a jobation on the subject of racing . . . The Tuesday and Thursday at Ascot have always been looked upon as the great days, as there is the Procession in your carriages up the course, which pleases the public and is looked upon by them as a kind of annual pageant. The other days are, of course, of minor importance, but when you have guests staying in your house they naturally like going on those days also, and it would I think look both odd and uncivil if I remained at home, and would excite comment if I suddenly deviated from the course which I have hitherto adopted. . . .

'I am always most anxious to meet your wishes, dear Mama, in every respect, and I always regret if we are not quite *d'accord*—but as I am past twenty-eight and have some considerable knowledge of the world and society, you will, I am sure, at least I trust, allow me to use my own discretion in matters of this kind . . .'[1]

BERTIE did not confine his gaieties merely to England. Every year he went to Paris on a spree, accompanied

[1] *The Letters of Queen Victoria.*

only by an equerry, which gave rise to plenty of fresh gossip concerning his weakness for women. There were stories of orgies. People whispered that in his private dining room at the Café Anglais, the demi-mondaine, Cora Pearl, had been served up on a huge, silver platter. And everyone knew that he was intoxicated by the beautiful actress, Mlle Schneider, who was playing the leading role in *The Grand Duchess of Gerolstein.* Night after night he visited her dressing room.

But although Bertie's infatuations were intense, they were never long-lived. Too many pretty women were eager to please him, to keep his attention on one. With a group of friends from the Jockey Club he liked to roam Paris paying unexpected calls back-stage. 'With wavy whiskers and curly hair, square monocles set in the eye, towering stove-pipe hats on their heads, the fast young men of the day drifted along the passages to knock at the little iron door which gave access to the wings of the stage.'[1]

Most of these young men were friends of Sarah Bernhardt, who at the time was playing in Sardou's *Fedora.* During one scene the actress had to weep by the bedside of a murdered prince. A number of Parisians amused themselves by playing for one night this mute and invisible part, and the Prince delighted French society by taking his turn at filling the role.

He allowed nothing to spoil his evening's amusement. Once when he was just setting out for the theatre he received a message that a distant but royal relative had died. His friends wondered whether the evening was ruined. 'What shall we do?' they asked him. 'Put on black studs and go to the play,' he replied.

In England weekly journals like *The Tomahawk,* denounced as scurrilous but widely read by the smart set, were now commenting freely on his private life. In the late sixties a series of devastating cartoons made

[1] *King Edward and His Times:* André Maurois.

their appearance. One, just before the Prince had left for Egypt on an official tour, showed Miss Britannia, as an abandoned *houri*, weeping and tugging at his coat tails while he was walking toward Miss Egypt, who was welcoming him with a very seductive look. Another showed Bertie moving toward the ghost of the Prince Regent while his level-headed Comptroller, Sir William Knollys, in the role of Horatio, tried vainly to hold him back. Underneath were the words: 'I'll follow thee.' A third, and perhaps the most devastating of all, depicted a young lady rouging before her looking-glass. On her dressing table was an invitation to Buckingham Palace and on her bed the Prince of Wales' cigarette case. The caption read: 'She Stoops to Conquer.'

Rumours of the Prince's dissipations did not escape Queen Victoria's ears, and she was growing increasingly angry and disturbed. In 1870 it suddenly seemed as if her worst fears might materialise, for it looked as though Bertie had landed himself in serious trouble. Sir Charles Mordaunt filed a petition for divorce against his twenty-one-year-old wife, Harriett, naming as co-respondents two of the Prince's friends, Viscount Cole and Sir Frederick Johnstone, and 'others'. The 'others' were believed to include the Prince himself, for it was known that Lady Mordaunt had mentioned him in her confession to her husband. Sir Charles' counsel subpoenaed him as a witness and his own lawyers advised him that his only hope of clearing his name was to answer the summons. No Prince of Wales had ever entered the witness box before.

The case opened in February 1870. From the very start it was a labyrinth of complications. Most of Sir Charles' evidence came from the hysterical declarations of Lady Mordaunt who, distraught by the fact that her first child was threatened with blindness, called her husband to her and said: 'Charlie, I have deceived you; you are not the father of that child.' Sir Charles said nothing. 'I believed,' he said, 'it was an observation made on account of some illness consequent on confinement . . . On the 8th the nurse sent for me again. I waited for my wife to begin the conversation. She appeared distressed but composed. She said, "Charlie, you are not the father of that child; Lord Cole is the father of it, and I am the cause of its blindness". She was silent for a quarter of an hour, then burst into tears and said, "Charlie, I have been very wicked; I have done very wrong". I said, "Who with?" She said, "With Lord Cole, Sir Frederick Johnstone, the Prince of Wales and others, often, and in open day." '[1]

The various nurses who had attended Lady Mordaunt during her confinement, and even the vicar's wife who had come to see her, took the stand, and declared that she had made the same confession to them. Then, Sir Charles claimed, he had looked through his wife's desk and found hotel bills that incriminated Lord Cole and Sir Frederick Johnstone, and he had also come across a series of letters from the Prince of Wales and a Valentine.

But before the truth of any of Sir Charles' accusations could be established, it had to be decided whether or not Lady Mordaunt was in her right mind. Her father, Sir Thomas Moncreiffe, had filed a counter-petition declaring that she was hopelessly insane and had been so ever since the birth of the child.

A number of doctors took the stand and swore that she had lost her mind and was suffering from 'puerperal mania'. Their evidence was so overwhelming that even Sir Charles Mordaunt's counsel, Mr. Sergeant Ballantine, threw up the sponge on this particular point. But was she insane, Ballantine asked, when the divorce petition was served on her a few weeks after she had made her revelations to her husband? He claimed that she was in

[1] *The Times*, February 19, 1870.

sound mind when her child was born, and her indiscretions were not an hallucination.

So although the divorce petition could not be considered until the question of Lady Mordaunt's sanity was cleared up, witnesses were brought forward to try and prove that she had spoken truthfully in her outburst to her husband. Among them was a hotel manager, a ladies' maid, a butler, a footman and a housekeeper. They stated that when Lady Mordaunt had stayed by herself in an hotel in London Sir Frederick Johnstone frequently came to dinner and stayed very late; that Lord Cole had been a constant visitor at her house in the country when her husband was away, and once had taken a train trip with Lady Mordaunt in a private carriage.

But what about the Prince of Wales? The ladies' maid took the stand first. 'Sir Charles,' she said, 'usually went out in the afternoon to his Parliamentary duties. The Prince of Wales called two or three times in 1867 at that time of day, and in 1868 more frequently. In 1868 he usually came about four in the afternoon, and stayed from one to one and a half or two hours. Her Ladyship was always at home and saw him. No one was in the drawing room at the time. The Prince did not come in his private carriage. I do not remember that Sir Charles was ever at home[1] when the Prince called in 1868.'[2]

Then the butler took the stand. 'In 1867 and 1868 the Prince of Wales called at Sir Charles' London house—in 1868 about once a week but one week twice. He came about four p.m. and stayed one to two hours. I received him. Sir Charles was in the House of Commons or out pigeon shooting. Lady Mordaunt gave me directions that when the Prince called no one was to be admitted.'[2]

[1] It was established that Sir Charles had been at home on one occasion when the Prince called.

[2] *The Times*, February 21, 1870.

Sir Charles Mordaunt painted the picture of the Prince as darkly as he could. He told the court: 'I was aware that the Prince of Wales had an acquaintance with my wife. I had spoken to his Royal Highness, but was never intimate with him. I was aware that he was on visiting terms with her family. He never came to the house at my invitation. I warned my wife against continuing the acquaintance with his Royal Highness for reasons which governed my own mind. I told her I had heard in various quarters certain circumstances connected with the Prince's character which caused me to make that remark. I did not enter into particulars. At that time I had seen the Prince once at my house . . . I was not aware till after my wife's confinement that the Prince had been a constant visitor at my house, nor that any correspondence existed between them . . .'[1]

What about this correspondence? How damaging was it? London was buzzing with gossip; then a provincial paper printed the letters in full, and *The Times* reprinted them the next day. A sigh of relief went up from the friends of the monarchy. The correspondence, in the words of *The Times*, consisted of 'simple, gossiping, everyday letters'. Certainly in context they were innocent enough; the only suspicion lay in the fact that they were written at all. Here is one of them. 'Dear Lady Mordaunt. I am sorry to find by the letter that I received from you this morning that you are unwell, and that I shall not be able to pay you a visit today, to which I had been looking forward with so much pleasure. Tomorrow and Saturday I shall be hunting in Nottinghamshire; but if you are still in town, may I come to see you about 5 on Sunday afternoon? And hoping you will be yourself again, Believe me, Yours ever sincerely, Albert Edward.'

Then the Prince of Wales entered the box for question

[1] *The Times*, February 19, 1870.

ing. But not by Sir Charles' counsel; by his own counsel in order to clear any lingering aspersions against his name.

I believe your Royal Highness has for some time been acquainted with the Moncreiffe family—I have.

Were you acquainted with Lady Mordaunt before her marriage?—I was.

On her marriage did your Royal Highness write to her and make her some wedding presents?—I did.

Previous to her marriage had she visited at Marlborough House when your Royal Highness and the Princess of Wales were there?—She had.

And has she gone to the theatre with both your Royal Highnesses?—She has.

We are told that she was married at the end of 1866. In 1867 did you see much of her?—I did.

And in the year 1868?—I did also.

Were you acquainted with Sir Charles Mordaunt?—I was.

Have you frequently met him?—I have.

With Lady Mordaunt?—With Lady Mordaunt.

Your Royal Highness knows Hurlingham?—I do.

Have you been in the habit of meeting Sir Charles there?—I have.

On one occasion, I think in June, 1868, there was a pigeon match there between Warwickshire and Norfolk?—There was.

I believe your Royal Highness and Sir Charles were captains of each county?—I believe so.

Was Lady Mordaunt there?—She was.

With her husband?—With her husband.

Does your Royal Highness remember the date?—I think it was about June.

Did Lady Mordaunt score for one side?—For both sides I think.

And in the course of that match did you speak to Lady

Mordaunt at times when Sir Charles was by?—I believe so.

We have heard in the course of this case that your Royal Highness uses hansom cabs occasionally. I do not know whether it is so?—It is so.

I have only one more question to trouble your Royal Highness with. Has there ever been any improper familiarity or criminal act between yourself and Lady Mordaunt?—There has not.

The Times reported that 'there was a burst of applause which was at once repressed. Mr. Sergeant Ballantine said he had "no question to ask his Royal Highness".' The Prince, said *The Times*, 'then bowed to His Lordship and retired, amid another attempt at applause, which was as before, promptly repressed'.[1]

As far as the Prince was concerned, the unpleasant episode was now closed. Sir Charles Mordaunt's petition for divorce was dismissed on the grounds of his wife's insanity, and he did not secure a divorce until five years later, when he successfully named Lord Cole as co-respondent.

After his appearance in the witness box, Bertie wrote his mother: 'I trust that by what I have said today the public at large will be satisfied that the gross imputations which have been so wantonly cast upon me are now cleared out.' Congratulations poured in, and Mr. Gladstone commented on the Prince's 'frank and firm demeanour' in court. Even Queen Victoria seemed satisfied. But the public was more exacting. It appeared to echo the disapproval expressed in *Reynolds' Newspaper* which regretted that His Royal Highness had not been put to a severe cross-examination. Why, asked *Reynolds*, should a young married man be so eager to pay weekly visits to a young married woman when her husband was absent if it was all so innocent?

[1] *The Times*, February 23, 1870.

The Times ran a leader adjuring the Prince to walk in his father's footsteps and to avoid even a semblance of levity; and on Ludgate Hill hawkers sold penny pamphlets entitled *The Infidelities of a Prince*, bearing the Prince of Wales' feathers on the cover—inside were extracts from Parliamentary papers dealing with George IV.

Alexandra stood loyally by her husband, but people noticed that she was lacking her usual buoyant spirits. The night the trial ended she accompanied him to dinner with the Prime Minister and Mrs. Gladstone, an engagement which had been fixed many weeks in advance. One of the guests, Lady Frederick Cavendish, wrote in her diary, 'The dinner and evening went off very well; the Princess looked lovely, but *very* sad when she was not exerting herself.'[1]

The Prince tried to resume his life with his usual sangfroid. But the warm, safe, admiring atmosphere which prompted thousands of loyal subjects to sing 'God Bless the Prince of Wales' had altered. At the theatre he was hissed, and when he visited the racecourse he was booed. A hostile wind was blowing.

[1] *The Diary of Lady Frederick Cavendish.*

CHAPTER FIVE

THE REPUBLICAN MOVEMENT

THE Monarchy was in trouble and it was not all Bertie's fault. If the Prince was criticised for staying at home too little, the Queen was even more strongly criticised for staying at home too much. Ever since Albert's death she had lived in seclusion. The public had waited patiently for the period of mourning to pass, but as the years rolled on Victoria showed no sign of abandoning her sorrow. At Windsor the Prince Consort's rooms were kept exactly as he had left them, and every night his clothes were laid out and his basin filled with water, as though he were still alive. The Queen's note-paper carried the black band of grief, and people dropped their voices in her presence. The glitter of royal life was utterly repugnant to her, and she refused flatly to don her robes of State and to take any part in the pageantry of the Throne. Her black bonnet had become a permanent fixture.

She avoided London whenever possible and alternated between Osborne, Windsor and Balmoral. And since Balmoral was the most remote, it became increasingly attractive to her until she was spending six months of the year there. It was hideously uncomfortable. The Queen hated fires, and the granite walls and Gothic windows added their own bitterness to the damp cold. The rooms were furnished with tartan curtains and chair covers, and some even had tartan linoleum on the floor and more tartan on the walls, all of which had been designed by the Prince Consort. When the Queen's

Private Secretary, Sir Henry Ponsonby, asked Lady Dalhousie if she thought the house pretty she replied: 'A frank question requires a frank answer and I will tell you I never saw anything more uncomfortable or that I coveted less.'[1] Sir Henry also noted in his diary that 'Lady Mandeville, who called later, blue with cold, was equally sour in her remarks on our Highland Palace.' This was no surprise to the long-suffering Ponsonby, who himself remarked: 'Every private house strikes me as so comfortable after the severe dreariness of our palatial rooms here.'[1]

The atmosphere was scarcely less chilling than the temperature. Although the Queen was sometimes unseen for days at a time, except by her servants and Ladies-in-waiting, her presence was felt by everyone down to the most remote regions of the Castle. She communicated with her household by the written word, and all day long messengers were scurrying through the draughty passages carrying her instructions. Everything was controlled and regulated to the smallest detail. 'Anyone who thought that life at Balmoral meant a relaxation from Court etiquette, where an easy-going informality might be enjoyed, made a great mistake,' wrote Sir Henry. 'The date of the arrival and departure of each member of the household was decided by her. The four dinners [the Queen's, the Household, the upper servants, the lower servants] were supervised by her. The Equerry was not allowed to give orders to the stables or to the Highlanders. The Maid of Honour was not allowed to go out with the gentlemen without a chaperone. The room in which the Household might sit after dinner was fixed by her. The eighteen ponies were strictly divided into five categories, each one apportioned to particular people. Anyone not fitting into one of the categories had to ask for special permission . . .'[1]

[1] *Henry Ponsonby: His Life from His Letters:* Arthur Ponsonby.

At the Queen's table, politics were absolutely taboo, and sometimes meals were passed in silence save for an occasional murmur or a cough or the clatter of the plates removed by the servants. 'Cabinet Ministers tried to find excuses,' continues Ponsonby. 'Lord Hartington pleaded a party for Newmarket and the Queen was annoyed that he should think that more amusing than coming to Balmoral. Lord Carlingford said he felt his return to waiting like a prisoner getting back into his cell again. Lord John Manners declared: "Yes, this is a very curious place and more curious things go on here than I should have dreamt of." And Lord Salisbury unlike some other ministers did not "attempt to conceal his disgust with the place" and was "heartily glad" when the time came for him to get away. Campbell-Bannerman in a letter to his wife wrote: "It is the funniest life conceivable: like a convent. We meet at meals and when we are finished, each is off to his cell." '[1]

The Queen's two alternating Prime Ministers were compelled to make regular visits to Balmoral and complained bitterly behind her back. 'Carrying on the government of a country six hundred miles from the Metropolis doubles the Labour,' wrote Disraeli; and Gladstone told Lord Rosebery, 'The Queen alone is enough to kill any man.'

If Victoria noticed disgruntled expressions she ignored them. At Balmoral she felt closer to Albert than anywhere else. She liked the freedom of the rough Highland countryside, and she liked the companionship of her strange, uncouth servant, John Brown.

The Queen's relationship with John Brown caused wide-spread gossip, yet the bond was obvious. Brown had been employed by Albert as a ghillie when Balmoral had been rebuilt in 1855. The royal couple were amused by his *farouche* look, and his blunt, coarse manners which

[1] *Henry Ponsonby: His Life from His Letters:* Arthur Ponsonby.

seemed to indicate a disarming sincerity. When Victoria found herself a widow she declared herself utterly cut off since she felt she was unable to treat her courtiers as equals, and the idea of allowing her children to become more intimate horrified her. Only with the rough, outspoken John Brown did she feel completely at ease. Soon he had become her inseparable companion, and soon he was taking liberties that no one else had ever dared to take with the Queen. He bullied her, and commented on her clothes; he took charge of all the sport and fishing and made sure that he had the best; he was disobliging to the royal children, uttered caustic comments on anything that came into his head, and delivered rude messages to the most august personages in the land. And Victoria was delighted with him. Her sons and daughters detested Brown, and so did most of the courtiers but everyone was careful not to run foul of him, because the Queen always took his side. Even the fact that Brown was addicted to the whisky bottle did not upset her. Once when a Maid of Honour saw a picnic basket being put into the Queen's carriage she asked if it was tea. 'Weel, no,' said Brown, 'she don't much like tea. We take oot biscuits and sperruts.'[1] On another occasion when the Queen was going out for a drive she sat waiting in her carriage for Brown to take his place on the box. Ponsonby went up to the ghillie's room and found him lying on the bed, drunk. Ponsonby returned and without a word to the Queen himself mounted the box. She made no comment.

So great was John Brown's hold over the Queen that Disraeli was always careful to send his regards to 'Mr. Brown'. Less wise was General Sir John McNeill, who asked Brown to wait outside the room after the latter had delivered a message, instead of offering him a chair. The next day Sir John received a message from the Queen

[1] *Henry Ponsonby: His Life from His Letters:* Arthur Ponsonby.

suggesting that he leave the Household and take an obscure command in India. It required much tact on the part of Sir Henry Ponsonby to put the matter right. On another occasion General Sir Lyndoch Gardiner, who somehow had got in Brown's bad graces, enquired after the Queen's health. 'The Queen's very well,' replied the ghillie. 'It was only the other day that she said to me, "There's that dommed old fool General Gardiner coming into waiting and I know he'll be putting his bloody nose into everything that doesn't concern him." '[1] The sequel to this story is unknown.

Apart from her afternoon drives, one of the Queen's few recreations was the annual ghillies' ball, organised by John Brown. At these affairs, where much whisky was consumed and the room rang with shouts and laughter, the Queen was very fond of dancing reels. The ball became such an important event she refused to leave Balmoral before it had taken place, no matter how pressing the affairs of state.

It is not surprising that the newspapers and magazines were growing critical. 'We humbly submit,' said *The Tomahawk* sarcastically, 'that it cannot be a very much greater exertion to entertain persons of your Majesty's own rank, than to preside at balls and other amusements of Scotch ghillies and their families.'[2] But Victoria insisted that it was. She explained to her secretary that at ghillies' balls she was not required to make conversation which she would certainly have to do among people of her 'own rank'.

Whispers about John Brown grew more pernicious. There were even rumours that the Queen had married him secretly, and a scurrilous pamphlet was published entitled *Mrs. John Brown.* In August 1867 *The Tomahawk* printed a cartoon showing John Brown leaning non-

[1] *Recollections of Three Reigns:* Sir Frederick Ponsonby.
[2] *The Tomahawk,* June 8, 1867.

chalantly against the throne, and entitled 'A Brown Study'.

Victoria paid no attention to these stories. It simply confirmed her opinion of the wickedness of the aristocracy. She wrote to Lord Charles Fitzroy that the malicious talk was '*merely* the result of *ill-natured* gossip in the higher classes' because of a natural love of 'ill-natured finding fault'.[1]

THE Queen's advisers were anxious, not so much because of John Brown, as the fact that the Queen flatly refused to emerge from her seclusion and lead a 'royal' life. The newspapers were becoming increasingly critical, and in June 1867 *The Tomahawk* came out with a leader that reflected popular sentiment:

'We have waited patiently, in company with many of your faithful subjects, for the time when it should please your Gracious Majesty to throw off the gloom and apathy which were the natural fruit of your great sorrow . . . It would be presumptuous in us to point out to Your Majesty that there should be a limit to the period during which those of us in this world, who have important duties to perform, can afford to indulge in lethargic grief for those, however dear to us, whom Death may have called away . . . We humbly submit that there may be as much selfishness in a prolonged indulgence in sorrow, as there is in levity or thoughtless hilarity . . . We would urge on your majesty that those who enjoy the power which belongs to a high position in the State have no right to neglect the duties and responsibilities attaching thereto . . .'[2]

[1] *Victoria the Widow and Her Son:* Hector Bolitho.
[2] *The Tomahawk*, June 8, 1867.

Picture Post Library

King Edward VII

Queen Victoria
the Prince Cons

Picture Post Library

The Empress Frederick at the time of her marriage, 1858

Picture Post Library

Picture Post Library

'Skittles' (Catherine Walters)

re Post Library

Mrs. Langtry

Sarah Bernhardt

Picture Post Library

Picture Post Library

Baron Stockmar

Picture Post Lib

The 8th Duke of Devonshire

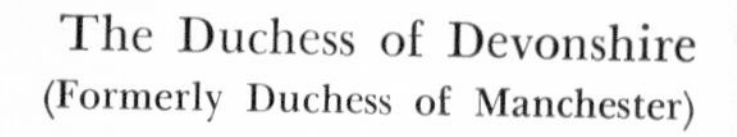

The Duchess of Devonshire
(Formerly Duchess of Manchester)

Picture Post Library

Picture Post Library

Edward and Alexandra, Prince and Princess of Wales, with Queen Victoria on their wedding day, March 10, 1863

Queen Victoria on the Riviera, with John Brown

Picture Post L

The Prince of Wales and other guests at a house party

Picture Post Library

Lord Charles Beresford

Lady Randolph Churchill

Picture Post Library

Picture Post Library

Sir Charles Dilke

Picture Post Library

Lord Randolph Churchill

Picture Post Library

Lord Hardwicke

Picture Post

Mr. Henry Chaplin
(Later Viscount Chaplin)

Sir William
Gordon-Cumming

Picture Post Library

Sir Frederick
Johnstone

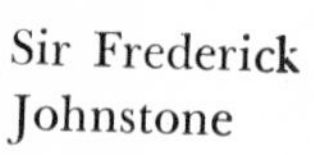

Picture Post Library

Alexandra, Princess of Wales

Picture Post Library

The Prince of Wales in 1876

Picture Post Library

Picture Post Li

The Prince of Wales leading in Persimmon at the Derby, 1896

The Prince of Wales in 1899 w Mr. John Monta and his car

Picture Post Library

From 'Things New and Old' by Max Beerbohm

'The rare, the rather awful visits of Albert Edward, Prince of Wales, to Windsor Castle'

Picture Post Library

Daisy, Princess of Pless

Picture Post Libr

Lady Warwick

Picture Post Library

William II, Emperor of Germany

Picture Post Li

Sir Ernest Cassel

ueen Victoria in 1897

Picture Post Library

King Edward VII and Queen Alexandra

Photographed after their Coronation, August 9, 1902

Picture Post Library

Picture Post Library

Shooting party at Windsor

On the left, the Kaiserin with King Edward and Queen Alexandra; in the background, the Kaiser with the Duke of Connaught

Group of Kings and Queens at Windsor

Left to right: The Queen of Spain, King Edward VII, the Kaiserin, the Kaiser, Queen Alexandra, the Queen of Portugal, the King of Spain, Queen Maud of Norway

Picture Post Library

Picture Post Library

Queen Alexandra

Mrs. Keppel

From a drawing by Ellis Roberts

Picture Post Library

The Czar and Czarina of Russia

Picture Post Library

The Queen was indignant at the tone of the press. Did her subjects not realise that she spent hours at her desk reading cabinet papers, writing memoranda, sending instructions, giving advice, in other words *governing*? As early as 1864 she had impulsively picked up her pen and in her own hand written a letter to *The Times* explaining that a Sovereign had other obligations besides showing herself to her people. 'The Queen heartily appreciates the desire of her subjects to see her,' the letter began, 'and whatever she *can* do to gratify them in this loyal and affectionate wish, she *will* do . . . But there are other and higher duties than those of mere representation which are now thrown upon the Queen, alone and unassisted—duties which she cannot neglect without injury to the public service, which weigh increasingly upon her, overwhelming her with work and anxiety.'[1]

Very occasionally, perhaps once or twice in a decade, the Queen opened Parliament, and she did so with deep resentment. In a letter to Lord Russell she made her attitude abundantly clear. 'The Queen *must say* that she does feel *very bitterly* the want of feeling of those who *ask* the Queen to go to open Parliament. That the public should wish to see her she fully understands, and has *no* wish to prevent—quite the contrary; but why this wish should be if so *unreasonable* and unfeeling a nature, as to *long* to *witness* the spectacle of a poor, broken-hearted widow, nervous and shrinking, dragged in *deep mourning*, ALONE *in* STATE as a *Show*, where she used to go supported by her husband, to be gazed at, without delicacy or feeling, is a thing *she cannot* understand, and she never could wish her bitterest foe to be exposed to! . . . It is hard, when she works and slaves away all day and till late at night, not to be spared at least such trials.'[2]

This is what she wrote in 1866 and what she still felt in 1871. But by 1871 the situation had deteriorated

[1] *The Times*, April 6, 1864. [2] *The Letters of Queen Victoria.*

greatly. The newspapers had dropped their pleading tone and were now openly hostile. They had begun to accuse the Queen of 'hoarding'. The Civil List provided her with a large sum of money to maintain the splendour of the throne, to entertain distinguished visitors, in short to act the part of a monarch, and she was not using it as intended. A pamphlet was published entitled *What Does She Do With It?* And even *Punch* was mischievous. If foreign royalties chose to come to England uninvited, the Queen saw no reason why she should leave Balmoral and entertain them at Buckingham Palace. As a result they stayed at hotels like ordinary tourists and *Punch* sang out derisively:

> '*We don't like to see the crowned heads*
> *That visit us charged for their carriages*
> *Forking out for their dinners and beds*
> *At Mivart's, at the Grosvenor, or Claridge's.*'[1]

Queen Victoria was well aware of the criticisms but she ignored them. Adamantly she refused to change her ways. 'We think she is getting to like to be still more alone,' wrote Sir Henry Ponsonby despairingly, 'and see no one at all, governing the country by means of messages through footmen to us.' 'The Queen will talk,' said Sir Thomas Biddulph, the Keeper of the Privy Purse, 'as if she were Mrs. Jones and might live just where she liked.' 'A meaner cause for the decay of thrones cannot be conceived,' lamented Gladstone, who was growing seriously concerned by the rising tide of unpopularity. 'I don't much care for the papers alone,' wrote Lord Halifax, the Lord Privy Seal, to Ponsonby, 'but one cannot meet anybody who does not tell the same story and one finds from this that the papers do express the common feeling and opinion.

[1] *Punch*, July 29, 1871.

'It matters less what Society thinks in London though even what *they* say does harm, but the mass of the people expect a King or a Queen to look and play the part. They want to see a Crown and a Sceptre and all that sort of thing. They want the gilding for their money. It is not wise to let them think that for all the Queen *apparently to them* does, there is more than paid and that they could so without a sovereign who lives at Osborne and Balmoral as any private lady might do . . .'[1]

THE reason for the increased agitation on the part of the Queen's advisers, was the fact that in 1871 a Republican Movement had begun to take shape. This alarming development had been nourished by events across the Channel. When the Prussians had conquered France in 1870 the Emperor Napoleon III had toppled from his throne and the Third Republic had been established.

England felt the repercussions. The disgruntled eagerly lined up behind the new, exciting banner. The Movement attracted the same paradoxical assortment of idealists and malcontents, of rebels and prigs, of pacifists and revolutionaries, which was to distinguish Britain's left-wing parties for many generations to come. Some of these 'republicans' talked about better working conditions for the poor; some about fewer privileges for the rich; some about the independence of Ireland; others about the immorality of the Prince of Wales; still others about the theoretical advantages of Republicanism.

The Movement was far from unified in its methods of attack, and the public figures who supported it were almost as diverse. There were Sir Charles Dilke, a Liberal

[1] *Henry Ponsonby: His Life from His Letters:* Arthur Ponsonby.

M.P., Joseph Chamberlain, a Radical Birmingham politician, George Odger, leader of the Trade Union Junta and known as 'the communist cobbler'; there was Professor Fawcett, a blind lecturer at Cambridge, Charles Bradlaugh, an atheist and radical, and Swinburne, the poet. Needless to say these warriors did not always see eye to eye. On April 16, 1871 the Government permitted a Republican demonstration in Hyde Park, but on this occasion the extreme wing of the movement had taken control, for the speakers, mostly artisans and shopkeepers with socialist sympathies, spoke contemptuously of their moral liberal-minded colleagues as 'tuppenny lecturers'. *The Times* described the affair as a 'signal failure' with the audience 'making sport of the proceedings from beginning to end'. The crowd, it continued, was made up of three classes, 'the roughs, domestic servants, and the trading classes; but the roughs only manifested a desire to obtain a close acquaintance with the Red Republicans, and they effected their purpose by climbing up trees which they broke in a shameful manner, and where they kept up continuous sport, while the other classes stood for a time afar off . . .'[1]

Nevertheless Republican Clubs were springing up in London, Birmingham, Aberdeen, Cardiff, Plymouth and many other towns. In the House of Commons Dilke attacked the expenditure of the Civil List and 53 M.P.s voted for a reduction in the annual allowance of £15,000 granted to Queen Victoria's youngest son, Prince Arthur.

Sir Charles carried his campaign to the hustings. In a famous speech at Newcastle on November 6 he criticised the organisation of the monarchy declaring that many of the posts connected with it were extravagant, unnecessary and utterly archaic. In the course of

[1] *The Times*, April 7, 1871.

his speech he stated: 'It is said that some day a commonwealth will be our government. Now, history and experience show that you cannot have a republic unless you possess at the same time the republican virtues. But you answer: Have we not public spirit? Have we not the practice of self-government? Are we not gaining general education? Well, if you can show me a fair chance that a republic here will be free from the political corruption that hangs about the monarchy, I say, for my part—and I believe that the middle classes in general will say—let it come.'[1]

This part of the speech caused a furore of indignation. Sir Charles' words were twisted and many newspapers alleged that he was 'threatening to overthrow the monarchy'. Charges of treason were levelled against him on the grounds that he had defied his oath of allegiance as a Member of Parliament. At a meeting at Bolton three weeks later a gang of 'Tory toughs' tried to break up Sir Charles' meeting, and tempers became so violent that a man was killed. Eight of the ringleaders were arrested, but Sergeant Ballantine, the most fashionable Q.C. of the day, made such play with 'Citizen' Dilke's unpopular opinions that the jury felt as loyal men they must acquit the prisoners, and promptly did so.

Queen Victoria never forgave Dilke for his utterances, and in the years to come she consistently did her best to prevent his inclusion in the Government. After all, Sir Charles' father had helped the Prince Consort organise the Great Exhibition of 1851 and had been rewarded with a baronetcy for his labours. Why should his son have republican views? Indeed, the Queen had once met the small boy, Charles, and she recalled to a friend that 'she remembered having stroked his head and supposed she had stroked it the wrong way'.[1]

[1] *The Life of Sir Charles Dilke:* Gwynne and Tuckwell.

BUT the onslaught was not all directed at Victoria. While Charles Dilke attacked the Civil List, Charles Bradlaugh concentrated on the Prince of Wales. This fervent radical, who later became a Member of Parliament and stood out as one of the individualists of the day, had prepared a pamphlet entitled *Impeachment of the House of Brunswick*. In this work he endeavoured to show of what inferior clay the royal family was fashioned and how this had been so for over a hundred years.

At the same time that Dilke was speaking in Newcastle, Bradlaugh was lecturing the Republican Club in London: 'Many of you are aware that I have lately repeatedly declared my most earnest desire that the present Prince of Wales should never dishonour this country by becoming its King. My opinion is that if four or five years of political education are allowed to continue in this land, that worthy representative of an unworthy race will never be King of England. My thorough conviction is that neither his intelligence nor his virtues, nor his political ability, nor his military capacity—great as all these are for a member of his family—can entitle him to occupy the throne of Great Britain. I am equally opposed to his ever being Regent of England. I trust that he may never sit on the throne or lounge under its shadow.'[1]

Like Dilke's speech these remarks raised a tremendous journalistic attack. One paper recommended a pillory and a flogging, and others distorted what he had said, as they had done with Dilke, wildly asserting that he had threatened the safety of the Prince of Wales. Fortescue adopted this line when he declared that Bradlaugh had made 'an impudent and disloyal announcement that he and a certain number of his friends would take care that the Prince would never come to the throne.'

In December an anonymous booklet was printed,

[1] *Charles Bradlaugh:* Hypatia Bradlaugh Bonner.

ridiculing the Prince of Wales and his 'fast' life. It was a parody on Tennyson's *Idylls of the King* which was greatly in vogue at the time, and entitled *The Coming K——*. The Prince was depicted as 'Guelpho the Gay' and when a young man named Sileas asked to become one of his 'Knights of the Dinner-table', Guelpho explained that times had changed since King Arthur's Knights of old.

> *Said Guelpho. 'You must know.*
> *My Knights are of a very different kind*
> *We don't ride forth redressing wrongs; we find*
> *It is enough to dress ourselves, young man.*
> *We don't in damp old chapels vigils keep,*
> *Or ride a-tilt, or put on casques or greaves;*
> *We do not rescue maidens in distress——*
> *Our motives might, you see, be misconstrued*
> *Mine* have *been, once or twice unpleasantly,*
> *I would not that such trouble came again.*
> *And much more careful am I than I was;—*
> *One illness and one witness-box's enough.'*

The young man then asks:

> *'What must I do then to be a knight of thine?'*
> *Then Guelpho bade him sit, and poured him out*
> *A glass of brimming ripe old burgundy,*
> *And said, 'Well, Sileas, I suppose you smoke?'*
> *And Sileas answered, 'Sire, I cannot say*
> *I do, although I own I've tried.' At which*
> *The Prince his head did shake, and murmur low,*
> *'Ah much, I fear me, he has much to learn.'*
> *Then loudly, 'Do you know your way about?'*
> *And Sileas flushed again, and shook his head.*
> *'But,' said he, 'I have bought a guide and map.'*
> *At which rejoinder Guelpho fairly yell'd.*

'By way about,' he said, 'I meant to ask
If you were up to all the tricks of town;
Whether you knew the way to go the pace;
The "O.K." thing, you know.' And Sileas stared,
So blankly that Guelpho yelled again,
And said, 'Methinks that you are rather green.
Say, have you e'er ta'en supper at Cremorne?
You've not? Nor been at all behind the scenes?
Still no? Come, come, young man. You've much to do.
I'll warrant one you're not in debt a bit,
Don't know a pretty horse-breaker nor make
A book upon the races. Sir, you must
Reform; you've time and money, go then forth
And win your spurs; then hie you back to me
When, if you kindly take to our gay life,
I'll dub you of my Dinner Table Knights.'

No one could tell how deep the feeling against the monarchy lay. In those days a Member of Parliament sometimes represented 13,000 electors; sometimes only 1,300. It was impossible to gauge public opinion with any accuracy. However, many eminent men of the day were convinced that Republicanism was only around the corner. Joseph Chamberlain wrote to Dilke: 'At the rate we are moving it will come in our generation. The greater is the necessity for discussing its conditions beforehand, and for a clear recognition of what we may lose as well as what we shall gain.'[1]

Gladstone wrote the Queen and the Prince many grave letters, and Lord Selborne, soon to become Lord Chancellor, told Victoria quite bluntly that if the new Republic of France succeeded, the British public was likely to seek the same goal.

Then came an event which no one could have fore-

[1] *The Life of Sir Charles Dilke:* Gwynne and Tuckwell.

seen. The Prince of Wales contracted typhoid fever and fell dangerously ill at Sandringham. The reports were so alarming that members of the royal family, and even the Queen herself, hastened to his bedside. On the ninth of December many people had given up hope. On the tenth the churches offered special prayers; and on the eleventh the leading article of *The Times* began: 'The Prince still lives, and we may still therefore hope; but the strength of the patient is terribly diminished, and all who watch his bedside, as, indeed, all England watches it—must acknowledge that their minds are heavy with apprehension.'

The altercations between mother and son were temporarily forgotten. Queen Victoria remained resolutely in attendance, but the long anxious hours did not prevent her from adhering to her habit of writing each night in her Journal. She gives us a gruelling account of the crisis, which is also peculiarly revealing, for the Queen's thoughts returned repeatedly to Albert, while the thirty-year-old Bertie, even in the throes of death still remained in pathetic awe of his mother.

'11th December—This has been a terrible day. At half past five I was woke by a message from Sir William Jenner saying dear Bertie had had a very severe spasm, which had alarmed them very much, though it was over now. I had scarcely got the message before Sir William returned saying there had been another. I saw him at once, and he told me the spasm had been so severe, that at any moment dear Bertie might go off, so that I had better come at once. I hurriedly got up, put on my dressing gown, and went to the room, where I found Alix and Alice by the bedside, and Dr. Gull and the two devoted nurses. It was dark, the candles burning, and most dreary. Poor dear Bertie was lying there, breathing heavily, and as if he must choke at any moment. I remained sitting behind a screen . . . After a little while he seemed easier, so the doctors advised us to go away, and I went back to my room, breakfasted, and dressed . . .'

'13th December—This really has been the worst day of all, and coming as it has so close to the sad 14th,[1] filled us, and, I believe, the whole country with anxious forebodings and the greatest alarm . . . Returned to Bertie's room, and, whilst there, he had a most frightful fit of coughing, which seemed at one moment to threaten his life! Only Alix and one of the nurses were there, and the doctors were at once hastily summoned. But the dreadful moment had passed. Poor dear Alix was in the greatest alarm and despair, and I supported her as best I could. Alice and I said to one another in tears "There can be no hope." I hardly left the room, as I was so terribly anxious, and wanted to be of any little use I could. I went up to the bed and took hold of his poor hand, kissing it and stroking his arm. He turned round and looked wildly at me saying, "Who are you?" and then, "It's Mama." "Dear child," I replied. Later he said, "It is so kind of you to come," which shows he knew me, which was most comforting to me. I sat next to the bed holding his hand, as he seemed dozing. Then once more he said, "It's so kind of you to come," and "Don't sit here for me." Dr. Gull and Sir William Jenner were so thankful for this, as was I. I left again when Alix and Alice came in, who had been resting a little.

'When I returned I found dear Bertie breathing heavily and with great difficulty. Another symptom which frightened me dreadfully, was his clutching at his bed-clothes and seeming to feel for things which were not there. The gasping between each word was most distressing. We were getting nearer and nearer to the 14th, and it seemed more and more like ten years ago, and yet it was very different too . . .'[2]

[1] This was the anniversary of the Prince Consort's death.

[2] *The Letters of Queen Victoria.*

But the fatal fourteenth, which for ten years the Queen had observed in the deepest gloom, proved this time to be a day of thanksgiving. The crisis passed and there was a spontaneous outburst of joy from one end of the country to the other. The show of feeling was so sudden and so startling in its intensity that even the Government was taken aback. Republicanism seemed to have been swept away overnight, with the monarchy emerging stronger than ever. In response to the public emotion, Mr. Gladstone felt that a special service should be held at St. Paul's, with the Queen and her son riding in open procession.

Victoria, of course, protested. She said she did not believe in making religion 'a vehicle' for a public demonstration. But here the Princess of Wales firmly stepped in. 'I quite understand your feelings,' she wrote to her mother-in-law, 'but . . . the whole nation has taken such a public share in our sorrow, it has been so entirely one with us in our grief, that it may perhaps feel it has a kind of claim to join us now in a public and universal thanks-giving.'[1]

The service took place and the Queen and the Prince rode together in a carriage through the streets of London, receiving a great ovation all the way. The Poet Laureate, Tennyson, obliged with an appropriately sentimental verse:

Bear witness, that rememberable day
When, pale as yet, and fever-worn, the Prince
Who scarce had plucked his flickering life again
From halfway down the shadow of the grave,
Past with thee thro' thy people and their love,
And London rolled one tide of joy through all
Her trebled millions . . .

[1] *King Edward VII:* Sir Sidney Lee.

The monarchists were delighted at the turn of events. Lord Henry Lennox, a leading member of the Conservative Party, wrote to Disraeli: 'What a sell for Dilke this illness has been.' And the Duke of Cambridge wrote to his mother: 'The Republicans say their chances are up—thank God for this! Heaven has sent this dispensation to save us.'

The Duke was not far wrong. The Republican movement struggled on for another two years, then petered out.

CHAPTER SIX

GERMANY

LIKE many other great ladies of the day, Princess Alexandra looked upon her husband's indiscretions as proof of his abounding manhood. She did not ask questions or make scenes when he disappeared from a ball and failed to turn up until the small hours of the morning; and she took it for granted that he would not be at home from *cinq à sept*. This was a feat of discipline, for she loved him, and in his fashion he loved her too.

He was tremendously proud of her beauty. He liked to watch the heads turn in genuine admiration when she entered a room and he often referred to her as 'the prettiest lady in London'. But Alexandra's social activities were curtailed in the sixties by incessant child-bearing. During the six years from 1864 to 1870 she gave birth to five children. She was very motherly and spent a good deal of time in the nursery. This room was directly over her own wing and she had a hole cut in the ceiling of her bedroom so that a sleeping infant could be lowered on a tray for a rapturous glance without awakening it.

Alexandra was not in the least clever. She had a simple, almost childish mind. She did not understand politics and had very little taste for either literature or art. Like many of her contemporaries she revelled in practical jokes, and she loved dancing. But her great point was her kind and affectionate nature. She was so gentle and uncomplicated that even Queen Victoria could find nothing to criticise, and always referred to her as 'dear, sweet Alix'. This goodness was a powerful weapon.

Her tears were sufficient to influence profoundly Bertie's political outlook; and Bertie's outlook was destined to help shape the forces which reached their fearful climax in the 1914 war.

Eight months after Alexandra became the Princess of Wales her father ascended the throne of Denmark. A few weeks later the Prussians handed him an ultimatum demanding the surrender of the Schleswig-Holstein duchies. The new King refused to capitulate and Prussia, aided by Austria, launched its long-expected attack on Denmark. Despite Queen Victoria's warnings Alexandra found it impossible to hide her feelings. She was so distraught she could neither sleep nor eat, and Bertie, in outraged sympathy, lost his head. He told everyone he met exactly what he thought of the Prussians. He urged excitedly that England should send its fleet to the Baltic, arguing that this gesture would frighten the Prussians into a peaceful settlement.

Bertie was not alone in his sentiments. There was a wave of sympathy throughout the country for 'little Denmark'. The Queen's subjects remembered the thousands of Danish flags that had fluttered in the breeze when Alexandra had arrived to become a member of the British royal family, and they regarded the assault on Denmark almost as an attack on themselves. Even Lord Palmerston, the Prime Minister, and Lord Russell, the Foreign Secretary, declared themselves outraged, and loudly denounced the 'brutal attacks'. But much to Bertie's disgust they did nothing, and contented themselves with abusive words. 'This horrible war will be a stain for ever on Prussian history,' Bertie wrote to Mrs. Bruce, on February 17, 'and I think it is *very* wrong of our government not to have interfered before now. As to Lord Russell's everlasting Notes nobody cares two pence about them on the continent, and the Foreign Ministers to whom they are addressed probably only light their cigars with them.'[1] Three months later, on May 5, he wrote in the same vein to Lord Spencer, his Groom of the Stole, 'I always say that if we had sent our Fleet to the Baltic at the beginning, all this bloodshed might possibly have been avoided, and we should cut a much better figure in Europe than we do.'[1]

NEEDLESS to say Queen Victoria was angered and annoyed by her eldest son's partisanship. She had no intention of allowing Britain to be drawn into the Prussian-Danish war, and spent long hours at her desk composing stern notes to her ministers, reminding them repeatedly that British interests were not involved, and they must not plunge England into a fracas that was not her concern. The Queen, of course, was pro-Prussian. She still clung to Albert's dream of an English-Prussian Europe; besides, she felt that Alexandra's father had behaved foolishly, and that there was a lot to be said for Prussia's demands. She could understand Alexandra's loyalty to her father, and Bertie's sympathy for his unhappy bride. On the other hand, what about Bertie's sympathy for his eldest sister, dear, darling Vicky, the Crown Princess of Prussia, whose husband was leading his troops at the front? In a letter to Lord Clarendon the iron-willed Queen observed critically that it 'is fearfully dangerous for the heir to the throne to take up one side violently', and added with astonishing coldness that he was 'bound by so many ties of blood to Germany, and only quite lately, by marriage, to Denmark.'[2]

Uncle Leopold did not help to ease matters between mother and son. He insisted on dotting the i's and cross-

[1] *King Edward VII:* Sir Sidney Lee.

[2] *The Letters of Queen Victoria.*

ing the t's. 'I cannot help saying a few words about Bertie and Alix,' he wrote to Victoria. 'You will recollect when first Albert spoke to me about Alix that he said, We take the Princess but *not* her relations. That might have remained as he wished for years, without the death of our cousin of Denmark. That of a sudden gave us a *Danish* Princess, and the consequences of a Constitution which even the late King had *not* sanctioned. Our own *dreadful* loss put Bertie and Alix *forward*; he and wife are *constantly before the public in* EVERY IMAGINABLE SHAPE *and* CHARACTER, *and fill entirely the public mind.*

'The English are very personal; to continue to love people they must see them, and even in part touch them: this shows itself in the wish to get something that belongs or belonged to them; it must be palpable. This state of affairs gives the young couple great influence on all classes, and is even calculated to influence the Cabinet, and to strengthen the Opposition, which would be quite powerless on that question without the strong popular feeling.

'Vicky little dreamt in selecting a charming Princess, that she would become the source of difficulties for England, and perhaps the cause of a popular war against Prussia.'[1]

Although the Queen found Bertie tiresome, she was slightly nettled by Uncle Leopold's letter. It was ridiculous to think that her son and daughter-in-law were as popular as all that; why, Uncle Leopold was even suggesting that the young couple was supplanting the Sovereign in public esteem. She picked up her pen and told her uncle about a recent (and rare) drive through the park, 'in my *open* carriage and four; it was *quite unexpected*, and, though *very painful*, pleased people more

[1] *The Letters of Queen Victoria.* The King of the Belgians not only seems to have adopted the Queen's style of writing in this letter, but talks as though he were a member of the English Royal Family.

than anything. . . . Everyone said that the difference shown when *I* appeared, and [when] Bertie and Alix drive, was *not* to be described. Naturally for *them* no one stops, or *runs*, as they always did, and *do* doubly now, for *me*.'[1]

It was tragic that the Prussian-Danish conflict broke out when Bertie was only 22. A few more years, and he might have known how to use his influence discreetly so as not to anger his mother. His partisanship merely strengthened her conviction that Bertie was a foolish, irresponsible boy.

It was almost impossible for the Prince to improve his relationship with his mother, for the Queen refused to countenance any intimacy. She treated Bertie as she treated everyone else, communicating with him by a series of peremptory notes. He begged her to keep him informed of developments in the Prussian-Danish war, and even impulsively offered his services as a mediator. But she was determined not to allow him any inside knowledge. She fobbed him off by instructing Lord Clarendon, an Under-Secretary of State, to give him a vague outline, and very vague at that, of what was going on. She also instructed Lord Clarendon to tell him how dangerous it was for the heir to the throne to take a 'one-sided view' of Foreign Affairs. One would have thought that the Queen would have found it possible to deliver this sort of lecture to her son herself, instead of making her criticisms a subject of ministerial gossip. But she was determined to make it clear to her ministers that her son was not to have access to confidential information.

For Alexandra's sake, Bertie of course was desperately

[1] *The Letters of Queen Victoria.*

anxious to find out what was going on. He talked to Lord Russell, the Foreign Secretary, and found that the latter had no objection to showing him despatches; but the Queen heard about the project and quickly nipped it in the bud. She bade her secretary, General Grey, to write to Russell in the following terms: 'The Prince of Wales seems to be under some misapprehension about the communication of despatches from the Foreign Office; for he seems to think you would have no objection to communicate them to him direct, and thus to keep him acquainted with the policy of Her Majesty's Government. . . .

'But the Queen cannot help objecting to the *principle*, which would be thus admitted, of separate and independent communication between the Prince of Wales and her Government. . . .

'Were the Prince of Wales to be cognisant of the confidential discussions between the Queen and her Ministers, as to the course to be pursued by this country; and were he to take antagonistic views on any important question (as he probably would have done on the Danish question) great inconvenience, not to say injury, might be occasioned to the public service. . . .'[1]

This harsh and mistrustful pronouncement remained the Queen's creed for over twenty years. Bertie was not to be trusted with any secrets. Occasionally he could see state papers when they had been acted upon; but by this time the information was often in the newspapers.

THE Danish-Prussian war at last came to an end in the early weeks of the summer, and the Duchies came under the ægis of Germany. Alexandra was determined to

[1] *The Letters of Queen Victoria.*

return home to visit her family, and Bertie was anxious to accompany her. The Queen raised every possible objection, and it was not until the Prince had eaten humble pie and promised to observe the strictest neutrality that the Queen gave her reluctant consent.

The visit to Denmark passed off smoothly except for one incident. When the ship bearing the royal couple came into the neighbourhood of Schleswig-Holstein, Princess Alexandra was outraged to see that the captain had hoisted the Prussian flag. She demanded that it be taken down at once. The captain gently insisted that he was only following accepted maritime rules, but the Princess stamped her foot and said: 'The Duchies belong to Papa. I will not move one step from where I am until you do as I say.'[1] And she got her way.

In order to balance the Danish trip Queen Victoria had insisted that the Prince and Princess pay a visit to Germany on the way home. This was far less successful. Bertie had always been devoted to his sister, Vicky, but on this occasion he found her impossible. She had never possessed tact, and offended both her brother and sister-in-law by her gloating references to Germany's triumph, and her pride in the role her husband had played. 'It was not pleasant to see him [the Crown Prince] and his A.D.C. always in Prussian uniform,' Bertie wrote to Lord Spencer, 'flaunting before our eyes a most objectionable ribbon which he had received for his *deeds* of valour??? against the unhappy Danes!'[2]

Neither Vicky nor Frederick meant to be offensive; but the Crown Prince was weak, and the Crown Princess had an unhappy knack of saying the wrong thing. She had made herself acutely unpopular in Berlin by her outspoken criticism of German manners and customs,

[1] *The Private Life of Queen Alexandra:* Hans Madol.
[2] *King Edward VII:* Sir Sidney Lee.

and her constant references to England as 'home'. She was only twenty-four, and was continually torn between love for her native land and duty towards her husband's country. She handled the difficult situation so badly she derived the worst from both worlds. She was an Englishwoman in Berlin and a German in London.

Her fervent defence of Germany's action over Denmark did not help to improve her position. Her father-in-law, King William I of Prussia, did not like the hold she had over his son, Frederick. She had imbued the Crown Prince with her own passionate belief in parliamentary government, which her father, the Prince Consort, had instilled in her. The young couple were always pressing for a more moderate rule and, a few years earlier, the King had found his Court divided into two factions. For a single, fleeting moment he had thought of abdicating and handing over to Frederick; but Frederick and Vicky had wavered, and if the opportunity ever really existed, it was lost for ever. Instead, the King had sent a message to the German Embassy in Paris summoning the autocratic, iron-fisted diplomat, Count von Bismarck, who was destined to change the shape of Europe. Gone was the last hope of Prussian liberalism. Bismarck seized control eagerly, and in his first speech declared his distrust of peaceful democratic progress. 'It is not with speeches or with parliamentary resolutions that the great questions of the day are decided,' he asserted, 'but with blood and iron.'

First he designed the attack on Denmark; then two years later the attack on Austria (necessary to give Prussia a united Germany); then in 1870 the provocation to France which resulted in the Franco-Prussian war. These victories transformed the King of Prussia into the Emperor of Germany, and transformed Germany into the strongest power on the Continent.

The Crown Princess soon became one of Bismarck's

targets. He recognised her as a potential enemy; and since he controlled the press he gave orders that her position should be undermined. 'The Englishwoman', as she sneeringly came to be known, was depicted as a royal spy, working in connivance with her mother to defeat Prussia's glorious aims.

It is not surprising that Vicky hated Bismarck, and that she hated the dictatorship which he imposed on the country. What is surprising is that every time Prussia launched an attack, she became a fervent, rabid, almost hysterical partisan of Bismarck's blood and iron policy.

During the Danish war we have Vicky writing to her mother: 'The continual meddling and interfering of England in other people's affairs has become *so* ridiculous abroad, that it almost ceases to annoy . . . The highly pathetic, philanthropic, and virtuous tone in which all the attacks against Prussia are made has something intensely ludicrous about it. The English would not like, if they were engaged in a war, to be dictated to in a pompous style, how they were to conduct it; indeed I am sure they would not stand such interference. Why should we then be supposed to submit to it? . . .'[1]

Two years later, when the savage attack on Austria took place, known as the Seven Weeks War, the Princess began by deploring Bismarck's unscrupulous aggressiveness, but soon she was caught up in the national fervour. Despite the fact that many of her kinsfolk, including the husband of her sister, Alice, were on the Austrian side, she wrote to her mother, 'I feel that I am *now* every bit as proud of being a Prussian as I am of being an Englishwoman . . .'[1]

And four years after that, when Bismarck provoked war with France, when the Emperor Napoleon was taken prisoner, when revolution broke out and the Empress

[1] *The Letters of Queen Victoria.*

Eugénie fled to England, when Prussian troops marched to Paris, we have Vicky commenting ecstatically to her mother: 'What astounding news! Really I could hardly believe my ears when I heard it. Here the excitement and delight of the people know no bounds . . .' The next day she wrote again, in an increasingly smug and irritating vein. 'What will Bertie and Alix say to all these marvellous events? When I think of the Emperor and the Empress in the zenith of their glory, in '55 and at the time of the exhibition when all the Sovereigns in Europe paid them their court, and they were so amiable and courteous to all, it seems a *curious* contrast! Gay and charming Paris! *What* mischief that court, and still more that very attractive Paris, has done to English Society, to the stage and to literature! *What harm* to the young and brilliant aristocracy of London! It would be well if they would pause and think that immoderate frivolity and luxury depraves and ruins and ultimately leads to a national misfortune. Our poverty, our dull towns, our plodding, hardworking *serious life*, has made us strong and determined; it is wholesome for us. I should grieve were we to imitate Paris and be so taken up with pleasure that no time was left for examination and serious thought! . . .'[1]

VICKY, no doubt, had her brother Bertie in mind when she spoke of the corrupting influence of Paris on the English aristocracy. Yet the gay, pleasure-loving Bertie had shown far more prescience as far as foreign affairs were concerned than his erratic sister.

Despite all the pressures the Queen placed upon him, Bertie doggedly followed his own convictions. Whether

[1] *Letters of the Empress Frederick.*

it was Alexandra's tears, or the harsh memory of his German upbringing, Bertie's sympathies remained steadfastly with the antagonists of Prussia.

First he was the champion of Denmark, then the champion of Austria. Ten days before Prussia launched its attack on this unhappy country in June 1866, he sat next to the French Ambassador at dinner. Bertie had very clear ideas as to the course Britain should follow and told the Ambassador that the only hope of maintaining peace lay in an alliance between England and France. 'Complications could best be avoided,' he said, 'and the general interests of Europe could best be served by an Entente between England and France.'[1]

This suggestion was regarded as a startling idea. The notion of preventing war by collective action was new. When the Prince declared that he was a 'pro-Austrian' the French Ambassador reminded him that England was a friend of Italy, and Italy was a traditional enemy of Austria; this, he said, made it impossible for an Englishman to back Austria. The Prince waved the difficulties aside, and replied it was France's business to restrain Italy and England's business to back France and restrain Germany. The Prince's views were firm, sensible and prophetic, but he was many years in advance of his time.

The trust that France placed in the Prince was signified by an unprecedented act on the part of the Emperor Napoleon III. At the end of the Prussian-Austrian war the Emperor offered his services as a mediator, and was accepted. He instructed his French Ambassador in London to send the Prince a confidential report of the negotiations taking place at the Quai d'Orsay; so, despite Victoria's ban, Bertie was even better informed than the British Foreign Secretary.

Four years later, Bertie again found himself, in heart

[1] *Les Origines Diplomatiques de la Guerre 1870–71.*

and mind, against Prussia. This was when war broke out with France. For a third time he held opposing views to his mother and sister. Victoria took the same stand as her eldest daughter, declaring that Germany stood for 'civilisation, liberty, order and unity' while France stood for 'despotism, corruption, immorality and aggression'. Of course what really influenced her was the fact, as she declared, that the Prince Consort had foreseen 'the necessity that this vainglorious and immoral people [the French] should be put down'.[1]

It is very difficult to disguise strong feelings, and the German Ambassador in London made the most of the stories of the Prince's pro-French sentiments. He sent a despatch to Berlin declaring that at a dinner party at the French Ambassador's Bertie had expressed the hopes of a French victory. It was probably true, and Bismarck at once exploited the situation. The Princess Royal wrote angrily that her brother's words were 'quoted everywhere'. Bertie denied the story; he denied it to his mother, to the Foreign Secretary, Lord Granville, and to the Prime Minister, Mr. Gladstone. Gradually the commotion died down.

But very soon another squall blew up. When the French monarchy was overthrown in the hour of defeat, the Empress and her son fled to England for safety. Kind-hearted Bertie at once offered them Chiswick House, which had been lent to him by the Duke of Devonshire. The Lord Chancellor cried out in alarm, declaring that the new Republican Government might misunderstand the Prince's offer; Queen Victoria rebuked him impatiently, and the Foreign Secretary described the act as 'highly imprudent'. The Empress extracted the British government from its embarrassment by refusing Bertie's offer.

No harm would have come from it; for Bertie's touch was far surer than that of his mother's ministers. During

[1] *King Edward VII:* Sir Sidney Lee.

the next ten years he not only remained a firm friend of the French royalists and aristocrats, but he made friends among the Republicans as well.

THE biographers of Albert Edward invariably point out that the Prince of Wales seldom read a book. They state the fact as though it were a sort of phenomenon. The reverse, of course, is true. Since when have English princes of the blood royal been partial to reading books? Since when has an intellectual sat on the throne of England? Bertie was a gay, sociable prince who preferred talk to Letters. Yet a constant depreciation of his mental capacity, emanating from the Queen, spread outside the palace and built up a picture of a young man with a butterfly mind; one who could not concentrate on a subject for more than half an hour at a time. Colonel Ponsonby, the Queen's secretary, reflected the palace view when he wrote to his wife: 'Nothing can be more genial and pleasant than he [the Prince] is for a few minutes. But he does not endure. He cannot keep up the interest for any length of time and I don't think he will ever settle down to business.'[1]

This was the accepted impression of Bertie by those in the inner circle. It is therefore interesting to take notice of his determination. He not only maintained an independent view of foreign affairs in stubborn opposition to his mother's pro-Prussian leanings, but worked unflaggingly for over forty years to secure an Entente with France. There are few examples of such consistency among princes.

The fact that France had become a Republic, and Bertie was a passionate royalist, did not alter his con-

[1] *Henry Ponsonby: His Life from His Letters:* Arthur Ponsonby.

victions. First of all he hoped that the Republic was only a temporary measure; second, the Republican leaders continued to send aristocrats as ambassadors to London. Bertie always formed close friendships with the French ambassadors, and always urged them to press for closer relations with England. One of them, the Duc de la Rochefoucauld-Bisaccia, went so far as to sound the British Government on the subject. Here Victoria promptly stepped in. An Entente was not at all to her liking, and she made her objections very clear. 'A new intimate alliance with France,' she instructed her secretary, Colonel Ponsonby, to write to the new Foreign Secretary, Lord Derby, on August 17, 1874, 'especially with Republican France, the Queen would strongly deprecate. Germany, Austria, and even Russia are far more useful, natural and good allies for England; but we should always try to be on good and friendly terms with France. The Duke of Wellington used to say, when that great intimacy in the time of King Louis Philippe existed, "Plenty of friendship, but no love," and this is quite true.'[1]

These rebuffs did not deter Bertie and he continued to work for his cause. He did not always find it easy. When, in 1874, he announced that he was going to Paris the British Foreign Secretary told him that he must call on the French President, M. Thiers. Bertie's royalist feelings rebelled and he protested that it 'went very much against the grain'. Nevertheless he did as he was bidden and the President was enormously flattered by the Prince's courteous manners.

France was not an easy place to visit in the seventies. Politically it was a turbulent mass of opposing factions. But the Prince was so delighted to feel the boulevards under his feet that his amiability knew no bounds. It was not difficult to be tactful under such circumstances and

[1] *King Edward VII:* Sir Sidney Lee.

he soon found he was able to maintain friendships that cut across the warring camps. Soon he was entertaining Legitimists and Bonaparte pretenders; aristocrats and, finally, leaders of the Republic; and no one took offence.

Even so, when Bertie announced in 1876 that he was planning to make a tour of the French château country and visit a number of the great aristocratic families in turn, the Foreign Office expressed deep anxiety. This, they argued, was going too far; it was bound to upset the Republican leaders. But Bertie knew better. The tour was a glittering triumph. The French aristocracy was only too glad to find an excuse to fling open its ballrooms again. Tables sparkled with silver, and music echoed across the countryside. Chefs vied with one another to see who could provide the most delectable dishes, the best wines of France flowed in profusion, the women spent fortunes on their dresses. The Prince visited the Duchesse de Luynes at the Château de Dompierre; the Duc and Duchesse de la Tremoille at the Château de Serrant; the Prince and Princess Sagan at the Château de Mello; and the Duc and Duchesse de Nouchy at Nouchy-le-Châtel. Far from being resentful, the Republican leaders were only too thankful that the Prince was sampling the best that France could offer. Quixotically, the fact that he maintained his role in a truly royal fashion put them at their ease. He was a man of sincerity. They could trust him.

The Prince's aristocratic friends gave him good advice. The Marquis de Lau pointed out that it was obvious that the French Republic had become a permanent fixture. He urged the Prince to modify his views, and accept the régime as a *fait accompli*. His talk bore fruit, and in 1878 Bertie asked to meet M. Gambetta. This dark, squat little man with a cast in one eye was the father of the Republic. His courage had sustained it during the dark days of France's defeat, and for the past eight years he had been the giant of the Chambre des Députés. He was a brilliant, witty conversationalist and Bertie fell completely beneath his spell. The two men found they had much in common. They both detested Bismarck, feared Prussia, and hoped for an Anglo-French Entente.

Until Gambetta's death in 1882 the Prince and he met frequently. They always talked with complete frankness. On one occasion Bertie's friend, the Marquis de Gallifet, was present and recorded in his diary the following snatch of conversation.

The Prince: Monsieur Gambetta, allow me to ask you why you and your friends keep the French aristocracy divorced from affairs?

Gambetta: But, sir, there is no longer an 'aristocracy' in France. There are only dukes who have no army to lead and marquises who are not responsible for defending any 'marches'; the counts and viscounts and barons have neither lands nor authority nor influence.

The Prince: Let me rather say that I meant the nobility.

Gambetta: But they have no desire for employment . . . They just sulk—that is their definite occupation. They are only to be met with in the army and navy, and sometimes in the diplomatic service. In those professions they look very well, I quite admit.

The Prince: But why not do as in my country, where we take the most distinguished men in industry, science, literature, commerce, and so on? . . . We make them noblemen, and our nobility remains a genuine aristocracy.

Gambetta: With you that is possible, for some time still; with us, it is not. The 'Duke of Rockfount' would not be willing to rub shoulders with the 'Duke of Industry' and the 'Duke of Science' or the 'Duke of Arts' and so forth. As a Republic, we can have only one aristocracy, that of science and merit. It declares itself without any need of titles.

The Prince: You are a real Republican, Monsieur Gambetta.
Gambetta: Allow me to admit that, sir. I consider it logical that you, for your part, should be a royalist.[1]

ALL these years the Prince continued to plead with his mother to give him a job to do. When the Franco-Prussian war broke out he wrote to the Queen, begging her to make use of him, just as he had during the Danish conflict. 'I cannot bear sitting here and doing nothing, whilst all this bloodshed is going on. How I wish you could send me with letters to the Emperor and the King of Prussia, with friendly advice, even if it ultimately failed. . . .'[2] Victoria replied dampingly that she thought his anxiety 'highly creditable' but she was afraid his position 'would make it impossible, *even if he were personally fitted for such a very difficult task* (author's italics), to undertake such a mission!'[2]

The Prince realised that his only hope of a responsible job lay in the outside pressure he could bring on the Queen. He found a number of influential allies who genuinely believed that it was not only important for the Heir Apparent to have a serious occupation but that Bertie would acquit himself well. The Marquess of Hamilton, a Lord of the Bedchamber, approached Colonel Ponsonby, who relayed to the Queen an account of the conversation. 'Lord Hamilton said he thought that His Royal Highness wished to be attached to different offices of the government so that he might be taught the business of the different departments. . . .'[3]

This was only one of many letters on the Prince's behalf. But the trouble was that while men like Lord Hamilton could discuss the matter with detachment, most of the

[1] *King Edward and His Times:* André Maurois.
[2] *King Edward VII:* Sir Sidney Lee. [3] *The Letters of Queen Victoria.*

people who had the Queen's confidence were anxious to keep her from delegating any power which might detract from their own authority. The Prince was passionately interested in foreign affairs. He was related to half the sovereigns on the Continent, and he knew most of the statesmen in Europe. He got on well with people. He might have been enormously successful as a semi-official ambassador. But in whose interests was it that he should be given a job?

The Queen's ministers were very reluctant to see him play an important role. Colonel Ponsonby had a poor opinion of the Prince, and suggested he be sent to India; Lord Halifax, the Lord Privy Seal, thought Ireland would suffice. Mr. Gladstone wrote a rambling, meaningless letter proposing vaguely that he might devote himself to improving the 'moral tone' of society; and Mr. Disraeli, who was determined not to let anyone influence the Queen but himself, did his best to disqualify Bertie from any job. He nick-named him 'Prince Hal' and complained of his 'chitter-chatter'. He told the Queen that he must not be shown confidential papers as 'he lets them out and talks to his friends about them'.[1]

Was Disraeli's opinion of the Prince as poor as all that? In the late seventies when Disraeli decided to send Lord Salisbury abroad on a mission, Bertie suggested that the latter should stop in Paris, Vienna, Berlin and Rome and interview personally the rulers and chief statesmen. The permanent under-secretary at the Foreign Office, Lord Tenterden, branded the suggestion as foolish and most extraordinary. But Disraeli wrote to Lord Salisbury: 'I think on these matters H.R.H. is a better counsellor than Lord Tenterden. The Prince of Wales is a thorough man of the world and knows all these individuals personally . . .'[2]

[1] *Henry Ponsonby: His Life from His Letters:* Arthur Ponsonby.

[2] *King Edward VII:* Sir Sidney Lee.

But it was not in the Prime Minister's interest that the Prince should exercise an influence in Foreign Affairs; and certainly the Foreign Secretary, Lord Granville, had no wish to have His Royal Highness reading despatches and making suggestions on how things should be done. When the Queen finally decided to act on Lord Hamilton's suggestion, and requested Granville to assign the Prince to one of the House of Lords' Committees, the Foreign Secretary picked out a particularly dull, and of course, non-political, committee which Bertie was bound to find immensely boring. Then he wrote to Colonel Ponsonby in an almost triumphant tone: 'He attended the first day. He then came to me to ask whether the Committee could not be adjourned for ten days. He had some engagements, and so on.

'I am afraid the Foreign Affairs question would be treated in the same way. If the Queen really desired his opinion, sent for him and consulted him he would probably get amused and interested. But if he only gets a few bones after they have been to the Prime Minister, and the Queen, and finds nothing but despatches telling him only what he has skimmed a week before in the paper, he will cease reading them. If all the drafts are to be submitted to him, the delay will be intolerable. . . . And as to really confidential matters, will they remain secret? He asked me to keep him informed during the [Franco-Prussian] war. One evening I got four messages from different friends, telling me to be careful. One of my first notes to him had been handed around a dinner party.

'All this will not prevent my doing anything in my power to co-operate. . . .'[1]

The final result of all this agitation was that the Prince mained unemployed.

[1] *Henry Ponsonby: His Life from His Letters:* Arthur Ponsonby.

CHAPTER SEVEN

THE MARLBOROUGH HOUSE SET: THE SEVENTIES

It would be wrong to give the impression that the Heir Apparent was unhappy. If he could not work, at least he could play, and he did this very well. He loved being royal. He revelled in the rank and authority and privilege and luxury that accompanied the role of Prince of Wales. There were radicals who liked to lampoon him, and courtiers who wanted to reform him. But there was a much bigger group, a rich, fashionable, powerful society who adored him, fawned on him, gratified him, and copied everything he did.

Paradoxically this adulation often increased the Prince's freedom of movement. A contemporary writer states that it was possible for the Prince of Wales to walk along Piccadilly, or St. James' Street or Pall Mall without being recognised. Why? Because photography was still undeveloped? Oh no. It was due to 'the curious fact that there are in society several gentlemen who bear an extraordinary resemblance to him, and who take some pride in dressing and moving exactly like him, so that it is often very difficult to identify him as he passes in the street on foot or in a hansom cab'.[1]

But the vogue of imitating the Prince did not stop at his beard, his clothes and his walk. Once when he had an attack of rheumatism in his shoulder, he was obliged to shake hands with his elbow pressed stiffly to his side. Immediately this peculiar hand-shake was adopted by fashionable London. And when Alexandra

[1] *The Private Life of the King:* By One of His Majesty's Servants.

had a severe illness in the late sixties, which left her lame for life, the smartest ladies in the land began to walk with a slightly halting gait, which became known as 'the Alexandra Limp'.

This aping of royalty was not considered vulgar. On the whole the Prince and Princess were amused and flattered by it, but every now and then someone went too far. On one occasion a rich manufacturer from the North drove in the Park with his horses wearing head-bands of the royal scarlet used exclusively by the Prince. The Heir Apparent did not attempt to hide his displeasure. His blue eyes grew cold, and his lower lip protruded in the famous Guelph pout. As a sharp lesson to the perpetrators of this unforgivably bad taste he drove in the Park the next day with his horses wearing black headbands. The manufacturer's wife and daughters could not fail to observe the significance of this slight, and left the Park in tears; and the Prince's friends congratulated him on his clever rebuff.

The Prince was not just 'a swell'. In the jargon of the day he was 'a heavy swell', and apparently there was a world of difference between the two terms. A swell was a rich young aristocrat who lived in extreme comfort; but a heavy swell added showmanship to the comfort and lived in a stylish luxury that even the French were obliged to envy. And of course the heavy swell was the acme of sartorial elegance.

The Prince did not in the least mind changing his dress half a dozen times a day. He loved clothes, and since whatever he chose to wear became the prevailing fashion overnight, he soon was regarded as an expert on the subject. His tailor-in-chief made a fortune. For many years he patronised a Mr. Poole. He discovered this gentleman by accident. He went to the theatre one night to see a well-known actor by the name of Fechter playing 'Robert Macaire'. As an impecunious adventurer

Fechter was obliged to wear a coat that was torn and dirty, but Bertie's expert eye noticed the elegant cut. At the end of the performance he asked Fechter for the name of his tailor, and Mr. Poole's future was assured.

The Prince had so many clothes he could never travel with less than two valets; and two more valets were left at home cleaning, brushing and pressing his vast wardrobe. There were suits and coats for every variation of every climate the world over. There were over a hundred pieces of headgear; and since Bertie was an honorary admiral and an honorary general of most of the countries of Europe, there was an entire room devoted to uniforms, sashes, epaulettes, belts, buckles, swords, feathers and other regalia.

As the years rolled on the Prince became an ever-increasing authority on dress. Tailors from all over Europe used to gather to study his clothes. Their favourite meeting place was Homburg, and later, Marienbad. Here they could catch a glimpse of the Prince half a dozen times a day, strolling along the promenade, or riding in an open carriage. Once Bertie dressed hurriedly and forgot to fasten the last button on his waistcoat; this became a permanent fashion.

British manufacturers were not slow to realise what an asset they had in the Heir Apparent and kept a vigilant eye on his movements. Once, one of them declared in outraged tones that he was buying his gloves in France. A storm blew up of such proportions that the Prince's secretary, Sir Francis Knollys, was forced to make a statement to the press. First, he declared that the Prince always had his gloves made in England, and second (and this was calculated to silence the critics) that His Royal Highness was very economical in the use of gloves and only found it necessary to order two dozen pairs a year.

Men's clothes became of such importance that new

shops sprang up like mushrooms in Savile Row, Clifford Street and Bond Street. Most of the Prince's innovations were inspired by comfort and convenience. He altered the cut of the evening dress waistcoat, he shortened the tails on the tail coat, he left his frock coat open (due to an increasing girth), he introduced the black homburg, and he attended race meetings, not in the frock coat hitherto *de rigueur*, but in tweeds. He tried having his trousers creased down the sides rather than the front and back, in order to hide his bandy legs, but this idea did not catch on, and he soon discarded it himself. But the Prince was not the only arbiter of men's fashions. The band of 'heavy swells' who followed his lead gave him plenty of competition. Lord Raglan and Lord Petersham invented coats which are still named after them, Lord Dupplin the dinner jacket and Lord Cardigan the button-up sweater. But Lord Hardwicke made the most spectacular contribution. Men's silk hats were made of beaver which was left in its original rough, shaggy state. Lord Hardwicke polished his hat until he could see his face in it, and consequently was known as 'Glossy Top'. He is responsible for the top hat as we know it today.

THE Prince made innovations in other fields besides dress. First and foremost came the subject of smoking. Queen Victoria had an absolute horror of this vice. At the royal residences smoking was strictly prohibited. It was believed that the nicotine which clung to the clothes and skin might very well poison a lady of delicate susceptibilities. 'I remember, on a visit to Windsor,' wrote Baron von Eckardstein, 'seeing Count Hatzfeldt, who could not live without a cigarette, lying in his pyjamas on his bedroom floor, blowing smoke up the chimney.'[1] There was a back passage, dark and cold, where Bertie's brother, Prince Alfred, sometimes led his friends to indulge in the awful vice. On one occasion a courtier wrote Victoria a letter while he was smoking. He received an icy reply from the Queen, who began by thanking him for 'his enclosure'. He could not think what on earth she meant, but some time later he was informed that the cigarette ash had dropped into his letter.

In the seventies it was the custom for the men to sit at the dinner table, after the ladies had left, drinking their port, but never smoking. When they finally gathered in the drawing-room the hostess would ask one of her female guests to entertain the company by playing the piano or singing. The young lady always demurred, with little, fluttery protests, saying that she had forgotten her music, but in the end she was prevailed upon, and perhaps treated the guests to 'The Grandfather Clock'.

The gentlemen could not hope to smoke until the ladies had departed. Then, if they were guests in a country house, they went to their bedrooms, donned thick, padded smoking jackets, and smoking hats to keep the odour from contaminating their hair, and descended to the most remote room in the house, usually the icy-cold gun-room.

The Prince of Wales put a stop to all this. In spite of the outraged protests of the Queen, he allowed smoking at his dinner table. As soon as the ladies had left the room, cigars and cigarettes were passed around. And since brandy and tobacco mixed better, port became less fashionable.

THE Prince was not the sort of man to put up with 'The Grandfather Clock'. Nor did shy, conventional young girls

[1] *Ten Years at the Court of St. James:* Baron von Eckardstein.

amuse him, or dull, over-polite young men. At Marlborough House he was determined to provide lively evenings. In the first place dinner was too long. He did not want to curtail the amount of food consumed, but he insisted that the service should be quickened up, plates removed as soon as people were finished, and that the whole meal should take place within the hour. Secondly, he had no wish to sit endlessly at the table over the brandy. He liked the company of pretty women and he had no intention of depriving himself of it.

The large formal dinner parties at Marlborough House had to follow a fixed pattern. After dinner whist tables usually were set up, or perhaps everyone went on to a ball. But the 'small evenings' were far from conventional. They seldom ended before dawn. Sometimes the carpets were flung back and an impromptu dance took place; sometimes the young men amused the company by tobogganing down the stairs on trays; sometimes there were hilarious parlour games; sometimes spirited battles with soda syphons; and always a few practical jokes. Soapsuds on somebody's sweet instead of whipped cream, or medicine in the wine glasses, was enough to convince everyone that the party was wildly gay.

As the reader can see, the innovations and changes the Prince introduced sprang entirely from his own fads and fancies. He liked to be comfortable and he hated being bored. He insisted on pretty women and entertaining men. He was amused, for instance, by the Marquis de Soveral, an attaché at the Portuguese Embassy, whose strange, dark, ugly looks won him the sobriquet 'The Blue Monkey' and who was regarded as the greatest wit of the day. He was also amused by tall, lugubrious Christopher Sykes, who filled the role of court jester because of an exaggerated deference to the Prince which was regarded as very humorous. Apparently Bertie and his friends used playfully to pour brandy over Christopher's head merely to hear him solemnly say: 'As your Royal Highness pleases'.

The Prince enjoyed the company of Sir Frederick Johnstone and of Lord Hardwicke, both experts in the pursuit of light amusement; and he liked the Duke of Sutherland who adored trains and fire-engines and occasionally persuaded Bertie to disguise himself with a fireman's hat and accompany him to a fire. But of all his men friends, the man with whom he probably felt the closest tie over the longest number of years was Lord Hartington.

'Harty-Tarty', as he was known to his intimate circle, was unmistakably an English eccentric. Although he did not become the Duke of Devonshire until 1891 he was immensely rich, and as a result unconcerned with material possessions. He was slow and vague and ponderous, but he had the rare virtue of common sense. He was a member of the Liberal Government for years, then joined the Liberal Unionists over Home Rule. Lord Randolph Churchill said he was apt to pigeon-hole a paper for months, but if he ever could bring himself to read it, his judgment was infallible. He was famous in the House of Commons for his sleepy expression. Once he yawned heavily in the middle of one of his statements, explaining that what he was saying was 'so damned dull'.

He liked to preserve an illusion of indifference toward his vast properties. When he became Duke of Devonshire he often disconcerted visitors to Chatwsorth, who hoped to please him by ecstatic observations, by replying, 'It's a rummy old place.' Once a friend of Mr. E. F.

Benson went down to stay with him at Compton Place near Eastbourne, and left London early, in order to visit the imposing ruin of Pevensey Castle, which belonged to the Duke. 'He told his host that evening what he had been doing, and how deeply impressed he was by Pevensey. The Duke was vaguely interested . . . "Pevensey?" he said. "Whose is Pevensey?" '[1]

Lord Hartington sometimes surprised his colleagues by his shabby clothes. 'Yesterday Lord Hartington came to see me,' wrote Mr. Smith, the Liberal-Unionist leader, from Aix-les-Bains, 'dressed as a seedy, shady sailor. . . .' On another occasion the fashionable ladies of London society decided that they were tired of the decrepit hat that he had worn for so many years. On his birthday they flooded him with headgear ranging from flannel cricket caps to the smartest toppers.

Lord Hartington's political career was attributed largely to the influence of the strong-willed and beautiful Duchess of Manchester. This young woman was a German by birth, Countess Louise von Alten, who had come to England as the bride of the Duke of Manchester. Her husband soon proved wild and unstable, and she formed a liaison with Lord Hartington, which lasted thirty years and ended in marriage. 'Lottie', as she was known to her friends, was very imperious. Once she took two companions for a drive. They stopped to inspect the scenery and as she was climbing back into the wagonette one of the horses moved. It was immediately checked, but she was thrown on to her knees in the carriage. She took her stick and hit the coachman sharply across the back, and then, without a flicker of an eye, seated herself and resumed her conversation, 'As I was saying . . .'

Lottie was ambitious, and she was quick to see Lord Hartington's political possibilities. 'Why are you not in the Cabinet?' she asked him critically one day. 'Ah,'

[1] *As We Were:* E. F. Benson.

he replied in some surprise. 'Well, why not? Hang it, Lottie. You have given me an idea. Perhaps it will be good fun.'

Throughout the thirty years of their *affaire* Lord Hartington and the Duchess of Manchester preserved the greatest decorum. No one ever heard them refer to each other except by their titles. But the great lady did not always find her admirer easy to handle. There was the period when he was infatuated with the beautiful demi-mondaine, Skittles. He left the Duchess of Manchester for over two years; indeed, there were many rumours that he had married the glamorous, disreputable lady on whom he had bestowed the finest carriages and ponies in England. But the gossip was unreliable and one day Lord Hartington returned to the Duchess' doorstep. She was having tea in the drawing-room. Once again she did not betray a flicker of emotion. 'Do you still like two lumps of sugar in your tea, Hartington?' she said.

It was not surprising that the Prince of Wales was attracted to Lord Hartington. The two men had many tastes in common. They both disliked books, adored shooting and racing, and were appreciative of the attractions of pretty ladies. Besides, Hartington was always so sensible and dependable. He was always ready to give the Prince sound advice and help him out of scrapes; and he never tried to lecture him. Occasionally Bertie could not resist playing a joke on his friend. Once Lord Hartington was scheduled to attend a civic reception in the north of England. He was to be the guest of the city corporation for several days. When he arrived the Mayor proudly showed him a bowling alley which had been erected in Hartington's honour. The latter looked dumbfounded, until the Mayor added: 'We were informed by the Prince's equerry that your lordship was very fond of skittles.'

The Prince liked people. He also liked comfort. If a man was rich and agreeable, and very eager to entertain him, he saw no reason to deprive him of the honour. In this category came the Rothschilds. Up to now they had not been received in royal circles. In 1869 Mr. Gladstone had tried to secure a peerage for Baron Lionel, a second-generation Rothschild who had become head of the great banking firm. But the Queen refused, saying that she could not think 'that one who owed his wealth to contracts with foreign governments for loans, or to successful speculation on the Stock Exchange could fairly claim a British peerage'.[1] And that was not all. She wrote Lord Granville: 'To make a *Jew a Peer* is a step the Queen *could not* consent to.'[1]

The Prince had no such feelings about Jews. Here were the Baron Lionel's sons and daughters and nephews with fabulous mansions and unlimited wealth, willing to spare no expense in providing him with amusement. Why not? Their great, massive houses, clustered along Piccadilly and Park Lane, were the wonders of the Victorian age. They were a blaze of marble and carved wood and red plush and gilt. A wit remarked that the chairs offered gilt-edged security.

The Prince had met Nathaniel at Cambridge, and soon the Rothschilds were frequent guests at Marlborough House, and in return the Prince was wined and dined on a magnificent scale and in whatever company he dictated.

The two most socially-minded Rothschilds were Alfred and his cousin Ferdinand. They vied with each other to see who could give the most elaborate dinners and balls, and the competition led to fantastic excesses of hospitality. Alfred paid unheard of sums to bring the most famous singers and musicians of the day to London to entertain his guests. These included de Reszke, Liszt,

[1] *The Magnificent Rothschilds:* Cecil Roth.

Melba and Rubinstein. But Ferdinand outdid him when he entertained the Crown Prince Rudolph of Austria and offered his lady guests new dresses from Doucet in Paris. However, rich men have their idiosyncrasies. Mrs. Langtry ordered a petticoat to go with her gown, and promptly received a bill for it with a message that the Baron Ferdinand had not 'authorised' it.

These two cousins both built houses in Buckinghamshire, and built them on the lines of French châteaux. Alfred's was Halton Hall, near Wendover, which he finished in 1884. He had an enormous house-warming party, but his efforts did not arouse the admiration for which he had hoped. Algernon West described Halton as 'an exaggerated nightmare of gorgeousness and senseless and ill-applied magnificence'. Eustace Balfour wrote: 'I have seldom seen anything more terribly vulgar. Outside it is a combination of a French château and a gambling house. Inside it is badly planned and gaudily decorated. . . . Oh, but the hideousness of everything, the showiness! the sense of lavish wealth thrust up your nose! the ugly mouldings, the heavy gilding always in the wrong place, the colours of the silk hangings! Eye hath not seen nor pen can write the ghastly coarseness of the sight.'[1]

The hospitality was as lavish as the decoration. The nearest station was at Tring, some miles away. In order that he should be informed the moment his guests arrived, Mr. Alfred posted men at intervals all along the road who signalled ahead with lanterns as the carriages progressed. When the visitors departed their broughams were packed with hot-house flowers and fruit, and delicacies of every kind. The only complaint of the guests was that they found it difficult to sleep at night due to the heavy tread of the night watchmen,

[1] *The Magnificent Rothschilds:* Cecil Roth.

employed to keep an eye on their host's priceless treasures.

Ferdinand was more successful with his house than Mr. Alfred. Waddesdon Manor was built nearly ten years earlier, and aroused a storm of admiration; the smart world considered it the last word in beauty and elegance. Like Alfred, Ferdinand spared no expense to give his guests pleasure. Once Lady Warwick arrived in a thunderstorm and was dismayed to find that the masses of red geraniums had been beaten down by the storm. She happened to arise very early the next morning and looked out of the window to see 'a truly amazing sight. I saw an army of gardeners at work, taking out the damaged plants and putting in new ones, that had been brought from the glass-houses in pots.'[1]

Ferdinand owned a thousand acres of land. He was very fond of shooting but he never knew what to do with the pheasants. Even after he had supplied his friends generously with them, there were always thousands left over. Finally, he and his cousin Leo (who had a large estate near Leighton Buzzard and apparently was faced with the same problem) concocted a plan. At Christmas every carriage driver and busman who passed the Rothschild doors in Piccadilly was given a brace of pheasants. This practice became an institution. Soon the whips of all the drivers and the bell-cords of all the conductors were decorated with blue and amber ribbons . . . the Rothschild racing colours. And when, at the end of the century, 'Ferdy' died, the drivers paid their tribute by entwining mourning ribbons with the rest.

Long before Ferdy died Queen Victoria had changed her mind about Jews. No doubt this was largely due to her enchanting Mr. Disraeli. In 1885 she bestowed a peerage on Nathaniel, the head of the family, and in

[1] *Life's Ebb and Flow:* Lady Warwick.

the same year she visited Waddesdon to see the magnificence of which she had heard so much. On this occasion Lord Hartington, as vague as ever, was present, and upset the Queen considerably by absent-mindedly shaking her hand instead of kissing it.

VICTORIA's change of mind did not take place until nearly a whole generation after Bertie first received Rothschilds into his house. The storm the Prince raised by this revolutionary step was fierce and prolonged. Until that time the landed aristocracy had reigned supreme. Rich men were in demand if they had their money in the right place, but the right place was the land. Self-made 'City men' were beyond the pale. The only way an outsider could enter Society was by some brilliant service to the Sovereign—such as becoming Prime Minister.

The fact that the Prince of Wales opened the doors to bankers and stockbrokers was considered too vulgar for words. And Jews at that. There must be some explanation for this curious and outrageous act. Soon there were whispers that the Prince was enormously in debt; that he had received a large sum from the Rothschilds in return for an entrée into Society.

There was no doubt that the £100,000 a year allowance which had seemed so satisfactory to Bertie when he had first married, now barely met the bills. Many of the Prince's friends, like the Rothschilds, were far richer than he, yet his tastes were every bit as expensive.

For instance, his two favourite sports were racing and shooting. Under the Prince's supervision Sandringham, the 11,000-acre estate in Norfolk, which he had bought from his Duchy of Cornwall revenue just before his twentieth birthday, boasted an excellent stud farm and the best shooting in the country. Neither were modest pastimes. The shooting was soon organised on the largest scale in England. Practically the whole 11,000 acres were given over to it. Dozens of cottages were erected for gamekeepers, and 10,000 pheasants were hatched each year and fed on grain. They were let out when they were full-grown.

Several times a year a 'battue' was arranged. The day before, notice was given all over the estate, and to the neighbouring farms, that work must stop. 'Soon after dawn', wrote an eye-witness, 'a number of lads and farm hands, with blue and red flags, are taken to their places by the keepers, who wear the Royal livery of green and gold. The beaters wear smocks, with a hatband of scarlet, to distinguish them from any stray yokel who may try to intrude himself into the day's proceedings. Mr. Jackson (the head gamekeeper) goes over the whole ground on a sturdy cob to see that the men are properly disposed. Game carts are sent betimes to the various spots where the fire is expected to be hottest, and by about eleven o'clock, when all is ready, the wagonettes and country carts containing the Prince and his guests arrive on the scene. The Prince's party seldom exceeds eight or ten guns, and it is needless to say that they are chosen by him for their skill. Every sportsman works with two loaders, and from two to four guns.'[1]

Anything from two to three thousand head of game would be shot. From 1870 to 1880 the season's result averaged between seven and nine thousand; but in the winter of 1885 the Prince reached the unprecedented record of sixteen thousand.

The Prince's tastes were not only expensive in the way of sport. He loved entertaining and when he was in

[1] *The Private Life of the King:* By One of His Majesty's Servants.

residence at Sandringham the house was always filled with guests. Every afternoon a train known as 'The Prince of Wales' Special' waited at St. Pancras Station to take his friends to Norfolk. He gave several large balls a year at Sandringham, and several more at Marlborough House. Of course there was an endless round of dinners, garden fêtes and even 'breakfast parties'; and trips to Paris, Homburg and the South of France, with the endless tipping and the shower of presents that was regarded as a normal obligation of royalty. It was all very costly. Besides, there were the gambling debts incurred abroad at the casinos and at home at the card table and on the race track. In those days no 'heavy swell' thought it worth while to bet less than a hundred pounds on a horse.

As the Prince's expenditure rose, the whispers increased about the Rothschilds' paying his debts. There was never any proof of it. On the other hand Bertie would have been stupid not to secure the advice of those shrewd bankers on investing his money; and it is hardly likely that the shrewd bankers would care to inform him if their tips failed to produce profitable results. No one knows what transactions took place.

The Radicals made the most of the rumours. They criticised Queen Victoria for hoarding her money and not being more generous with her son, and drew a picture of a distraught Bertie at the mercy of the wicked Jewish moneylenders.

A vicious parody on both the Prince and Shakespeare, entitled *Edward VII*, appeared in 1876. One of the scenes shows the worried, debt-laden Bertie in a room with his rich, tight-pursed mother, who has fallen asleep by her desk. He looks into her account books, and sees that her only expenditure is marked 'A.M.', which he knows means money for Albert's memorials. In anguish he cries:

'Oh, that I could muster up resolution; tell her all,
And claim full payment for the work I do!
Tell all or not tell all, that is the question:
Whether it is better of the Jews to borrow,
To take the cash of base-born, low-bred men
Who out of my necessities would make
A ladder up to peerages, who claim
My notice, 'cause I take their ill-gained coin
Who whine for invitations to my house,
As though the cad who sells them gold deserved
More notice than the ones who sell you hats,
Or build you coats, or fashion you your boots;
Nay, not so much, for these are honest men——
Whether 'tis better their demands to suffer
Or make clean breast of it; declare my debts
And pay off all the Jewish herd in full
With money that now fills the Royal purse:
Methinks I will.'

THE Rothschilds were useful for other things besides financial advice. The Prince's chief amusement in life continued to be pretty women, and the banking Barons took care that when he visited their houses he was never disappointed. Besides, they always did as they were bid. When Sarah Bernhardt came to England, the Prince was anxious that people should make a fuss over her. In those days actresses were not received in Society, but the Rothschilds obediently entertained her and soon she was 'taken up' by many influential people. However, the more conservative element of the aristocracy fumed with anger. On July 6, 1879, Lady Frederick Cavendish wrote in her diary: 'London has gone mad over the principal actress in the Comédie Française who are here: Sarah Bernhardt—a woman of notorious, shameless character. . . . Not content with being run after on the stage, this woman is asked to respectable people's houses to act, and even to luncheon and dinner; and all the world goes. It is an outrageous scandal!'

Sarah Bernhardt was not the Prince's only eccentricity. Considered even stranger was his *penchant* for American heiresses with fierce, Middle-Western accents. Bertie was greatly struck by Miss Chamberlayne, from Cleveland, Ohio. This superb beauty was doing a Grand Tour of Europe accompanied by her mother and father. The Prince met her at Homburg and followed her to Cannes. Apparently he could never see her alone, so he entertained mother and father as well. American reporters gathered, and wrote columns for their newspapers. They interviewed the parents who said how 'homely' the Prince was, indeed he was 'the most agreeable' gentleman they had ever met. And they interviewed the daughter and reported that this fine specimen of American womanhood required for breakfast two eggs, a fried sole, a beefsteak and plenty of potatoes.

Encouraged by this romance *Punch* came out with a series of cartoons. One was entitled: 'An Enamoured Briton On A Ship Talking To An American Belle.'

'It must be awfully jolly knocking about like this all over Europe with your mother and sister. But why didn't you take your father with you?'

'Oh! Pa don't voy'ge—He's too fleshy.'

The Prince's flirtation with Miss Chamberlayne ended when the young lady returned to America, where she eventually married. Some years later a Mr. Rae, a prominent member of the Reform Club, wrote a novel entitled *Miss Bayle's Romance*. This was a merry skit on Miss Chamberlayne, but the surprising feature of the book is that the author introduces real people as characters. Not only does the Prince of Wales play a prominent part, but Mr. Disraeli appears, Lord Randolph Churchill, and even Queen Victoria.

Like everything else, the Prince of Wales' admiration for American ladies started a vogue. Soon there was an epidemic of marriages between members of the English aristocracy and daughters of wealthy American business men, a fashion which continued for nearly half a century. One of the earliest of these alliances took place between Lord Randolph Churchill and Miss Jennie Jerome.

This lady had two sisters, and all three Jeromes caught the fancy of the Prince. 'I don't know why,' wrote Jennie's sister, Clara, in June 1875, 'but people always seem to ask us whenever H.R.H. goes to them. I suppose it is because Jennie is so pretty and you have no idea how charming Randolph can be when *il fait des frais*! And I don't want to be conceited but I think I make myself agreeable too as they could easily ask them without me.'[1]

This friendship with the Prince, of which the sisters were so proud, was broken off in 1876 through no fault of their own. It was due to a scandal that set London agog. The story began when the Prince departed on a tour of India in the autumn of 1875. When the trip was first proposed Queen Victoria was very much against it. She did not like Bertie representing her. She made all sorts of excuses, saying it would be difficult for the Viceroy, for who would take precedence over whom?

She also objected to the retinue the Prince proposed to take with him. Some of his companions were serious men, but sandwiched among them were half a dozen of the gayest members of the Marlborough House Set. These included Lord Charles Beresford, Lord Carrington, the Duke of Sutherland and the Earl of Aylesford, generally known as 'Sporting Joe'.

The Queen tried to dissuade Bertie from including

[1] *The Fabulous Mr. Jerome:* Anita Leslie.

these companions in his entourage but he was adamant. It was left to Sir Henry Ponsonby to smooth away the difficulties between Marlborough House and Balmoral, and he was finally able to write: 'The Queen has agreed in my observations far more than I expected but maintains she should express her dislike of those going as she cannot truthfully approve. I have suggested that instead of saying anything more against these she might regret that he had not selected more distinguished men more eminently qualified to act as guides in India.'[1]

The Prince breathed a sigh of relief, as he was determined to have his friends with him. He was counting on 'Sporting Joe', one of the best riders in England, to organise the polo and the pig-sticking. Besides, according to the gossips, the Prince had been paying very marked attention to Joe's pretty wife, Edith Aylesford, and the malicious-minded said Bertie was afraid to leave the Earl behind for fear he might learn the truth.

But Lady Aylesford apparently had a fickle temperament, for no sooner had husband and admirer sailed away than she allowed Lord Blandford, the elder brother of Lord Randolph Churchill, to move his horses to an inn not far from her house and settle down for a winter's hunting.

Lord Blandford's interest in women was notorious. His name had already been linked with several scandals, and he sometimes managed to shock even his sophisticated friends. The older generation compared his reckless nature to that of his grandfather, the sixth Duke of Marlborough, recalling how the latter had lured a Miss Susan Law into a marriage ceremony which was nothing but a hoax performed by a member of the Guards Brigade impersonating a parson. It was not until the lady had produced several children that she discovered her predicament. The Duke then legally married the

[1] *Henry Ponsonby: His Life from His Letters:* Arthur Ponsonby.

daughter of the Earl of Galloway, and Miss Law was given an annual income to make amends for her unfortunate plight.

Lord Blandford had inherited his grandfather's impulsiveness. Even though Lord Aylesford was his closest friend, he could not resist the blandishments of the charming wife. But clouds soon began to gather, for someone wrote 'Sporting Joe' a letter telling him what was happening, and he broke off his trip with the Prince and came hurrying back from India.

The Heir Apparent was furious. It was inconvenient losing Aylesford. How dare Blandford seduce the Countess when her husband had sailed off in the service of his Prince? When he returned to England he made it plain what he thought of such behaviour. There was a good deal of talk about 'a best friend's wife'; and here Lord Randolph Churchill stepped in. Who was the Prince of Wales to pass strictures? What about his own shortcomings?

And then Lord Randolph did the unforgivable. He declared he had a packet of love letters written by the Prince to Lady Aylesford. Some said he had climbed in a window and stolen them; others said the lady had let him have them. Whatever the truth of the matter, Lord Randolph declared that unless the Prince stopped criticising his brother, he would see that the letters found their way into print.

His Royal Highness' fury knew no bounds. This was practically blackmail. He sent Lord Knollys to challenge Lord Randolph to a duel, suggesting Rotterdam as a suitable place. 'Even Jennie's iron nerves began to grow frayed,' writes one of the Jerome descendants. 'She passed sleepless nights until Randolph appointed Lord Falmouth as his second and dispatched him with a message to say he would fight any nominee, but could not lift sword against his future Sovereign.'[1]

[1] *The Fabulous Mr. Jerome:* Anita Leslie.

No duel was fought, and the storm gradually died down. But the Prince's fury remained. He made it clear that he would not set foot in any house that continued to receive the Churchills. And since Society regarded Bertie's word as law, ostracism was complete. The Duke of Marlborough reluctantly decided to accept the post of Viceroy of Ireland in order to provide a new home for his son. Lord Randolph took his wife and his two-year-old son, Winston, with him and spent nearly six years of his life in virtual exile.

It was no small thing to arouse the Prince of Wales' displeasure.

CHAPTER EIGHT

PROFESSIONAL BEAUTIES: THE EIGHTIES

BY the eighties hostesses were finding it increasingly difficult to keep the worldly, forty-year-old Prince amused. They were always searching for novelties in the form of new jokes, new games or new beauties. They drew a sigh of relief when Lillie Langtry appeared on the scene.

This stunning creature with the rounded figure, the Grecian profile, the alabaster skin and the pale gold hair took London by storm. She had been brought up on the island of Jersey where her father was a clergyman. Before she was out of her teens she had set her cap at an Irish widower by the name of Mr. Langtry, whose chief attraction was the fact that he owned a comfortable yacht. A few months after their honeymoon they made a visit to London. They knew no one and spent most of their time at art galleries and museums. But one day when they were visiting the Aquarium they ran into an old acquaintance, Lord Ranelagh, whom they had known one summer in Jersey. Lord Ranelagh asked them to a tea party where they met more people, and a Lady Sebright invited them to an evening gathering at which many stars of the literary and art world were present.

That evening marked the beginning of Lillie's spectacular success. Lady Sebright's distinguished guests included Henry Irving, John Millais and James Whistler, all of whom begged to take her to supper. The next day her rooms were filled with cards and invitations to lunch and dine. Her first dinner was with Lord and

Lady Wharncliffe. Lord Randolph Churchill was a guest, and he wrote to his wife, Jennie, 'I dined with Lord Wharncliffe last night, and took in to dinner a Mrs. Langtry, a most beautiful creature quite unknown, very poor, and they say has but one black dress.'[1]

Thus the news of Mrs. Langtry's astonishing beauty began to spread. At a reception at Lady Jersey's, people stood on chairs to get a good look at her. Photographers, whose art was at last beginning to develop, implored her to sit for them and soon the shops were full of her pictures. Her face was becoming familiar to the London crowds, which had certain disadvantages. One Sunday afternoon she was sitting on a bench in the Park near the Achilles statue. 'Someone,' she wrote, 'raised the cry that it was I, people rushed toward me and, before the police could interfere, I was mobbed to such an extent that an ambulance finally conveyed me, suffocating and unconscious, to St. George's Hospital.' She goes on to say, 'It would be difficult for me to analyse my feelings at this time . . . to find myself not only invited to, but watched for at all the great balls and parties; to hear the murmur as I entered the room, to be compelled to close the yard gates in order to avoid the curious, waiting crowd outside, before I could mount my horse for my daily canter in the Row; and to see my portrait roped round for protection at the Royal Academy[2]—surely, I thought, London had gone mad.'[3]

By this time talk of Mrs. Langtry's beauty was becoming world wide. It is not surprising that royalty began to prick up its ears. The first member of Queen

[1] *The Reminiscences of Lady Randolph Churchill.* Mrs. Langtry only owned one dinner dress, not because of poverty but because until now she had only needed one.

[2] This was the portrait by Millais showing Mrs. Langtry with a Jersey Lily in her hand, which henceforth became her sobriquet.

[3] *The Days I Knew:* Lillie Langtry.

Victoria's family to pay marked attention to the Jersey Lily was the Heir Apparent's brother, Prince Leopold. He called very frequently and hung a sketch of her by Frank Miles over his bed. Sometime later Queen Victoria spied the drawing, dragged forth a chair, climbed up and removed it.

The young Prince soon acquired competitors. One was the new King of the Belgians, who began to pay calls on Mrs. Langtry at the odd hour of nine in the morning. Then there was the saucy, unstable Crown Prince Rudolf of Austria, who deluged her with flowers and invitations. But none of these admirers could stand up to the competition of the Prince of Wales. Day after day he rode in the park with Mrs. Langtry, and every hostess who had visions of luring the Prince of Wales to dinner, had to secure Mrs. Langtry's acceptance first.

The Lily was liberal with her favours. One of her first admirers was Morton Frewen, who later married one of the Jerome sisters. He gave her Redskin, the horse that she rode in the Park. But he, apparently, was discouraged by the competition for he wrote, somewhat ungallantly, that he had found it 'quite impossible to compete with Prince Rudolph much less the Prince of Wales, but I had the joy of seeing her riding my horse when out exercising with H.R.H. Anyway lilies can be dreadfully boring when not planted in a bed!'[1]

Queen Victoria was seldom enthusiastic about Bertie's activities and his friendship with Mrs. Langtry was no exception. Nevertheless the Queen was curious. She wanted to see for herself what this woman was like that all London raved about. So suddenly the Lily found herself in possession of an invitation to one of Her Majesty's Drawing Rooms. It was rare for the Queen to appear; and even more rare for her to remain through the whole afternoon. But Mrs. Langtry was near the last to be

[1] *The Fabulous Mr. Jerome:* Anita Leslie.

presented, so there was nothing to do but wait. 'Queen Victoria,' wrote Mrs. Langtry, 'looked straight in front of her, and, I thought, extended her hand in rather a perfunctory manner.' No doubt she did. Curiosity was satisfied, but what she thought of the lady's charms she never revealed.

In the meantime what about Mr. Langtry? He appears to have hung about, protesting, for some time. Occasionally he made scenes. Once he discovered the contents of a love letter his wife had written, by holding the blotter up to the mirror. The Lily was reduced to tears and her host, the famous diplomat, Lord Malmesbury, found her sobbing out her heart. When she told him the story he stormed at the servants. They had, he said, strict orders to change the blotting paper every day just so that sort of thing could not occur!

Eventually Lillie separated from her husband, and went on the stage. When she performed, the theatre was always packed, thanks to the patronage of the Prince of Wales. But she was not very effective. She refused to use any grease paint or make-up for fear of spoiling her skin, and as a result she had a curious washed-out look. Besides, she had little talent as an actress. A current quip was, 'What is the difference between Madame Modjeska (the great Polish star) and Lillie Langtry?' 'One is a Pole, and the other a Stick.'

Eventually Mrs. Langtry married Sir Hugo de Bathe and took up racing. The Prince's infatuation had ended long before, but he remained on friendly terms with her for many years.

DURING the height of the Lily's vogue, beautiful Society ladies copied everything she did. They wore their hair in a 'Langtry knot', they bought 'Langtry shoes' and 'Langtry hats'; above all they followed Mrs. Langtry's example in the matter of photography. They posed for hundreds of pictures against every conceivable kind of background in every conceivable kind of outfit. Most of them were nauseatingly sentimental. 'Some smothered themselves in furs to brave photographic snowstorms; some sat in swings; some lolled dreamily in hammocks; others carried huge bunches of flowers (indigenous to the dusty studio and looking painfully artificial), and one was actually produced gazing at a dead fish. I myself, on one occasion only, foolishly gave his head to the photographer, who represented me with a dead bird in my hand and an expression of grief on my face. . . .'[1]

Among the ladies whose photographs were 'best-sellers' were Mrs. Luke Wheeler (another also-admired-by-the-Prince), Lady Randolph Churchill, Lady Dudley, Lady Helen Vincent and Mrs. Cornwallis-West. These ladies became known as 'The Professional Beauties', and soon the music halls were ringing with skits on their activities. One of the most popular was:

'I have been photographed like this,
I have been photographed like that,
But I have never been photoed
As a raving maniac.'

A large section of Society disapproved of the 'Professional Beauties'. They regarded publicity as exceedingly vulgar and were shocked that 'ladies' could lend themselves to such a disgraceful fad. They attributed it to the

[1] *The Days I Knew:* Lillie Langtry.

insidious decay that was undermining Society by the admission of Jews and City men and Americans into the best houses of the land. And this was due entirely to the Prince of Wales' influence.

Worse still, they felt that moral standards were deteriorating. Every few years some lurid divorce case was printed in *The Times* and the participants always seemed to be members of the Prince's inner circle. In the late seventies Joe Aylesford sued his wife for divorce, but the Queen's Proctor intervened and revealed how he himself frequented the Cremorne night after night and carried on 'vulgar amours' with women of the lowest type. In 1883 Lady Blandford divorced her husband, and the evidence showed how Lord Blandford and Lady Aylesford had lived openly in Paris for several years as Mr. and Mrs. Spencer. Then in 1885 Valentine Baker, Colonel of the 10th Hussars and one of the darlings of the Marlborough House Set, made fairly drastic advances towards a pretty girl in a railway carriage travelling from Midhurst to London. She pushed him away and became so hysterical that she jumped on to the footboard and clung to the door screaming for help. No help came, however, until the train reached Esher. Then the station guards hurried up, and after hearing the girl's story, detained Baker. He was eventually tried for indecent assault and found guilty. He was sentenced to a year's imprisonment and, of course, cashiered from the army.

All these things were very disturbing and a committee of indignant ladies called to discuss the alarming trend with the Archbishop of Canterbury. The delegation was led by the Duchess of Leeds, and included the Marchionesses of Tavistock, Bristol and Ailsa, the Countesses of Aberdeen, Zetland and Haddington, Countess Stanhope, and the Ladies Mount-Temple, Muncaster, Harriet Ashley and Welby-Gregory. 'They had come,' the

Archbishop's son wrote many years later, 'to ask my father if he could do nothing to stop the moral rot which, they affirmed, was ruining London. Girls newly "come out", they said, of high tone and upright intentions, were speedily corrupted by it, and what they had been brought up to regard as evil they soon regarded as natural and inevitable, young married women had no standard of morality at all, and the centre of the mischief was the Marlborough House Set. They wanted my father to start a sort of moral mission for women of their class and to hold devotional meetings for them at Lambeth, thus creating a powerful and influential nucleus of those who aimed at high ideals and could not tolerate the looseness of life that was becoming general. They thought it would give impetus to the movement if the Princess of Wales would come to these meetings: it was no use trying to get the sympathy of the Queen, for that would have no effect as "she was not smart enough". Finally they all agreed that my father should talk to the Prince about the harm that was going on "for he would listen to no one else".'[1]

The Archbishop did not think it was his business to lecture the Prince on hearsay reports of his private life. But he consented to hold the Lambeth meetings, and the ladies wrote to Princess Alexandra asking her if she would like to attend. The Princess replied that she must consult the Queen. The idea of prayers in the middle of the week struck Victoria as 'most extraordinary'. 'I can't understand,' she said, 'why Princesses should want to go to Lambeth meetings. It's all sacerdotal. I can't think what it's all about.'

The Princess of Wales did not attend, but the other ladies did, and prayed solemnly that Society would become more exclusive again, and people would behave themselves better all round.

[1] *As We Were:* E. F. Benson.

ALTHOUGH the Queen disapproved of prayers in the middle of the week, she shared the view of the ladies' delegation regarding her eldest son. She wrote to the Prince repeatedly asking him to lead a more serious life. When she sent him the manuscript of a continuation of her Highland Journal, entitled *More Leaves*, which contained frequent references to John Brown, he wrote back, suggesting that perhaps some of the chapters were too personal to publish.[1] Victoria's indignation knew no bounds. She sent a note to her secretary enclosing the Prince's letter, 'which she thinks he will think strange considering how much talk and want of reticence there is in his home and how little he keeps anything to himself and how continually he lives in Society. . . . It is very strange that objections should come from that quarter where great strictness as to conduct is not generally much cared for.'[2]

Queen Victoria was worried by the Prince's 'gadding about'. Why couldn't he stay at home, as Albert did, and spend quiet, satisfying evenings improving his mind? For a long time she had hoped that his restlessness would diminish with his youth, but in middle-age his fever for diversion seemed to be increasing. When he was not at Ascot or Goodwood or Cowes, when he was not at Sandringham, when he was not at Homburg or Marienbad or Cannes, he was paying visits from one end of England to the other.

No other Prince of Wales, before or after Albert Edward, has ever graced so many private houses with his presence. There was scarcely a stately home in the Kingdom whose hospitality the Prince did not sample at one time or another. He visited the Duke of Portland at Welbeck, the Duke of Devonshire at Chatsworth, the Duke of Richmond at Goodwood, the Duke of Beaufort

[1] Many of these references were finally deleted.

[2] *Henry Ponsonby: His Life from His Letters:* Arthur Ponsonby.

at Badminton, the Duke of Westminster at Eaton Hall, the Duke of Norfolk at Arundel, the Duke of Sutherland at Dunrobin. He visited the Pembrokes at Wilton, the Desboroughs at Taplow Court, the Lansdownes at Bowood, the Alingtons at Crichel, the Warwicks at Warwick Castle. He visited Mr. and Mrs. Lewis Harcourt at Nuneham, Mrs. William James at West Dean Park, Mrs. Bankes at Kingston Lacy. He visited all the Rothschild houses in turn.

These visits were very opulent. Elaborate preparations were made to see that the Prince, and the Princess who frequently accompanied him, had every comfort. A suite of rooms was usually redecorated for the occasion, and a post office installed in the house.

A whole wing in the staff quarters was set aside for the royal servants, for the Prince always travelled with a large retinue. Besides his two valets, he always brought his own footman, who wore the royal livery, stood behind his chair at meal time and served him with his food. If there was any shooting the Prince brought two loaders with him; any hunting and he brought his horses and two grooms. He usually travelled with a gentleman-in-waiting and one or two equerries.

Enormous efforts were made to provide special entertainment; sports, cards, lively dinner companions, and perhaps a ball. Even so, the long stays, usually stretching from Monday to Saturday, had their moments of tedium. Fortunately for the hostess the elaborate and lengthy meals made 'resting' an absolute necessity; then the fact that everyone had to change their clothes several times a day accounted for more hours.

In spite of all the preparations, the highlights of the stay were often provided by the practical jokers. Both the Prince and the Princess adored practical jokes. Indeed these 'larks', as they were called, were smiled upon by Society for nearly thirty years. All the memoirs of the day refer to them. We have Lillie Langtry boasting of how she told her host the soup was cold, and how he angrily took a large swallow and badly burnt his mouth. We have the ex-Duchess of Marlborough telling us how her mother-in-law once gave a dinner party and put small bits of soap among the real pieces of cheese; and how on another occasion she tied an ink-pot over a door which emptied its contents on her husband's head.

We read of apple-pie beds, leaking hot-water bottles, and how Lady de Grey once bought a whole set of china so that the footman could drop it and make Lord de Grey think he had lost his priceless collection. Lillie Langtry tells us how she dressed up like a hawker and sold matches on the street; and Daisy, Princess of Pless, was so used to 'larks' that she once mistook an earthquake for a joker under her bed.

The Prince loved the fun of house-parties and himself initiated many of the escapades that took place. But of course no one would have dreamed of playing a practical joke on him. He liked to enjoy himself in what he called an easy fashion, yet never for a single minute did he forget that the blood royal ran through his veins. He was not the least pompous, but as a fervent believer in the monarchical principle he regarded the gulf between the ruler and the ruled as immutably fixed.

Once he was asked whether he did not think an English duke should take precedence over a minor Indian rajah, and he replied indignantly, 'Certainly not'. On another occasion he aroused the anger of the German Embassy in London by insisting that the Kalakua, the King of the Cannibal Islands, should take precedence over his sister's husband, the German Crown Prince. 'At a party given by Lady Spencer at the South Kensington Museum,' wrote Sir Charles Dilke in his diary, 'Kalakua marched along with the Prince of Wales, the Crown Prince of Germany following humbly behind; and at the Marlborough House Ball Kalakua opened the first quadrille with the Princess of Wales. When the Germans remonstrated with the Prince, he replied, "Either the brute is a King or else he is an ordinary black nigger, and if he is not a King, why is he here?" which made further discussion impossible.'[1]

The Prince was able to regard his infatuations as part of the royal tradition. By the middle-eighties people could no longer attribute the Prince's indiscretions to youthful exuberance. The Heir Apparent was now forty-five, and it was obvious that his pursuit of.women was no passing fancy. The flame of desire burned within him as brightly as ever, and promiscuity had to be accepted as an inherent part of his nature. Miss Margot Tennant, who made her debut in 1885 and met the Prince shortly afterwards, described him as 'a professional love-maker'. 'Men did not interest him,' she wrote, 'and like Disraeli, he delighted in the society of women. He was stimulated by their company, intrigued by their entanglements, flattered by their confidence, and valued their counsel. . . .'[2]

The Prince had the agreeable quality of being a friend as well as a lover, and was extremely generous in the presents he bestowed upon the ladies he fancied. After meeting Miss Tennant only once he sent her a gold shark-skin cigarette case with a diamond and sapphire clasp. There were, of course, malicious tongues which claimed that the Prince of Wales did not like taking 'no' for an answer; that ladies who rejected his advances found themselves excluded from the Marlborough House Balls. But either the Heir Apparent was irresistible, or the Marlborough House Balls were considered worth any inconvenience, for there is no reference to this type of ostracism in the memoirs of the day.

[1] *The Life of Sir Charles Dilke:* Gwynn and Tuckwell.

[2] *More Memories:* Margot Oxford.

Throughout the years Princess Alexandra put up with her husband's flirtations with remarkable generosity. Sometimes she was a little piqued; she nick-named Miss Chamberlayne 'Chamberpots' and poked good-natured fun at her. But on the whole, she regarded his passion for pretty women as a sort of hobby; she managed to take the same detached view of it that one would toward a connoisseur of first editions. She adored him, and on her birthday in 1878 she wrote gaily to her mother-in-law, 'My Bertie quite overloaded me with lovely presents.'[1]

The Prince never embarrassed Alexandra in public, and was always watchful to see that every courtesy was shown her. Once, when the Duchess of Marlborough attended a dinner in honour of the Prince and Princess of Wales, and wore a diamond crescent in her hair instead of the prescribed tiara, the Prince eyed her disapprovingly. 'The Princess has taken the trouble to wear a tiara. Why have you not done so?'[2]

Alexandra was simple, unaffected and high spirited. Perhaps it was her sense of humour that allowed her to treat her husband as indulgently as a small boy. She understood his devotion to her, but she also understood his need for a light hand. She never accompanied him on his trips to Paris and Homburg, and she often allowed him to make his expeditions to the great houses of England by himself.

But her gradual withdrawal from the full round of social life was influenced by other considerations as well. Ever since the late sixties she had been afflicted by a slowly increasing deafness which she had inherited from her mother. As a result she preferred the company of people she knew well, rather than new faces.

But more important still was her passionate devotion

[1] *The Letters of Queen Victoria.*

[2] *The Glitter and the Gold:* Consuelo Balsan.

to her children. Alexandra had been brought up in a close family circle, and considered it natural to pour unrestrained affection on her sons and daughters. They, in turn, worshipped their mother. When the 15-year-old Prince George embarked on a two-year world cruise he wrote a heart-breaking farewell letter. 'My darling Motherdear, I miss you so very much and felt so sorry when I had to say goodbye to you and sisters and it was dreadfully hard saying goodbye to dear Papa and Uncle Hans. It was too rough yesterday to go to sea, so we stopped in here for the night . . . I felt so miserable yesterday saying goodbye. I shall think of you all going to Scotland tonight and I only wish we were going too. Lord Colville will take this letter and he has to go, so I must finish it. *So goodbye once more my darling Motherdear*, please give darling Papa and sisters my very best love and kisses and very much to dear Uncle Hans. I remain your very loving son Georgy. *So goodbye darling Motherdear, dearest Papa and sisters*.'[1]

Although the children were more in awe of their father than their mother, the Prince gave his sons a warmth and intimacy he himself had never known. In 1886, a few months before Prince George's twenty-first birthday, he spent a few days alone with the boy at Cannes. When the young Prince rejoined his ship the father wrote, 'On seeing you go off by the train yesterday I felt very sad and you could, I am sure, see that I had a lump in my throat when I wished you goodbye.'[1] The letter crossed one from the son: 'I cannot tell you how much I miss you every minute of the day, because we have been together so much lately. It was so kind of you coming all the way to Mentone to see me off the other day. I felt so very low at saying goodbye to you. . . .'[1]

The Prince was usually very gentle with his children.

[1] *King George V:* Harold Nicolson.

When he died many years later Prince George wrote broken-heartedly in his diary: 'I have lost my best friend and the best of fathers. I never had a word with him in his life. . . .'[1] Nevertheless, the boys sometimes caused him anxiety. When George and Eddy, aged 15 and 16 were on their world cruise, they visited the Botanical Gardens in the Barbados and sniffed the white lilies. They returned to the ship their faces stained yellow, and an enterprising journalist at once telegraphed home with the report that they had had their noses tattooed. The Prince of Wales was horrified and immediately sent stern messages. But Alexandra rocked with laughter. 'How could you,' she wrote to Prince George, 'have your impudent snout tattooed? What an object you must look, and won't everybody stare at the ridiculous boy with the anchor on his nose! Why on earth not have put it somewhere else?'[1]

The Rev. J. N. Dalton, who was in charge of the boys, quickly put the parents' minds at rest. 'The Princes' noses are without any fleck, mark, scratch or spot of any kind whatever. The skin is as white as the day they left home.'[1]

QUEEN Victoria, of course, was often critical of her grandsons' upbringing. Despite her dissatisfaction with Bertie it never occurred to her that any mistakes had been made as far as *his* education was concerned. In a letter to Mr. Dalton she mentioned Baron Stockmar. '*No one*', she said, 'gave us better and wiser advice on the education of our Children.' She remembered with pride how Bertie had been prevented from associating with companions of his own age and added, 'I have a great

[1] *King George V:* Harold Nicolson.

fear of young and carefully brought up Boys mixing with older Boys and indeed with any Boys in general. . . .'[1]

Bertie and Alexandra were polite, but they had their own ideas about bringing up children. They received the Queen's strictures with patience and replied as judiciously as possible. In 1880 Victoria declared that the "fast and fashionable" friends who visited Sandringham were not fit company for the boys. 'I must also return most earnestly and strongly to the *absolute necessity* of the children, all of them, *not* mixing with the society you are constantly having. They must either take their meals *alone*, or you must breakfast and lunch *alone* with them and to this a *room* must be given up wherever you are.'[1]

The Prince reassured his mother that the children were not mixing 'in what you call "fashionable society", and we hope and think that they are so simple and that those who have come in contact with them have such tact with them that they are not likely to do them any harm.'[1]

THE Queen's disapproval of nearly everything Bertie did had become a vicious circle. She continued to complain of his friends and his frivolity and his endless travelling; yet she still refused to give him responsibility or provide him with any interesting work. The House of Lords committees had not proved successful. The Foreign Secretary had leaned over backwards to select committees of a non-political character for the Prince to attend, with the result that Bertie found himself deliberating first the Plague of Cows and second the Scarcity of Horses. Neither riveted his attention.

The subject in which he was whole-heartedly and

[1] *King George V:* Harold Nicolson.

passionately interested was Foreign Affairs. He had visited half the countries of the world; he spoke French and German almost as well as English; he had met all the rulers (most of whom were his relations) and all the leading political figures in Europe. He was wonderfully equipped to serve the Government as an unofficial ambassador. He had an undisputed flair for diplomacy, and, according to Mr. Gladstone, 'No royalty I have ever met has such charm and tact as the Prince of Wales.'

Yet the Queen was adamant. She not only flatly refused to make use of his experience, but she continued to deny him access to confidential Foreign Office papers. She allowed documents which had been acted upon to be sent to him, and précis of a general nature to be prepared for him, but if she suspected Foreign Office officials were providing him with more than she intended, she promptly rapped them on the knuckles, and put an end to it. Sir Julian Pauncefote, the Permanent Under-Secretary at the Foreign Office, found the situation very confusing. On January 25, 1887, he wrote to the Queen's secretary:

'I am sorry to find from your note to Barrington (returning the Italian Draft) that the Queen disapproved of its being sent to the Prince of Wales as it is marked "Very Confidential". I have of course directed that the Draft should not go to His Royal Highness, but I should be extremely obliged if you could *privately* and without troubling Her Majesty on the subject, give me some indication as to where to draw the line in selecting the Documents to be sent to the Prince. I was greatly pleased to think that, when you last wrote on the subject, I was authorised to use a free hand in the matter and I have accordingly sent to him all despatches of real interest whether marked "Secret" or not. I hope I may continue to do so as I think it most important at this critical juncture that he should see what cards are in the hands of the players in the great European game which is going on, and how they are being played.'[1]

The Queen had no intention of allowing Bertie to see how the cards were 'being played', and Sir Henry Ponsonby's reply was brief and to the point. 'Quite right to let H.R.H. know what is going on—but as the direction of affairs is not in his hands it does not appear to be necessary to submit confidential drafts for his consideration before they take effect.'[1]

Those close to the Queen did not trouble to hide the fact that one of the reasons Her Majesty refused to allow the Prince to read the secret papers was because 'he lets them out'. Bertie smarted under these accusations. They never reached him openly, only in whispers, and it was difficult to deny vague rumours. Besides, he probably had committed indiscretions, but the cure for that, his friends believed, was responsibility. He complained bitterly that even the Ministers' secretaries had keys to the cabinet boxes, but he was trusted less than anybody.

The battle over the confidential papers raged throughout the eighties with the Queen stubbornly refusing to yield an inch. As a result the Prince was obliged to obtain his information by word of mouth; and the two politicians he chose to make his confidants were the two men whom the Queen disliked more than any others. One was Sir Charles Dilke, and the other Lord Randolph Churchill.

As far as Victoria was concerned Sir Charles Dilke was absolutely beyond the pale. He was a Radical Liberal and had incurred her undying dislike by voicing Repub-

[1] *Henry Ponsonby: His Life from His Letters:* Arthur Ponsonby.

lican sentiments in the seventies; he also had had the impertinence to attack the Civil List. According to the Queen he was a thoroughly reprehensible character and she would have nothing whatsoever to do with him.

Unlike Victoria, who found it difficult to tolerate anyone who disagreed with her, the Prince often was intrigued by men with independent views. He had gone out of his way to charm Joseph Chamberlain when that young man was Mayor of Birmingham and at the height of his Radical career. In the seventies the Prince had entertained the French Republican leader, Gambetta, at dinner; and had invited the English Radical M.P., Henry Labouchère, to garden parties at Marlborough House; now it was Sir Charles Dilke. The Prince could see nothing odd in it.

As for Dilke, he had nothing to lose by the Prince's friendship, and possibly a good deal to gain. His personal magnetism had won him a great following in the House of Commons. He was erudite, witty and voluble. In 1880 he was made Under-Secretary for Foreign Affairs. He could see no harm in keeping the Prince well informed as to what was going on. In the first place he agreed with Bertie as to the desirability of an Anglo-French Alliance. In the second, it was impossible to incur the Queen's displeasure any more deeply than he already had, and perhaps the Prince could be useful in helping him to implement his policies.

So the friendship developed, and for the next five years the two men saw each other frequently. 'It is worth talking seriously to the Prince,' Sir Charles wrote in his diary. 'One seems to make no impression at the time . . . but he does listen all the same, and afterwards, when he is talking to somebody else, brings out everything that you have said.'[1]

This was a little patronising of Sir Charles, but he

[1] *The Life of Sir Charles Dilke:* Gwynn and Tuckwell.

was a very conceited man. Nevertheless they both benefited from their association. Sir Charles not only supplied the Prince with fascinating details on Foreign Office policy, but later was responsible for the Prince's appointment as a member of a Royal Commission set up to investigate the housing conditions of the poor. The Prince was very flattered at being given this work, and managed to attend 16 out of the 38 meetings.

He also worked hard behind the scenes for Sir Charles' promotion to the Cabinet. Queen Victoria's open detestation of the man was a stumbling block. In 1882 Gladstone wanted to make Dilke Chancellor of the Duchy of Lancaster, but the Queen refused, saying that place had always been 'a purely personal one'. It became apparent that no important office of State could be given Dilke because of Victoria's opposition; Gladstone finally appointed him President of the Local Government Board, which required very little contact with the Sovereign.

Nevertheless Sir Charles continued to enhance his political standing until it became obvious, even to the Queen, that he was likely to succeed Mr. Gladstone as a Liberal Prime Minister. Victoria was worried over this horrid prospect; then, to her intense relief, came a scandal which ruined Dilke's career, and removed him once and for all from the Queen's notice.

Sir Charles returned home one evening in 1885, after dining at the Reform Club, and found a message from his friend and colleague, Donald Crawford, M.P., saying that he had an urgent matter to discuss with him. The upshot was that 22-year-old Mrs. Crawford had confessed to her husband that she had been having an affair with Sir Charles for the past three years.

This began one of the most baffling cases involving an eminent public figure ever heard in a British law court. Mr. Crawford sued his wife for divorce, naming Dilke as co-respondent; and Dilke emphatically denied the charge. Mr. Crawford, in giving his testimony, said that he had no reason to suspect Sir Charles until he received an anonymous letter saying 'Beware of the Member for Chelsea'. This meant nothing to him, other than the fact that Sir Charles represented Chelsea; he threw the paper into the waste basket. At this time Mr. Crawford was worried about his wife's association with a certain Captain Forster, who seemed to be calling on Mrs. Crawford much too frequently. Then a second letter arrived, saying: 'The first person who ruined your wife was Sir Charles Dilke. She has passed nights in his house and is well known to the servants.'

Mr. Crawford read this note to his wife. She coloured, clenched her hands; and walked up and down the room and said, 'That's mother; that woman is a fiend.' Of course she denied it. Shortly afterwards came a third note, but this one was to do with Captain Forster. 'Your wife has been seen at the Metropole on Monday with Captain Forster. Are you a fool?'

By this time poor Mr. Crawford was desperate. He had always suspected Captain Forster, but he was baffled by the allusions to Dilke. Mrs. Crawford's sister was married to Charles Dilke's brother, and as a result the Crawfords had always been on friendly terms with the Dilke family. He had never seen or heard anything that could cast the slightest suspicion on Sir Charles' behaviour; on the other hand he was constantly worried by Captain Forster's relationship with his wife. Finally, there came a fourth and last note. 'Fool, looking for the cuckoo when he has flown having defiled your nest. You have been foully deceived and dare not touch the real traitor.'

Upon reading this message, Mr. Crawford went upstairs and found his wife in bed. He told her what was in the letter. 'She took the matches, struck a light, and stood beside the bed looking at him. He asked her whether it was true she had defiled his bed. She replied, "Yes, it is true. It is time that you should know the truth. You have been on the wrong track. You suspected those who were innocent and never suspected those who were guilty." Mr. Crawford replied, "I never suspected anyone but Captain Forster." She said, "It was not Captain Forster; the man who ruined me is Sir Charles Dilke. He seduced me three and a half years ago. He called on me at Bailey's Hotel after our wedding trip and made love to me and kissed me, but nothing more." She added, "He called two or three days after we came to London in 1882. I met him at a house in Tottenham Court Road the same day and he seduced me there." '[1]

Mrs. Crawford's affair with Sir Charles had been very desultory. Over the past three years she had committed adultery with him not more than a dozen times. Twice, she told her husband, they had visited the house off the Tottenham Court Road: several times he had called to see her at her own house; and perhaps half a dozen times she had visited his house at 11.15 in the morning.

Nevertheless the case had certain shocking aspects to it. Mr. Crawford's lawyer claimed that Mrs. Crawford, in her confession to her husband, 'told him that Sir Charles Dilke made her go to bed with Fanny, who lay beside them. He asked her who Fanny was, and she replied that Fanny was a woman he had there as his mistress. She said she did not like it at first, but she did it because he wished it . . . she said he had taught her every French vice and had taught her all she knew . . . and that Sir Charles Dilke told her he took her because she was so like her mother and that he used to say when they were together, "How like you are to your mother just now." '[2]

[1] Testimony reported in *The Times*, February 13, 1886.
[2] *The Times*, February 13, 1886.

These allegations did not place Sir Charles Dilke in a very attractive light, yet his counsel advised him against going into the box. They knew that Crawford was bound to get his divorce, for in those days a wife's confession was considered sufficient evidence. They also knew that since no witnesses had been called against Sir Charles, the judge would be bound to dismiss the case against him. In this respect they were right. 'The unsworn statement of a person in the position of Mrs. Crawford,' said the judge, 'is not entitled to be received or even considered in a Court of Justice as against the person she is alleged to have committed adultery with. . . . Under these circumstances, I have no hesitation whatsoever in saying that counsel have been well-advised in suggesting the course they have induced Sir Charles to take, and the petition as against him must be dismissed, with costs.'

But neither the judge nor Sir Charles' lawyers had taken into account the force of public opinion. The readers of *The Times* newspaper, which reported the case in full, felt that Dilke had escaped on a technicality. How could you declare that a wife had committed adultery with a third party, and at the same time declare that the third party had not necessarily committed adultery with the wife? The public believed that Dilke was both guilty and depraved, and such strong feeling arose against him that Gladstone felt himself unable to include the rising politician in his new government.

By this time Dilke was frantic to be allowed to go into the witness box in the hope of clearing himself; but it was difficult to find a legal loop-hole which would permit it. Finally Dilke's friends, led by Joseph Chamberlain, persuaded the Queen's Proctor to intervene on the flimsy assertion that the divorce had been procured contrary to the interests of justice.

So the case was re-opened. But this time it was not a question of Mr. Crawford proving his wife *had* committed adultery with Sir Charles, but Sir Charles proving that he *had not* committed adultery with Mrs. Crawford. This was impossible to do.

Both Mrs. Crawford and Sir Charles gave sworn testimony, and to this day doubts remain as to which one was speaking the truth. Mrs. Crawford repeated the same evidence as before. But she was forced to admit that she had committed adultery with Captain Forster as well as Dilke, and with another man whose identity was not revealed. Could her 'confession' to her husband merely have been an attempt to protect the name of her true lover? Although she declared that Sir Charles' servants could corroborate her evidence, and that two of them had seen her in Dilke's bedroom, the servants denied these assertions. The eminently respectable J. E. C. Bodley, who was Sir Charles' private secretary, testified that he had an office on the half-landing, that his door was always open, and that it would have been impossible for any lady to have gone upstairs without his seeing her.

But what about the anonymous letters? Who could have written them? Twice Sir Charles was asked whether he had been the lover of Mrs. Crawford's mother, and he declined to answer. Gossip of the day declared that the mother, smarting under the role of rejected mistress, had decided to ruin both Dilke and her daughter, and herself had sent the letters. But what about the servants? Why had they not given evidence against Sir Charles? Mrs. Crawford claimed that the head housemaid, Sarah, was a former mistress and was interested in protecting him. It also came out in Court that the girl, Fanny, who Mrs. Crawford declared went to bed with them, was Sarah's sister. Where was Fanny now? If Mrs. Crawford's charges against her were untrue, why did she not come forward and deny them? Sarah claimed somewhat lamely that she had no idea of Fanny's whereabouts.

She had recently been married and had disappeared with her husband as he did not wish her to get mixed up in the affair.[1]

The refusal of Fanny to give evidence under oath on Dilke's behalf was damaging to Sir Charles; also damaging was Mrs. Crawford's identification of the house off the Tottenham Court Road, and the discovery that this house was run by a woman who had once been in Dilke's service.

The jury took only a quarter of an hour to come back with the verdict: 'We find it (the decree of divorce) was not procured contrary to the justice of the case.' And the next morning *The Times* announced: 'The jury in Crawford *v.* Crawford has found that Mrs. Crawford has spoken the truth and Sir Charles has not.'

Throughout the trial the Prince of Wales reasserted his faith in Dilke, and wrote him encouraging notes. To the end of his life the latter declared his innocence, but his career was smashed. Queen Victoria did not try to hide her satisfaction at the outcome of the affair and, of course, struck Dilke's name off the Court lists. But the Prince never ceased to befriend the stricken man. And when Albert Edward finally became King of England, he once again opened the door of Buckingham Palace to him. No one could accuse the Prince of being a fair-weather friend.

As Sir Charles Dilke's political prospects collapsed, Lord Randolph's star began its meteoric climb. In 1883 the Prince of Wales patched up his bitter long-standing quarrel with this younger son of the Duke of

[1] *The Times*, July 19, 20, 21, 1886.

Marlborough. It began when Queen Victoria insisted that invitations should be sent to the Churchills to attend a Drawing Room. Shortly afterwards the Prince and Princess consented to be the guests of honour at a dinner given by Lady Randolph. Other guests were Mr. Gladstone and Lord Salisbury.

That evening marked the renewal of a friendship which gradually became close and durable. It is stout testimony to the fascination of Lord Randolph's impulsive, paradoxical nature that he could make the Prince forget the past. The story has often been told of how this strange, explosive man became Chancellor of the Exchequer at the age of 37; how he resigned six months later believing that Lord Salisbury would be forced to call him back and give him his head; how the Prime Minister succeeded in forming a Government without him; and how his political career lay for ever ruined.

Queen Victoria was outraged by Lord Randolph's behaviour. She took umbrage at the fact that he wrote his letter of resignation to Lord Salisbury while he was staying at Windsor Castle—and wrote it on Windsor Castle paper. That apparently was a crime. She also was outraged because he disclosed the information prematurely to *The Times*, so that she had the shock of reading it in the newspaper before her Prime Minister could inform her. That, too, was a crime. Although Lord Randolph wrote to the Prince explaining his conduct, and Bertie sent the letter to his mother, hoping to make things better, it did not have the desired result. 'The Queen', she informed her secretary, 'thought the proceeding so strange of the P. of W. to send her this most objectionable and incorrect letter from Lord Randolph. . . . It is most undesirable and even dangerous for the P. of W. to be in communication [with him].' [1]

The Prince refused to desert his friend. He liked to

[1] *Henry Ponsonby: His Life from His Letters:* Arthur Ponsonby.

discuss foreign affairs with Lord Randolph; the two men saw eye to eye on many important points. They shared the belief that Britain should try to overcome her long-standing antagonism toward Russia and reach some sort of understanding with her. Now that Lord Randolph was out of office he conceived the notion of visiting Russia, and the Prince asked Alexandra to give him a letter to her sister, who was married to the Czar.

Lord Randolph's trip caused a sensation. His critics said it was outrageous that he should air opinions on Foreign Policy which were anathema to the Queen and her advisers; and since the Prince had made it possible for his friend to reach the Czar, and was in constant communication with Lord Randolph, he, too, was implicated. He was obviously a party to the whole affair.

Today Lord Randolph's actions seem harmless enough. All he did was to inform the Czar that he believed Russia and England had an identity of interests, and report back to England that the Czar was filled with an 'extreme desire' for an Anglo-Russian understanding. The Prince forwarded his letters to the Queen, but she took exception to the whole business. She informed him angrily that she could not understand his 'high opinion of a man devoid of all principle, who holds the most insular and dangerous doctrines on foreign affairs, and who is so impulsive and utterly unreliable'. [1]

The truth was that Britain's foreign policy was based on two beliefs: one was on a friendly Germany and the other on an unfriendly Russia. 'We must try and not alienate all our best allies,' the Queen wrote to Bertie coldly, 'and we are, I am thankful to say, on the best of terms with Germany, Austria and Italy [i.e. the Triple Alliance] which is, as you well know, of the utmost importance and the only means of keeping Russian aggression in check. . . .'[1]

[1] *The Letters of Queen Victoria.*

But the Prince did not believe that Russian aggression was the only danger. He felt strongly that Germany was an even greater threat. He felt that an understanding first with France and secondly with Russia might be desirable safeguards. And in spite of Queen Victoria's insistence, he refused to change his mind.

CHAPTER NINE

HIS NEPHEW, THE KAISER

THE estrangement between the Prince of Wales and his sister Vicky, caused by Germany's military attacks on her neighbours, did not last for long. A few years after the Franco-Prussian war, the Heir Apparent was again visiting the Crown Princess and she was writing glowingly to her mother: 'Dear Bertie is *all* kindness, so considerate, so amiable and affectionate. . . . He is as amiable a guest as he is a host, and this is saying a *great* deal!'[1]

The Prince of Wales was very fond of his gentle brother-in-law, Fritz, and he believed that when the latter ascended the throne he would be able to steer Germany on to a liberal, constitutional path which would make it possible for her to walk in harmony with England. Both Vicky and Fritz shared the Prince's detestation of Bismarck. The Iron Chancellor had recognised the strong-willed Crown Princess as an enemy and through the years he continued to employ every means, fair and foul, to counteract her influence. He misrepresented her words; he accused her of intrigues; and he depicted her consistently as an alien working hand in glove with her mother for the aggrandisement of England and the impoverishment of Germany.

These actions cut Vicky to the quick. Life in Germany was never very congenial to her. She disliked the provincialism, the lack of taste, the five o'clock dinners, and the filthy habit of spitting into the finger bowls. But

[1] *Letters of the Empress Frederick.*

no matter how much she longed for the more cultivated atmosphere of England, she was intensely loyal to her adopted country. Years later, when she was at a party, she asked Bismarck for a glass of water. When he handed it to her she turned to her lady-in-waiting and said: 'He has caused me as many tears as the water in this glass.'[1]

As it became obvious that the aged William I, who was born in 1797, was nearing the close of his life, it seemed as though Vicky's tribulations soon would be brought to an end. But in 1887 sinister shadows began to fall. The Crown Prince complained of a soreness in his throat. All the best doctors in Germany were summoned, and some of them believed it might be a malignant growth. Then a London specialist was called, at the request of the other doctors, and he was more hopeful. He refused to diagnose it as cancer but declared that it was too early to tell.

While Vicky was torn with anxiety and forebodings, other ominous shadows began to fall. The Crown Princess' eldest son, William, was behaving in an off-hand, even hostile manner. As a youth, the son had been very close to his mother. The fact that his arm had been injured at birth had drawn forth a flood of tender feelings from her. When the boy was twelve she had written to Queen Victoria: 'I watch over him myself, over every detail, even the minutest, of his education, as his Papa has never had the time to occupy himself with the children. These next few years will be very critical and important for him, as they are the passage from childhood to manhood. I am happy to say that between him and me there is a bond of love and confidence, which I feel sure nothing can destroy.'[1]

Yet soon after William reached his twenty-first birthday a gradual estrangement took place. He married and established his own residence. He was a quick, clever

[1] *Letters of the Empress Frederick.*

boy, impulsive and emotional. He talked a good deal about Destiny, and he liked to dream of doing spectacular things in a spectacular way. Bismarck was quick to see his opportunity. It was not hard to flatter such a youth, and he began to wean him away from his parents' influence. He taught him to regard his father as an ineffectual visionary, and to look upon his mother as a misguided Englishwoman who could not appreciate the true and glorious rôle Germany was fated to play. Although William's father, the Crown Prince, was not allowed to read the Foreign Office despatches, in 1886 Bismarck allowed the son to have access to them. Soon his conceit, and his indifference to his parents, was growing almost unbearable.

Up to now Vicky had not complained. But that same year she wrote to her mother, relating how Willy was laid up with an ear-ache, and added: 'We met him in the garden and I thought him looking all right. He did not condescend to remember that he had not seen me for two months, or that I had been to England and to Homburg, or that his sisters had the measles. He never asked after them or you, or any of my relations in England, so that I felt hurt and disappointed as I had been tormenting myself so much about him. He is a curious creature! A little civility, kindess and *empressement* go a long way, but I never get them from him. However, now he is not so well I will certainly take no notice of his strange want of thoughtfulness. Still, it is very painful to a soft-hearted Mama to feel so plainly that her own child does not care whether he sees her or no. . . .'[1]

By the beginning of 1888 the doctors attending the Crown Prince agreed that he was suffering from cancer.

[1] *Letters of the Empress Frederick.*

They knew that the end could not be long. At the same time the old Emperor was sinking, and it became a macabre race between father and son to see who would die first. The Emperor finally expired on March 9, 1888, and the Crown Prince who by this time was in great pain and had lost the use of his voice, ascended the throne. He ruled for only a hundred days, then sank into the grave.

Throughout the period of mourning which followed, young William behaved with such cruelty and callousness to his mother, the widowed Empress, that impartial observers began to doubt his sanity. He lent himself to a whispering campaign which blamed the Empress Frederick and 'her English doctor' for his father's death; he surrounded her house with soldiers and said that no papers or documents were to be removed without his permission. He then informed her curtly that her residence, known as Friedrichskron, would revert to its old name of the Neue Palais. He seemed to go out of his way to show disrespect to his father's memory, and encouraged Bismarck to speak of the dead man in cruel terms. At the funeral the Prince of Wales was deeply shocked when Bismarck's son, Herbert, referred to Frederick as an 'incubus' and added coldly that 'an Emperor who could not talk was unfit to reign'.[1] And William himself, far from showing any sign of filial sadness, refused even to adhere to the convention of mourning.

Naturally none of these things endeared him to his English relatives. When Queen Victoria reproached him for inviting himself to St. Petersburg and Vienna immediately after Frederick's funeral, he replied airily that he was travelling in the interest of peace, and made an allusion to 'we Emperors'. But the Queen had her own methods of dealing with her self-confident grandson. Very haughtily she received the Kaiser's representative

[1] *King Edward VII:* Sir Sidney Lee.

who had come to announce formally the accession of a new sovereign. This, of course, was reported back to Berlin, and the British Military Attaché wrote to the Queen's secretary: 'The young Emperor spoke to me this morning of the cold reception his special Envoy, General von Winterfeldt, had received at Windsor. . . .' Victoria added a marginal note: 'The Queen intended it should be cold. She last saw him as her son-in-law's A.D.C. He came to her and never uttered one word of sorrow for his death, and rejoiced in the accession of his new master.'[1]

The Princess of Wales did not manage to keep so composed as the Queen. She had never liked the Germans anyway, and now William's behaviour to his mother made her boil with rage. 'Instead of William being a comfort and support to her,' she wrote in August 1888, 'he has quite gone over to Bismarck and Co. who entirely overlook and crush her. It is too infamous.'[2]

QUEEN Victoria had always been fond of Prince William. When he was five years old she had written to Uncle Leopold that 'Dear little William, Vicky's eldest boy, a sweet, darling, promising child, on whom my own darling *doted*, and who has that misfortune with his poor little left arm, it is who is come for sea bathing and a change of air . . . And this dear child remembers his dear *grandpapa*!' Throughout his youth he paid her many visits to Osborne and Balmoral. He was brash and impetuous, but she viewed him with surprising leniency. After all he had been her first grandchild, and she could never forget that the Prince Consort had 'doted' on him.

At this time the Prince of Wales also referred to his

[1] *Letters of the Empress Frederick.*
[2] *King George V:* Harold Nicolson.

nephew as 'a nice boy' but he gave him very little thought. He saw him on many occasions as he grew to manhood, but he had no idea of the jealousy and ambition that was rankling and swelling within him. The visits to England seemed to upset the German heir. He could not help being impressed by the majesty of his grandmother; by the solidity of the Court; by the stirring ceremonies and parades and reviews that proclaimed the might of the Empire; and above all by the magnificence of the British Navy. By the time he reached home the admiration had turned to envy, and he treated his entourage to a stream of polemics on his mother's native country. 'The Prince has taken up an attitude strongly against England,' Count von Waldensee wrote in his diary in 1884, 'a quite natural reaction against the efforts of his mother to make Anglo-maniacs of her children.'

Personally, Prince William was fond of his grandmother, and the affection was tinged with an awe which he never lost. But his Uncle Bertie aroused within him a savage resentment. It seemed unfair that this man should inherit an Empire whose power was feared from one end of the world to the other, while he, Willy, had to struggle to make people respect Germany's force and position. Wherever Uncle Bertie went the world of wealth and rank and privilege accepted him as their leader, while Willy was often treated as an unimportant Prince.

These tempestuous emotions caused the nephew to do very strange things. In 1883 Uncle Bertie sent him a costume of Royal Stuart tartan, with all the accoutrements of the Highland dress, to wear at fancy dress balls. Eagerly he arrayed himself in it, and had his photograph taken. He sent copies of the picture to all his friends, and on the bottom of each he wrote: 'I bide my time.'

The following year Prince William visited St. Petersburg for the sixteenth birthday of the Czarevitch. He spent much of his time trying to poison the Czar's mind against the Prince of Wales. This was also a curious thing to do, as the Czar was married to Princess Alexandra's sister, and the two wives carried on a close correspondence. Rumours of his behaviour drifted back to England. Nevertheless Prince William persisted and when the Prince of Wales came to Berlin later in the year he wrote to the Czar to inform him of the efforts he was making to confound 'the conspiracy' which he insisted his uncle was directing. 'The visit of the Prince of Wales has yielded and is still bringing extraordinary fruit, which will continue to multiply under the hands of my mother and the Queen of England.'[1]

The Prince of Wales paid little attention to the tales he heard. William seemed a long way from the throne. But when his nephew suddenly became an Emperor the disagreeable facets of his character were forcibly called to his uncle's notice. Indeed, the first incident occurred before the Emperor Frederick had been dead a week. Bertie attended his funeral with Princess Alexandra, and he remembered, sadly, how his dead brother-in-law had told him that when he reached the throne he would restore Schleswig to Denmark and Alsace-Lorraine to France. With a lack of tact which was rare for Bertie, he asked Herbert Bismarck if he believed that the Emperor would have wished to carry out this policy. Bismarck replied in the negative, and repeated the conversation to the Emperor. William said nothing but the next month he made a public speech. 'There are people,' he cried, 'who have the audacity to maintain that my father was willing to part with what he, in conjunction with the late Prince, gained on the battlefield. We, who knew him so well, cannot quietly tolerate, even for a single moment, such an insult to his memory. . . .'[2]

[1] *King Edward VII:* Sir Sidney Lee.

[2] *The German Emperor's Speeches:* translated by Louis Elkind.

This was only the beginning of the quarrel. The Emperor William knew that his uncle had accepted an invitation to join the Austrian Emperor at the mid-September manœuvres, and afterwards to shoot with his son, the Crown Prince Rudolf. He waited until the Prince of Wales had arrived in Vienna, then announced his own imminent arrival, stipulating that no other royal guest save himself should be present at the Viennese Court during his stay. He left no doubt as to the meaning of his action, for the British Ambassador had the unpleasant task of informing the Prince of Wales that the German Ambassador had been told to repeat to him the Kaiser's remark that he preferred his uncle's room to his uncle's presence.

The Austrians were afraid of offending the Emperor and the Prince had no option but to accept the rebuff and leave the country. He took refuge with the King and Queen of Roumania until his nephew had departed, then returned to Vienna to say good-bye to his host.

THE Prince returned to England in a fury, and for once Victoria shared his indignation. She regarded the affair not only as an affront to Bertie, but to the Queen of England. Lord Salisbury, the Prime Minister, sent her a report based on a memorandum by Bismarck, in which he stressed young William's complaint 'that the Prince treated him as an uncle treats a nephew, instead of recognising that he was an Emperor. . . .'

This was too much. 'As regarding the Prince's not treating his nephew as an Emperor,' she wrote to Lord Salisbury, 'this is really too *vulgar* and too absurd, as well as untrue, almost *to be believed*.

'We have always been very intimate with our grandson and nephew, and to pretend that he is to be treated *in private* as well as in public as "his Imperial Majesty" is *perfect madness*! He has been treated just as we should have treated his beloved father and even grandfather, and as the Queen *herself* was always treated by her dear uncle King Leopold. If he has *such* notions he [had] better *never* come *here*.

'The Queen will not swallow this affront.'

Before she finished her letter she added a more ominous paragraph. 'As regards the political relations of the two Governments, the Queen quite agrees that that should not be affected (if possible) by these miserable personal quarrels; but the Queen much *fears* that, with such a hot-headed, conceited, and wrong-headed young man, devoid of all feeling, this may at ANY moment become impossible.'[1]

The quarrel was finally patched up the following year when the Kaiser made it known that he would like to visit Cowes for the Regatta. Lord Salisbury impressed the Queen with the necessity of restoring harmonious relations, and an invitation finally was extended.

The Kaiser was in his most amiable mood. A naval review was held in his honour, and the Queen made him an honorary Admiral of the Fleet. 'Fancy wearing the same uniform as St. Vincent and Nelson,' he wrote jubilantly to Sir Edward Malet. 'It is enough to make me quite giddy.'[2]

The Prince of Wales found his enthusiasm a little disconcerting. One of the reasons he had wanted to visit Cowes, he said, was to inspect England's naval equipment. He pretended to have an expert knowledge of guns and armaments, and hinted more than once that one day his own Fleet would excel that of England.

There is no doubt that his imagination was fired by

[1] *The Letters of Queen Victoria.*

[2] *King Edward VII:* Sir Sidney Lee.

his visit and his new uniform. 'I now am able to feel,' he wrote to the Queen, thanking her for her hospitality, 'and take interest in your Fleet as if it were my own, and with keenest sympathy shall I watch every phase of its further development. . . .'

The Times newspaper doubted the wisdom of allowing the impressionable Emperor to make so free a study of Britain's naval organisation, but Lord Salisbury and the Foreign Office believed the interests of peace had been served.

THE Prince of Wales had not enjoyed the Emperor's visit. He found it increasingly difficult to like his nephew. The Princess did not improve matters, for she detested the young man, and no longer tried to hide her deep anti-German feelings from her family. When in 1900 her second son, Prince George, accompanied the Prince of Wales on a state visit to Berlin and was awarded the honorary command of a Prussian regiment by the Emperor William, she wrote: 'And so my Georgie boy has become a real live filthy bluecoated Picklehaube German soldier!!! Well, I never thought to have lived to see *that*! But never mind; as you say, it could not have been helped—it was your misfortune and not your fault—and anything was better—even my two boys being sacrificed!!!—than Papa being made a German Admiral—that I could not have survived—you would have had to look for your poor old Motherdear at the bottom of the sea, the first time he adorned himself with it!'[1]

Besides Alexandra's influence, the letters that the distraught Empress Frederick wrote did not help to endear Bertie to his nephew. The young Kaiser was so enthralled

[1] *King George V:* Harold Nicolson.

with his new position that he had little time for his mother. Her feelings were cruelly wounded and she made no attempt to hide her anguish from Queen Victoria. 'William considers any public mention of his father's name an offence to him! So they have succeeded in working him up and stuffing his head full of rubbish —mingling flattery with accusations against his parents —*il globe tout* because he is so green and so suspicious and so prejudiced.'[1]

A few weeks later she was writing again, 'William does not mean to distress and wound me as he does, I daresay, but it makes it none the less hard to bear. He has so little feeling himself that he does not know other people have, and a want of respect, courtesy, consideration and fairness, coming from him is an offence and keenly felt!'[1]

A year later the relationship between mother and son had not improved, and the letters are even more pathetic than before. 'When I was in Berlin I saw William three times . . . The whole time he was gay and merry, but quite indifferent, never asking me one question about myself, and not one sympathising or kind word was uttered!

'Their going to Friedrichskron is a pang to me I cannot describe! If one could think they went there with the right feelings it would be so different—if only it had been left one year uninhabited after all that happened! To think of the room our beloved one closed his eyes in now simply used as a passage,—strangers going to and fro and laughing, etc. All the rooms we inhabited and where I suffered such untold agonies, after one short year occupied by others, and the home ringing with noise, laughter and merriment before a year is out, pains me so bitterly! I know it is foolish, but I cannot get over it! . . . .'[1]

[1] *Letters of the Empress Frederick.*

Queen Victoria did her best to smooth away the irritations that rose between her grandson, and her son and daughter. But the Kaiser's megalomania seemed to be increasing. Restless, impatient, volatile, he craved always for the dramatic. His uniforms were growing increasingly splendid and he experienced a real sense of exultation when he mounted a charger and led his fine troops through the streets of Berlin. Nothing seemed to lie beyond him, and he made it clear to Prince Bismarck that he, and not his Chancellor, was the master of Germany. 'This young German Emperor,' wrote de Goncourt, in 1890, 'this neurotic mystic, this enthusiast for the religious and warlike operas of Wagner, this man who, in his dreams, wears the white armour of Parsifal, with his sleepless nights, his sickly activity, his feverish brain, seems to be a monarch who will be very troublesome in the future.'

In the same month that this was written the Kaiser astonished Europe by sacking Bismarck. The old Chancellor had wanted to renew his 'Re-Insurance' Treaty[1] with Russia, but the Kaiser who hitherto had enjoyed intriguing with the Czar was now tired of the game and impulsively said no. He sent a telegram to Queen Victoria announcing that the seventy-five-year-old Bismarck had retired because of failing health. Eight days later he wrote to his grandmother: 'I have been educated politically by the Prince [Bismarck] and now I must show what I can do.'

During this crisis the Prince of Wales and his son, Prince George, were in Berlin on a state visit. Bismarck invited them to luncheon and, in a furious denunciation of the Kaiser, made no effort to conceal what had happened. In London there was a feeling of uneasiness. Bis-

[1] This treaty provided that if one of the two powers should engage in war, the other power would remain neutral, except in the event of an attack by Germany on France or Russia on Austria.

marck had been no friend of England, but people said it was best to have 'the devil you know'. 'What do you say to the removal of the great German Panjandrum himself?' wrote Sir William Harcourt to John Morly. 'It is not a pleasant prospect to have Europe left at the mercy of a hothead who seems also to be a fool.'[1]

[1] *Life of Sir William Harcourt:* Gardiner.

CHAPTER TEN

FIN DE SIÈCLE

THE Eighteen-Nineties opened with a scandal. The British public was not shocked by the Prince of Wales' extravagant life, nor by his mistresses, nor by his bets on the race-track. These were British failings. But the rumpus that broke out in the early weeks of 1891 over a game of baccarat caused a sensation. Baccarat had a distinctly foreign flavour; it *must* be a vice.

The Prince had gone to Doncaster to stay at Tranby Croft, the home of a wealthy shipowner by the name of Arthur Wilson, for the St. Leger races. Mr. Wilson had a large party, and after dinner the guests amused themselves by playing baccarat. A table was improvised by putting three whist tables together. The Prince took the bank. He also produced the counters with which the guests played.

The game was not played for very high stakes. But on the first night the twenty-two-year-old son of the house, A. S. Wilson, who was one of the players, thought he saw Sir William Gordon-Cumming cheating. He seemed to be withdrawing or augmenting the stake he had placed on the table, under cover of his hand, according to the cards he drew. 'When Lord Edward Somerset, who sat immediately to the left of Sir William, was taking up the cards,' young Mr. Wilson later declared, 'I saw that Sir William had one £5 counter at the top of the notepaper (which lay in front of him) and he was sitting with his hands clasped over the counter . . . Sir William leant over to see what cards Lord Edward Somerset had got. I was also looking, and whilst doing so I saw something red in the palm of Sir William's hands, which I knew could be nothing else but a £5 counter. Lord Edward had a natural—a nine—and a court card. Immediately Sir William saw this he opened his hands and let drop on to the notepaper three more £5 counters and he was paid £20 for the coup.[1]

'After this I saw him again sitting in the same position as before. I cannot recall who was taking up the cards at this time. The cards were bad, and I think our side were nothing. Sir William was sitting with his hands advanced over the table as before, and when he saw the cards were bad he withdrew his hands and let some counters which were in his palm fall back on his own pile. I could not say how many.

'I was sitting next to Berkeley Levett, whom I knew to be a brother officer of Sir William. Immediately I saw the last incident I turned to Levett and said, "By God! Levett, this is too hot." He said, "What on earth do you mean?" "Why, the man next to me is cheating." He replied, "My dear fellow, you must have made some mistake; it is absolutely impossible!" "Well, just look for yourself." He did so and a few minutes afterwards turned to me and said, "It is too hot!" '[2]

After the game was over, Wilson went to Levett's room to discuss the matter. Levett was much shaken. He was a young man of twenty-seven, and a subaltern in Sir William's regiment. He had always been on friendly terms with the older man, whom he looked up to and admired. He threw himself across the bed and said, 'My God, to think of it. Lieutenant-Colonel Sir William Gordon-Cumming, Baronet, to be caught

[1] It was not wrong for Sir William to look at Lord Edward's cards since they were playing together against the bank; but bets could not be altered once the cards had been dealt.

[2] From the testimony given by Arthur Wilson as reported in *The Times*, June 4, 1891.

cheating at cards! He was my captain for a year and a half. For God's sake, don't ask me what is to be done.'

It was a tragedy that such a delicate situation should have been left in the hands of an inexperienced boy of twenty-two, such as Mr. Wilson. There was only one action that might have prevented the incident becoming public—that was, to confront Sir William immediately and tell him he must leave the house in the morning; then to keep quiet.

But Mr. Wilson hurried off to tell his mother all about it. She was not very helpful. Her only comment was 'For God's sake, don't let us have any scandal here.' Then he told his brother-in-law Mr. Lycett Green, and Mr. Green told his wife. So five people knew. The first mistake they made was to decide to play baccarat again the following evening. Mr. Wilson felt he could solve the problem by giving instructions to the butler to produce a real baccarat table, around which the usual chalk line could be drawn. The stakes would have to be placed across the line. Under these circumstances he felt it would be impossible for Sir William to cheat.

Mr. Wilson was unsophisticated. Cheating at baccarat is such a well-known failing the French even have a word for it; '*la poussette*' it is called. When the guests sat down to play, the Prince once again took the bank. Mr. Berkeley Levett, who was sickened by the whole business, refused to look in Sir William's direction. But Mrs. Wilson, Mr. Wilson and Mr. and Mrs. Green kept a careful eye on the colonel and when the game was over all of them told each other they had witnessed further instances of cheating. 'I saw him push a blue counter over the line (value £3) when the cards had been declared favourable to his side,' Mr. Lycett Green declared. 'The next thing I observed was that he was looking at Lady Coventry's hand, and then after the Prince had declared the card, he gradually pushed a £10 counter over the line. The Prince paid, I think £5, and Sir William said, "There is £10 more" and the Prince said to General Williams, "Pay him £10 more." When I saw this I was horrified, and my first impulse was to jump up and say, "Sir William Gordon-Cumming, you are cheating!" But I did not like to make a scene before ladies, and I retired and sent a note to my mother-in-law, Mrs. Wilson. The note has been destroyed but it contained these words, "I have distinctly seen Sir William Gordon-Cumming cheating twice." '[1]

At this point the five people who had seen the cheating told Lord Edward Somerset, Lord Coventry and General Owen Williams. The latter was a close friend of Sir William, and it was decided that he and Lord Coventry should confront the baronet with the evidence against him. Lord Coventry opened the conversation by saying, 'A very unpleasant thing has occurred; some of the people have objected to your manner of playing baccarat.' 'Good heavens, what do you mean?' replied Sir William. 'Yes,' said Coventry, 'it is the case; certain persons in the house have suggested that you caused a foul play at baccarat.'

Sir William heatedly denied the charge, but he did not ask the names of his accusers, or insist on being faced with them. Instead, he said, 'What do you advise me to do?' and begged to see the Prince.

At 10.30 that night the Prince consented to see him. The conversation was brief. 'I have asked for an interview with Your Royal Highness,' said Sir William, 'as I have heard that certain persons have brought a foul and abominable charge against me, and I have to emphatically deny that I have done anything of the kind insinuated. Your Royal Highness can see what a terrible thing this must be for a man who has attempted to live

[1] Testimony given by Mr. Green as reported in *The Times*, June 5, 1891.

for 25 years the life of an officer and a gentleman.'

'What can you do? There are five accusers against you?'

'My first impulse,' said Sir William, 'is to publicly insult these five people on the first occasion I meet them —if necessary on the race-course tomorrow.'

'What is the use of that as they are five to one?'

'Something must be done,' said Sir William, and left the room.[1]

Something was done. The Prince of Wales and General Williams questioned the five people who accused Sir William, and satisfied themselves that they could not have been mistaken. Then General Williams drew up a pledge for Sir William to sign, promising that he would never play cards for money again as long as he lived.

When Lord Coventry and the General confronted Sir William with this pledge later on in the same evening he again professed his innocence. 'Why, this would be tantamount to an admission of guilt,' he exclaimed. General Williams admitted that this was so but earnestly recommended him to sign, saying it was the only way of avoiding a scandal. If Sir William did not sign, the whole story would be told over the race-course the next day. If he did sign, everyone who knew about the matter would give his word of honour to maintain absolute secrecy. So Sir William put his name to the pledge and ten people added their names as witnesses, including the Prince of Wales. The paper was then sent to the Prince's secretary, to be filed away among his private papers.

Over a dozen people knew about the dramatic events at Tranby Croft. Although they had all pledged themselves to secrecy, could anyone really believe that no word of the affair would leak out? In a few weeks' time

[1] Testimony given by Sir William Gordon-Cumming reported in *The Times*, June 2, 1891.

the whole of fashionable London was buzzing with gossip. Sir William, who was in Paris, received an anonymous letter which showed him that the matter was becoming public knowledge. People were beginning to cut him, and he knew it would not be long before the War Office got wind of it. There was only one way in which his ruined reputation could be restored. That was to win a slander suit against his five accusers. It was a desperate gamble, but he decided to take it.

The case opened on June 1, 1891, and lasted seven days. The Prince of Wales was subpœnaed to appear as a witness for Sir William and was present in court every day. Sir William continued to deny his guilt, but under cross-examination could not give any convincing reasons as to why he had not at once demanded to be faced with his accusers, and why, if he were innocent, he had consented to sign the document presented to him. His only excuse was that he wished to protect the Prince of Wales from harmful gossip.

The accusers were all called, and testified to the specific acts of cheating they had seen. Then the Prince was called by Sir William's counsel to testify to a long and close friendship with Gordon-Cumming. Just as he was about to step down from the box a juryman intervened and asked His Royal Highness point blank:

'I understand you saw no foul play?'

'It is difficult for the banker to see the play, and moreover at the house of a friend you are not likely to expect foul play.'

'What was your opinion at the time as to the charges made?' persisted the juryman.

'They seemed so strongly supported—unanimously so—by those who brought them forward that I felt that no other course was open to me but to believe what I was told.'[1]

[1] As reported in *The Times*, June 3, 1891.

From that moment on, the case was decided in the minds of the jury. If the Prince, an old friend of Sir William, who knew the background and all the people involved, believed the man guilty, guilty he must be. Certainly the evidence against him was overwhelming. When the jury went out they took only ten minutes to reach their verdict. Sir William lost his case and was ordered to pay the costs.

Needless to say a colossal scandal arose. On the very day the case finished nonconformists all over the country were holding meetings. The Welsh Baptists declared that the Prince was fostering 'immoral habits', and the Wesleyans 'bitterly regretted that the Heir to the Throne should be given to one of the worst forms of gambling . . . and that he took about with him counters for the game'.

This was not all; bad enough was the baccarat and the counters and the Prince taking the bank and dealing the cards. But what about the fact that one of the Prince's most intimate friends was a cheat; and that his hostess, a woman no one had ever heard of before, had spied on one of her guests; and that someone who had given his word of honour to remain silent had blabbed? From start to finish the whole business was squalid.

Almost every paper in the country lashed out against the Prince. In the *Review of Reviews* the editor calculated that 880,000,000 prayers had been said for His Royal Highness since his birth and pointed out that the only answer from the Almighty seemed to be a baccarat scandal. *The Times* was more pompous. It was grieved to learn that the Prince's set was 'a gambling baccarat-playing set'. It was shocked that His Royal Highness carried counters about with him. It also made it plain that it did not like his friends or his pastimes, 'If the Prince of Wales is known to frequent certain circles; and to eschew others with a greater natural claim upon the notice of Royalty; if he is known to pursue on his private visits a certain round of questionable pleasures; the serious public—who after all are the backbone of England—regret and resent it. Sir William Gordon-Cumming was made to sign a declaration that "he would never touch a card again". We almost wish, for the sake of English Society in general, that we could learn that the result of this most unhappy case had been that the Prince of Wales had signed a similar declaration.'[1]

Even abroad, the papers blazed forth with acid comment. The spruce oak which the Prince had planted in Central Park, New York, was adorned anonymously with a sign saying BACCARAT. The German press carried a cartoon showing the great door of Windsor Castle decorated with the Prince of Wales' feathers, and underneath his motto changed from 'I Serve' to 'I Deal'. Almost the last straw was a letter from the Kaiser, informing his uncle of his displeasure that anyone holding the position of Colonel in the Prussian Hussars should embroil himself in a gambling squabble and play with men young enough to be his sons.

LIKE everyone else, the Queen was distressed by the 'Tranby Croft' affair, and after a series of acid notes to her son she finally extracted from him the promise that he would never again play baccarat. Despite this incident her attitude toward the Prince seemed to be softening. In her letters and diaries of the late eighties she begins to speak of him with a surprising new affection. He becomes 'dear Bertie' and once, no doubt impulsively,

[1] *The Times*, June 10, 1891.

she comments on what 'a good and dutiful son' he is. When he visited her in Balmoral in the autumn of 1887 she wrote in her Journal, 'An early luncheon, after which dear Bertie left, having had a most pleasant visit, which I think he enjoyed and said so repeatedly. He had not stayed alone with me, excepting for a couple of days in May in '68, at Balmoral, since he married! He is so kind and affectionate that it is a pleasure to be a little quietly together.'

There was no doubt that age was mellowing the Queen. These pleasant references to the Prince continue, spasmodically, throughout the nineties, yet they did not signify any fundamental change of heart. Victoria still treated her son like a child. She refused to allow any intimacy to spring up between them, and insisted on their personal differences being discussed, not by conversation, but by letter. Although the Prince was fifty years old in 1891 he still was not allowed to see the Cabinet papers; and although he took a passionate interest in foreign affairs, his mother did not pretend to place any value on his judgment. When he visited her at Cowes in 1892 his feelings were hurt at her off-hand manner. His secretary, Sir Francis Knollys, wrote to the Queen's secretary, Sir Henry Ponsonby: 'The Prince of Wales writes to me that there is not much use his remaining on at Cowes as he is not of the slightest use to the Queen; that everything he says or suggests is pooh-poohed and that his sisters and brothers are much more listened to than he is.'[1]

The Prince would not have dreamed of reproaching his mother directly. Even at fifty he still retained his childhood fear of her. A drawing by Max Beerbohm appeared in the nineties, showing the middle-aged Prince standing in disgrace in the corner of his mother's room. It was entitled, 'The Rare, the Rather Awful

[1] *Henry Ponsonby: His Life from His Letters:* Arthur Ponsonby.

Visits of Albert Edward, Prince of Wales, to Windsor Castle.'

During the Cowes Regatta of 1893 the Prince, on board his sloop *Britannia*, challenged a friend to a race. The German Kaiser raced alongside the two boats in his *Meteor*. In the late afternoon, when the yachts were off Sandown, the wind suddenly dropped, and it became obvious that unless the race was abandoned and everyone returned to Cowes by train, they would not be in time for the full-dress dinner the Queen was giving in honour of the Kaiser that night. The Prince consulted his suite and signalled the Kaiser: 'Propose abandon race and return by train, so as to reach Osborne in time for dinner.' But the Kaiser immediately replied: 'I object. Race must be fought out. It doesn't matter when we reach Cowes.'[1]

The Prince fumed, but there was nothing he could do about it. He asked Baron von Eckardstein, a German diplomat who was on board his yacht, whether he could not make his Emperor understand that the Queen would be deeply displeased. Von Eckardstein gave him a wry smile and the Prince laughed and said, 'I suppose if you did what I suggest you would wake up the day after tomorrow at the latest in the Legation at Timbuctoo?' So the matter rested; the race went on, and the Kaiser and the Prince and their equerries appeared at Osborne after the Queen had left the dinner table and had entered the reception room. The Kaiser kissed her hand and apologised breezily for being so late. But the poor Prince regarded it as an ordeal. He hurried into the room 'in full uniform, but took cover for a moment behind a pillar, wiping the perspiration from his forehead before he could summon up courage enough to come forward and make his bow. The Queen only gave him a stiff nod, and he retreated behind the pillar again.'[1]

[1] *Ten Years at the Court of St. James:* Baron von Eckardstein.

In spite of the Prince's apprehensions, the Queen continued to be increasingly indulgent toward him. When, in 1893, Mr. Gladstone became Prime Minister for the last time, he expressed the wish that the Heir Apparent should see the Cabinet papers. For once the Queen did not protest. So at long last, after thirty years of pleading and arguing, Bertie was allowed to observe the inner workings of Her Majesty's Government. When Lord Rosebery succeeded Gladstone the following year he continued the practice; and so did Lord Salisbury when he took office in 1895. The precedent was established.

The delectable possession of the Cabinet keys gave the Prince a new interest in life. He became more absorbed than ever in foreign affairs, and soon proved he could be useful. For eight years he had believed that steps should be taken to improve Anglo-Russian relations, and in 1894 an opportunity presented itself which he grasped eagerly.

Although Alexandra's sister was married to the Czar of Russia, the Prince had never had a very high opinion of the autocratic Alexander III. However, the Emperor's eldest son, Nicholas, seemed a charming, sensible boy, and it was well known that he was madly in love with the Prince's niece, Princess Alix. This twenty-one-year-old girl was the daughter of the Prince's second sister Alice, who had married Prince Louis of Hesse, and who had died in 1878.

The beautiful, golden-haired Princess Alix could not make up her mind about the heir to the Russian throne, because marriage would mean the changing of her religion. Early in 1894 she went to Coburg for a family gathering at which her grandmother, Queen Victoria, was present. The Czarevitch came too and the courtship continued under a smiling April sky. Then one morning came the 'beautiful, unforgettable day' when they went hand in hand to tell the Queen that they had reached an understanding. 'I was quite thunderstruck,' Victoria wrote in her journal, 'as, though I knew Nicky much wished it, I thought Alicky was not sure of her mind.'

In the following November, a few weeks before the wedding was scheduled to take place, news arrived that Czar Alexander was seriously ill. The Princess of Wales at once set off to comfort her sister, and Bertie went with her. The Czar died before they arrived.

The Prince of Wales had planned to spend only a short time abroad, but he now saw an opportunity to be of real use to the young Emperor. He cancelled his engagements in England and stayed in Russia a month. He attended the long funeral ceremonies, first in Moscow and then in St. Petersburg; and he was one of the witnesses at the wedding of his niece to Czar Nicholas, which took place very quietly in the chapel of the Winter Palace.

Russian opinion was deeply moved by the Prince of Wales' solicitude; over-night the whole tone of the traditionally hostile press changed. Between Nicky and the Prince there sprang up a warm personal friendship which lasted throughout Bertie's life-time. When the Prince finally arrived back in London, Her Majesty's ministers showered congratulations upon him. The Prime Minister, Lord Rosebery, wrote to him in glowing terms: 'Never has your Royal Highness stood so high in the national esteem as today, for never have you had such an opportunity. That at last has come and has enabled you to justify the highest anticipations, and to render a signal service to your country as well as to Russia and the peace of the world.'[1]

Unfortunately the good-will that the Prince's visit had engendered was not permanent. Soon the Russian press, inspired by ministers who saw that the British Empire remained a stumbling block to coveted riches in

[1] *King Edward VII:* Sir Sidney Lee.

Asia and the Middle East, began to re-sound its note of hostility. And Nicky, who had seemed such a sensible, agreeable boy, made a speech which shocked English liberal opinion. He denounced all schemes of popular government as 'senseless dreams' and made it clear that he would 'maintain for the good of the whole nation the principle of absolute autocracy as firmly and as strongly as did my late lamented father'.

Nevertheless the Prince continued to write to the young Emperor in terms of endearment; and his efforts were destined to bear fruit in the next decade.

IN the meantime, the Prince's relations were rapidly deteriorating with his other nephew, the German Kaiser.

At the end of the eighties William II was talking with increasing fervour of the importance of an Anglo-German understanding. If he could turn the Triple Alliance into a 'quadruple' arrangement by bringing in England, the peace of the world, he declared, would be assured. Things looked bright in 1890, for Britain agreed to cede Heligoland to Germany in exchange for the latter's protectorates in East Africa—Zanzibar, Witu and Somaliland. This deal benefited both parties; but the Kaiser was particularly ecstatic, for he interpreted it as Britain's first step toward entering the German orbit.

From then on, he decided that no stone must be left unturned to further his plans; and he also decided that no one was better qualified to negotiate a pact than himself. Starting in 1891, he visited England every year until 1896. He began these yearly trips by a State visit with the Kaiserin to Windsor; after that, he chose Cowes as his annual stamping-ground.

The Kaiser was always spectacular. He was well-read, artistic and quick-witted. He could make a brilliant impression when he chose, but his undoing was his almost neurotic exhibitionism. He could not resist theatrical effects. And since these effects were usually at someone's expense, and nothing creates bad blood more easily than wounded vanity, he usually succeeded in making more enemies than friends.

He always arrived at Cowes in his imperial yacht, the *Hohenzollern*. He dined twice with the Queen at Osborne; once formally, and once *en famille*. The rest of his time was spent largely in the company of his Uncle Bertie.

The Prince found this a great strain. The German Kaiser was imperious, temperamental and hard to please. Bertie made him a member of the Royal Yacht Squadron, and soon he seemed to think he owned it. He tried to outshine his uncle in every possible sphere. Matters were not improved by the fact that in 1893 he challenged the Prince's racing cutter *Britannia* with his *Meteor* and won the Queen's Cup.

The Prince took his defeat well, but he resented his nephew's manner toward him. The Kaiser delighted in demonstrating to the Prince's friends that he, as an Emperor, could treat his uncle as casually as he liked. He seemed to go out of his way to annoy. He chaffed him for never having seen action at the front; he slapped him on the back; he put forward his own ideas on the handicapping for the races, and aired his views freely as to how the Regatta could be better organised. The Prince murmured to his friends that the Kaiser seemed to think he was the 'Boss of Cowes'. William appeared unaware of the resentment he was arousing. He referred to his uncle behind his back as 'an old peacock'.

In the meantime the Kaiser was not idle on the political front. The *Hohenzollern* was turned into a floating Foreign Office. He always had a large suite aboard which included the German Ambassador to England, Count Hatzfeld. Immediately upon arrival he began bidding English Cabinet ministers to his presence. He was so eager to impress these statesmen with his force and clarity that he usually adopted an aggressive line. He rapped them on the knuckles for being rude to Germany; he lectured them on the dangers of Russia; he put forward a series of political and colonial proposals, and when they were not acted upon, complained bitterly of disrespect toward himself.

In 1895 the Kaiser's behaviour reached a climax of offensiveness. He steamed into Cowes escorted by two German naval cruisers, the *Wörth* and the *Weissenburg*, named after places in Alsace. He had timed his arrival to coincide with the twenty-fifth anniversary of the Prussian conquest of Alsace, and seized the opportunity to make a war-like speech to the sailors of the *Wörth*. Needless to say, this raised a storm of anger in France; and soon the English press joined the clamour, accusing the Kaiser of over-stepping the bounds of hospitality by attacking a friendly power in English waters.

Personal criticism was something new for the Kaiser; he took great umbrage, and from then on seemed to throw all discretion to the winds. A few weeks later he invited Lord Salisbury, the new Prime Minister, to visit him on the *Hohenzollern*. The latter was an hour late (through no fault of his own) and the Kaiser made no attempt to hide his anger. He received him so icily, friendly talk was out of the question, then berated him at length for not making more of an effort to bring the two countries together.

Lord Salisbury was not the only target for his bad temper that summer. He bullied his uncle, gave him orders, and even went so far as to try and run the Regatta for him. At this, the Prince demurred; and the Kaiser retaliated to the slight by protesting against the handicaps set for the *Meteor's* race against the *Britannia.* The Prince replied that they had been fixed by the Yacht Club Committee and could not be changed. So the Kaiser refused to take part in the race, leaving his uncle to sail the course alone. 'The Regatta used to be a pleasant recreation for me,' the Prince fumed to a friend, 'but now, since the Kaiser takes command, it is a vexation.'[1]

William II left Cowes unsmilingly, and no one was sorry to see him go. Some historians have tried to blame Germany's failure to secure an agreement with England to the Kaiser's bad relations with the future Edward VII. No one would deny that the two men were temperamentally incompatible, and that each disliked the other. But in this case, personal relations had little to do with the matter. The hard truth was that England had nothing to gain from an alliance with Germany.

In the nineties the situation in Europe was clear-cut. Britain possessed a mighty Empire which stretched from the Falkland Islands to China. The powers who would have liked to expand at Britain's expense were divided into two camps: Germany, with her allies Italy and Austria; and France and Russia who had signed a mutual defensive pact with each other. Lord Salisbury, Britain's Prime Minister, regarded the two blocs with satisfaction. When Russia or France threatened British interests she could lean toward Germany; when Germany threatened British interests she could lean toward Russia and France. The only real threat to her security would have been an understanding between Germany and Russia. But the Kaiser had tried for years to come to an agreement with the Russians and had always found them disconcertingly unreliable; besides, Russia's internal poverty and unrest was growing, which made her strength increasingly doubtful.

[1] *Ten Years at the Court of St. James:* Baron von Eckardstein.

Nevertheless it was a good thing for England to strengthen her influence with the new Czar in order to diminish German influence; and that was why the Prince of Wales was now taking so much trouble. But what use would an Anglo-German alliance be to England? A partnership with Germany would merely mean that Britain would have to agree to German colonial expansion at her own expense; in some cases she was willing to do this, but what if Germany went too far? A partnership would deprive her of a lever, in the shape of allies, by which she could apply the brakes. No; the present set-up was much the best. Britain must be free to throw her weight against the aggressor of the moment.

The Kaiser did not seem to understand the workings of the English mind. He returned to Germany saying bitterly that he was 'done with England'. He told his ministers that for seven years he had tried to bring the two countries together, but that his plans had been foiled by England's 'selfishness and lying'. He was in a very dangerous mood. When an opportunity suddenly arose, a few months later, to strike a blow at England, he grasped it eagerly.

For some time there had been friction in South Africa between the English settlers led by Cecil Rhodes, the Prime Minister of the Cape Government, and the Boer settlers (of Dutch and German extraction) led by Kruger, President of the Transvaal Republic. At the end of 1895 Rhodes encouraged a British official, by the name of Dr. Jameson, to raid Kruger's territory with an army of irregulars (who were employed by Rhodes' mining company) in an effort to overthrow the President's Government. The British Cabinet did not hear of the action until it had started, and immediately telegraphed its displeasure, ordering Jameson to quit the territory. In the meantime the plan had failed and Jameson and his men were taken prisoner.

The Kaiser and his advisers decided to give Britain a public slap. So they sent Kruger a telegram which caused an uproar, not only in London, but in all the Chancelleries of Europe. Today, to a generation nurtured on the crude insults of Hitler and Stalin, the telegram strikes one as very mild, but in the nineties words counted. Every diplomat knew how to assess a *double entendre* and the hint of a threat was sometimes enough to draw nations to the brink of war. This is what the Kaiser wired to Kruger: 'I express my sincere congratulations that, supported by your people *without appealing for the help of friendly Powers*, (author's italics) you have succeeded by your own energetic action against armed bands which invaded your country as disturbers of the peace and have thus been enabled to restore peace *and safeguard the independence of the country against attacks from the outside*' (italics again mine).

The British Government took some time to cool down; and the Prince wrote to his mother heatedly, suggesting that she give William a good snub. But the Queen had received a long letter from the Emperor expressing surprise that his innocent message had caused such indignation, and insisting that his words had been misconstrued. The Queen still had a grandmotherly feeling for William; and although she agreed that his telegram was 'outrageous' she wrote to Bertie that 'it would not do to give him a good snub. Those sharp, cutting answers and remarks only irritate and do harm, and in Sovereigns and Princes should be most carefully guarded against. William's faults come from impetuousness (as well as conceit); and calmness and firmness are the most powerful weapons in such cases.'[1]

But she did not urge him to come to England again, and for over three years he sulked in Germany. The Prince was relieved not to have him at Cowes, but

[1] *The Letters of Queen Victoria.*

William scored a minor triumph, even from afar. Before he quitted England he commissioned the architect who had built the *Britannia* for his Uncle Bertie to design him a new racing yacht on similar lines—only faster. The *Meteor II* was the result; despite the Kaiser's absence it was sent to Cowes in the summer of 1896 and easily outsailed the *Britannia.* The Prince's fun was spoiled. The next year he sold his yacht and gave up racing for good.

WHILE the Prince was courting the Czar and quarrelling with the Kaiser, he was also finding the time to enjoy the pleasures of Society. He still graced every important social event. He still went to Ascot and Goodwood and Epsom; he still patronised the opera and the theatre; he still gave the most brilliant balls of the season at Marlborough House; and he still had an eye for the ladies.

In the nineties, the beauty who claimed his most constant attention was Lady Brooke, whose husband in 1893 succeeded to the earldom of Warwick. This lady, known to her friends as 'Daisy', was much admired for her wonderful clothes and the lavish parties she gave at Easton Lodge. The Prince was often a guest. He found her irresistible; and when he was away from her, wrote to her regularly.

Rival hostesses were only too ready to repeat malicious gossip about the imperious, quick-tempered Lady Brooke; and the Tranby Croft affair gave them a splendid chance. They began to whisper that the Prince had told the secret of Gordon-Cumming's cheating to Lady Brooke; and that Lady Brooke, resentful of Mrs. Arthur Wilson's entrée into Society, had repeated the confidence.

So Lady 'Babble-brooke', as they promptly named her, was responsible for the scandal.

When this story came to the ears of the future Lady Warwick her indignation knew no bounds. She got in touch with a solicitor who issued a statement saying that his client had been in Scotland at the time of the Tranby Croft affair, and that if the rumours continued the perpetrators would be sued for libel.

Lady Warwick was an unusual woman. She reflected the troubled conscience that was to make itself felt under Lloyd George's leadership in the next decade. In 1895 she took a decision that shook the complacence of Society. She and her husband had just moved into Warwick Castle and she decided to give a fancy dress ball as part of the house-warming celebrations. The ball was spoken of as the 'event' of the winter. Neighbours arranged large house parties and the whole of fashionable London moved into the district.

At that time there was great distress among the poor, and Lady Warwick derived a certain satisfaction from the thought that the lavish preparations for her ball were providing a good deal of temporary employment. The party was a great success, and the newspapers stressed the charitable angle, with the exception of one obscure sheet called *The Clarion*. This paper did not reach the Castle until two days after the ball, and when Lady Warwick read the article, underlined by black lines, her gorge rose. The writer described her large expenditure as 'a sham benevolence' and scathingly attacked her for ignoring the desperate social conditions around her. She was so angry at the criticism that she left the Castle, which was still filled with guests, and without a word to anyone boarded a train for London. She took a cab to Fleet Street and drew up in front of the *Clarion* office which was at the top of a long dark flight of stairs. The editor's name, Robert Blatchford, was on the door. She walked in and found a middle-aged man with a cold, critical expression sitting at his desk. 'I remember thinking,' she wrote many years later, 'that the garment he wore, which was something between a dressing-gown and a lounge coat, was most undignified.'

She held out a copy of the offensive news sheet. 'How could you be so unfair, so unjust? Our ball has given work to half the country and to dozens of dressmakers in London besides,' she began. Blatchford rose. 'Will you sit down,' he said, 'while I explain to you how mistaken you are about the real effect of luxury?'

Blatchford then lectured her on economics. He told her that the labour used to produce finery was wasted; that the only productive labour was that which produced useful articles, which in turn helped labour to produce again. She was so fascinated by his conversation that she did not leave the office until late afternoon.

Robert Blatchford was a convinced Socialist, and he planted the ideas in Lady Warwick's head that finally led her to join the Socialist Party. Until the end of her days she preached Marxism to all who would listen; needless to say her friends did not take too kindly to the revolutionary views of this titled heiress, and she made many new enemies. But the Prince of Wales remained a friend. When she tried to talk to him about Socialism, he merely yawned and said soothingly, 'Society grows; it is not made.'

LADY Warwick's defection did not dampen the high spirits of her friends. The London season was never more brilliant than in the last years of the nineties. In 1896 the Prince of Wales had a series of spectacular successes on the Turf. His Sandringham-bred horse

Persimmon won not only the Derby but the St. Leger and the Jockey Club Stakes as well. The excitement of the crowds and the thunderous roar of approval when Persimmon carried the Prince's colours past the winning post was sure proof that as far as the public was concerned, all was forgiven and forgotten.[1]

From that moment the Prince's popularity never waned. He was the darling of the masses, and 'Good old Teddy' became a slogan from one end of the Empire to the other. He could go to theatres and operas to his heart's content; he could smoke cigars and entertain pretty ladies at late suppers; he could mix in frivolous company and travel abroad as much as he liked. Scarcely a voice was raised against him. Whatever he did was high fashion. He seemed to have broken through the sound barrier of convention and moved into a rarefied atmosphere where people are no longer condemned for not conforming, but admired for their individuality. As a result, his failings immediately became precious characteristics. 'The Prince of Wales is loved,' remarked Lord Granville, 'because he has all the faults of which the Englishman is accused.'[2]

The Marlborough House Set reaped the benefit of the public's new indulgence toward the Prince. For years this group had been frowned upon by the conservative element that surrounded the Queen. It was criticised for its racing and gambling and general 'looseness'. Even the Kaiser put in his oar and protested against an incident at a country house when his son, the Crown Prince, was present, 'where there had been unseemly

[1] The Prince was one of the few men in England to make racing pay over the years. He reckoned in later life that his purchase of Perdita II in 1887, the dam of his first two Derby winners, Persimmon and Diamond Jubilee, earned him a quarter of a million pounds within twenty years.

[2] *Memoirs:* Prince von Bülow.

romping in unlighted corridors, and one lady had even gone so far as to take off her slipper'.[1]

Of course the composition of the Marlborough House Set had changed over the years. For instance, Lord Charles Beresford (who later became an admiral) quarrelled with the Prince in 1891 over Lady Brooke. There was a terrible scene at Lady Brooke's house when Beresford, enraged because the beautiful Daisy had deserted him for her royal admirer, raised a clenched fist and advanced toward the Heir Apparent. The retreating Prince warned him in a last act of friendship, 'Don't strike me'. If the blow had fallen on the royal person, Lord Charles would have been dismissed from the Navy, and ostracised by Society. As it was, his naval career progressed but his friendship with the Prince came to a permanent close.

There were others who fell by the wayside, some through scandal, some through extravagance. In the last category came a number of heavy swells. Lord 'Glossy Top' Hardwicke dissipated his entire fortune and then died; Mr. Henry Chaplin was forced to sell his fine estates to escape bankruptcy; and the same applied to poor Mr. Christopher Sykes whose only failing was an inability to deny the Heir Apparent the splendid entertainments he craved. Indeed, it was the impoverished Sykes' failure to offer hospitality to the Prince for the St. Leger in 1890 that led to Bertie's visit to Tranby Croft.

There were always newcomers to fill in the gaps in the Prince's circle. The Heir Apparent had never tried to conceal the fact that he loved millionaires, but in the nineties he showed a marked predilection for the self-made millionaires of the business world. He seemed fascinated by the rise of obscure men to power and fortune. Besides, he revelled in City 'shop'. He liked the romance of foreign investment; the talk of deals in

[1] *Lord Lansdowne:* Lord Newton.

terms of millions; the rewarding fluctuations of the Stock Exchange; the creation of fabulous financial empires that spread across the globe.

In London he gave a warm welcome to the South African millionaires, mostly Jewish—the Beits, the Robinsons and Wernhers. But the two most important friendships he formed were with the Hungarian Jew, Baron Hirsch, who had amassed a colossal fortune by financing railways in the Balkans and Turkey, and the German Jew, Ernest Cassel, who had made an equally colossal fortune by financing railways in Sweden, America and Mexico.

The Prince had met Hirsch in Paris, and when he accepted an invitation to pay the Baron a twelve-day visit at his estate in Hungary, consternation was voiced in many quarters. Continental society had never accepted Hirsch, and the Austrian Ambassador pointed out that he was not received at Court. The Prince waved the protests aside, and in his honour the Baron arranged the largest shoot ever organised in Europe. Over 11,000 partridges were killed in five days.

When Hirsch came to England the Prince entertained him warmly and obedient hostesses reluctantly followed suit. The Baron took a liking to the vivacious Margot Tennant, and in a business-like way invited her to marry his son, Lucien, whom he described as a serious boy who liked books and collecting coins. She declined the offer and shortly afterwards the son died. Consequently the Baron left his vast fortune to an adopted son, the Baron de Forest.

It was Hirsch who introduced Ernest Cassel to the Prince, marking the beginning of one of the most important friendships in the future King's life. Like Hirsch, Cassel had started with nothing. He had begun work at the age of fourteen in a Cologne banking firm, then he was sent to a bank in Liverpool for a year, then to a branch in Paris. At the outbreak of the Franco-Prussian war in 1870 he returned to England and entered the financial house of Bischoffsheim and Goldschmidt in London. He was only eighteen at the time, and was paid a salary of £200; but his remarkable ability prompted his employers to raise his pay, before he had reached the age of twenty-two, to the unheard of sum of £5,000 a year. From then on, Cassel never looked back. After making a fortune in railways, he doubled his money by financing industrial developments in Egypt.

Cassel was not in the least interesting to the spirited members of Society. Although he copied the pattern of the aristocracy by buying a country estate, and establishing himself in an imposing London mansion, his houses were luxurious but ugly and he had notoriously uninteresting food. He had no gift for small talk, but the Prince found him fascinating. He liked to hear him discuss the great financial deals he was promoting; even more he liked the fact that Cassel took over the management of his money, with very gratifying results.

Cassel had an almost uncanny resemblance to the Prince. Consequently rumours began to spread that the new friendship was due to the fact that the two men were related! The old story was revived that the Prince Consort was the son of his mother's Jewish court chamberlain, and somehow the two men were endowed with common blood. No proof was ever produced to corroborate this tale.

The die-hards of Society protested against this new influx of 'City men' into their exclusive precincts, but there was no longer anything they could do about it. The Marlborough House revolution was complete. If the aristocracy wished to entertain the Prince, it had to accept the plutocracy on an equal footing. Albert Edward had achieved other changes as well; he had forced Society to accept acting as a respectable profession; and he had taught hostesses to invite opera stars to their houses. He also was the first Prince to form close friendships with foreign diplomats. He was on intimate terms with the Russian Ambassador, M. de Staal, the German Minister, Baron von Eckardstein, a whole string of French Ambassadors, and of course the Portuguese Minister, the Marquis de Soveral.

There was only one group that was absolutely taboo. That was writers and poets and anyone who styled himself an 'intellectual'. The Prince had a horror of highbrows. Some of his friends, like Lord Rosebery, were clever men, but the latter was sophisticated enough to avoid all mention of literature in favour of talk about politics or racing. 'As a class,' said Lady Warwick, 'we did not like brains. . . . We acknowledged that it was necessary that pictures should be painted, books written, the law administered; we even acknowledged that there was a certain stratum whose job it might be to do these things. But we did not see why their achievements entitled them to our recognition . . .'[1]

The prejudices of the Marlborough House Set were countered to some extent by 'The Souls', who sprang up in the latter part of the eighties and flourished for ten or fifteen years under the ægis of Margot Tennant and Arthur Balfour. They were, of course, society amateurs, but many of them had real talent, and they delighted in gathering at country houses where they could discuss books, recite poetry and take intellectual exercise in the form of paper and pencil games.

These activities did not impress the Prince, and he had the satisfaction of knowing that no matter how highbrow the Souls considered themselves, not one would fail to jump at an invitation to Marlborough House. He set the fashions more firmly than ever. Not only his food, his clothes, and his mannerisms were copied, but his idiosyncrasies as well. Because he was superstitious the

[1] *Afterthoughts:* Frances, Countess of Warwick.

smart world took infinite pains to see that mattresses were not turned on Fridays, that knives were not crossed on the table, and, of course, that no one sat down thirteen to dinner.

The Prince liked his food more than most men, yet he would rather forgo it altogether than defy this stricture. Once when a dinner was being given in his honour, the fourteenth guest was late, and he refused to leave the drawing-room. For twenty minutes the company awaited the delinquent, who was an army subaltern by the name of Winston Churchill. 'When I arrived at Deepdene,' wrote Mr. Churchill many years later, 'I found the entire company assembled in the drawing-room . . . The Prince had refused point blank to go in, and would not allow any rearrangement of two tables to be made. He had, as was his custom, been punctual to the minute of half-past eight. It was now twelve minutes to nine. There, in this large room, stood this select and distinguished company in the worst of tempers, and there on the other hand was I, a young boy asked as a special favour and compliment. Of course I had a perfectly good explanation. Oddly enough, it was one that I have had to use on more than one occasion since. I had not started soon enough! I put it aside. I stammered a few words of apology, and advanced to make my bow. "Don't they teach you to be punctual in your regiment, Winston?" said the Prince in his most severe tone. . . . It was an awful moment! We went in to dinner two by two and sat down an unexceptionable fourteen. After about a quarter of an hour the Prince, who was a naturally and genuinely kind-hearted man, put me at my ease again by some gracious chaffing remark.'[1]

Once, in Germany, a more serious situation arose. The Prince only learned when dinner was over that

[1] *My Early Life:* Winston S. Churchill.

there had been thirteen at the table. He fretted and fumed for nearly an hour, then suddenly his face became wreathed with smiles and he told his secretary, Sir Frederick Ponsonby, that it was all right after all. When Ponsonby asked why, he replied, 'Because Princess Frederick Charles of Hesse is *enceinte*!'

THE whole of Society joined together in 1897 to celebrate the Queen's Diamond Jubilee, which marked a reign of sixty years. From all over Europe came members of the royal houses; and from all over the Empire came princes and chieftains and ministers. Never was the pageantry more spectacular. There were sepoys from India, mounted cavalry from Canada, riflemen from Australia, tribesmen from Africa. The Queen rode through the dense, cheering, weeping crowds in an open carriage to St. Paul's, where a short service was held on the steps. That night she wrote in her diary: 'A never-to-be-forgotten day. No one ever, I believe, has met with such an ovation as was given to me, passing through those six miles of streets, including Constitution Hill. The crowds were quite indescribable, and their enthusiasm truly marvellous and deeply touching. The cheering was quite deafening, and every face seemed to be filled with real joy. I was much moved and gratified.'[1]

The brilliance of the Jubilee celebrations continued throughout the season. Louisa Manchester, who had at last married 'Harty-Tarty' and become the Duchess of Devonshire, gave the most spectacular fancy dress ball that London had ever seen. Three thousand invitations were sent out, and for weeks people pored over the history books to find some original and glamorous

[1] *The Letters of Queen Victoria.*

character they might impersonate. The Paris dressmakers were kept busy, and the men, as well as the women, spent three and four hundred pounds apiece on their costumes. The Prince and Princess of Wales went to the ball as the Grand Prior of the Order of St. John of Jerusalem and Marguerite de Valois, while the Duke and Duchess of Devonshire were dressed as Emperor Charles V and Zenobia, Queen of Palmyra.

All the memoirs of the day refer to this fancy dress ball as the most impressive gathering of rank and wealth and beauty ever seen at a private assembly. Years later Winston Churchill, who was enjoying a hilarious season, reflected on the past. 'The picture which remains in my mind's eye,' he wrote, 'is the Duchess of Devonshire's fancy dress ball in 1897. It reproduced the scenes upon which Disraeli dilated in his novels. Indeed it revived one of his most celebrated descriptions; for outside in the Green Park large crowds of people had gathered in the summer night to watch the arriving and departing guests, to listen to the music, and perhaps to meditate upon the gulf which in those days separated the rulers and the ruled.'[1]

ALTHOUGH the Kaiser did not visit England between 1895 and 1899, and the Prince was able to enjoy 'the pleasant recreation' of Cowes undisturbed, his nephew created plenty of trouble from afar. All sorts of petty quarrels developed between himself and his uncle. For instance, when the Kaiser heard that the Prince had accepted an invitation to go aboard Sir Thomas Lipton's yacht, he told people derisively that his uncle had 'gone boating with his grocer'. This story found its way

[1] *My Early Life:* Winston S. Churchill.

back to London and was repeated to the Prince. In the meantime the Kaiser's A.D.C. made frequent visits to England and always returned with malicious gossip. An allegation that the Prince was ridiculing both Germany and its ruler created such bad feeling that angry rebukes and denials went back and forth for nearly two years.

In the middle of this particular quarrel Mr. Chamberlain, the Colonial Secretary, who favoured an Anglo-German alliance, approached the Kaiser to explore the possibilities of an understanding, but the Emperor waved him away haughtily. Once his temper had cooled down, he began to regret his action, but by this time the English were annoyed and disinterested. And so it went, like a see-saw. One moment the Emperor was raging against England and saying he was 'through with it for ever' and the next he was putting forward impulsive new proposals.

The truth was that he was jealous. Germany could not expand her territories in Africa without the goodwill of Britain. Britain had the most powerful navy in the world and Germany knew her line of supply could be cut off. And since in those days, and for many years after, all nations thought of wealth in terms of square miles, Germany champed at the bit. She was determined to expand, and yet it was impossible without the consent of England. Hence the Kaiser's repeated proposals for an Anglo-German Agreement, and his furious outbursts against England for not falling in with his wishes. In 1898 Germany offered to surrender her claims on the Tonga Islands and the Samoan Archipelago in the Pacific if England would cede her Nyasaland in Central Africa and Walfisch Bay in South-West Africa. But Lord Salisbury decided that the territorial demands were 'too extensive to be acceptable'.

The Kaiser had many arguments on his side for expanding German interests; but his temperamental extravagances, coupled with his mischief-making in Moscow, did not endear him to the English Prime Minister. Lord Salisbury simply did not trust him, and, as a result, became the Kaiser's bugbear. In 1899, a dispute arose between England and Germany concerning Samoa. The Kaiser was indignant at the suggested settlement. He told the British Ambassador in Berlin that English policy was 'incomprehensible' to him. For years he had done everything he could to help her, and his only reward was base ingratitude. He picked up his pen and wrote Queen Victoria a letter in which he lashed out against Lord Salisbury. He referred to Samoa as 'a stupid island which is a hairpin to England compared to the thousands of square miles she is annexing right and left unopposed every year' and stated bluntly, 'If this sort of high-handed treatment of German affairs by Lord Salisbury's Government is suffered to continue, I am afraid that there will be a permanent source of misunderstandings and recrimination between the two nations which in the end may lead to bad blood.'[1]

The Queen kept calm as usual. She reproved him sharply in her own particular fashion—'I doubt whether any Sovereign ever wrote in such terms to another Sovereign, and that Sovereign his own Grandmother, about their Prime Minister'[1]—and then finished up her letter by saying that she would be glad to receive him at Osborne in the summer.

The Kaiser accepted the invitation but he did not come to England until November. By that time the Boer War had broken out. This war, which most people today regard as a bad blot on the British escutcheon, was engineered by Joseph Chamberlain to extend British authority in South Africa. England entered into the conflict believing it would be finished in three

[1] *Letters of Queen Victoria.*

months. But the Boers proved sturdy fighters, the English met with many heavy defeats and the war dragged on, drearily and expensively, for nearly three years.

The Kaiser paid his state visit. Members of the royal family and Cabinet ministers alike strained every nerve to avoid unpleasant incidents and the trip passed off successfully. But no sooner had the Kaiser returned to Germany than news arrived of new and serious reverses on the battle-front. The Kaiser began to write to the Prince of Wales suggesting improvements in British strategy and tactics. In one letter he advised against continuing the operations in South Africa until a larger concentration of troops could be assembled. But he added that he did not know whether the hostility of foreign powers would make this respite possible. If diplomacy could not guarantee a peaceful interim, he wrote, 'it would certainly be better to bring matters to a settlement. Even the best football club, if it is beaten notwithstanding the most gallant defence, accepts finally its defeat with equanimity. Last year in the great cricket match of England *v.* Australia, the former took the victory of the latter quietly, with chivalrous acknowledgement of her opponent.'[1]

Needless to say, the English did not regard their African war as comparable to a cricket match; and in cold terms the Prince of Wales informed his nephew of this fact.

The correspondence between uncle and nephew once again took place in terms of veiled hostility. Then, in December 1900 it became apparent that the health of the eighty-one-year-old Queen was failing. On January 18th the Kaiser received a message from the German Embassy saying that the Sovereign was seriously ill. He hurried from Berlin to Osborne to attend her death-bed.

[1] *Letters of Queen Victoria.*

There was no doubt that he was sincerely fond of his grandmother, who had always treated him with more indulgence than she had shown to any of her own children. He was deeply moved as her life ebbed, and stayed by her bed for long hours at a time.

The Queen died with all her children surrounding her. Her last word was 'Bertie'; but, ironically enough, she drew her final breath not in the arms of the son to whom she had always been so distant, but in the arms of the grandson Albert had found so engaging. Thus ended the triumphant reign which had lasted nearly sixty-four years.

PART TWO

AS KING

CHAPTER ELEVEN

THE NEW REIGN

'WE shall not pretend,' said *The Times* primly, 'that there is nothing in his [the new King's] long career which those who respect and admire him could wish otherwise. . . .'[1] Obviously aimed at apprehensive Victorian die-hards, the leader pointed out that the heir to the throne inevitably was 'followed, dogged, and importuned by temptation in its most seductive forms', and suggested that the heavy responsibility of Kingship would sober down the new, pleasure-loving monarch.

Whatever the future, the Sovereign began by asserting his independence. As Prince of Wales he had always signed his name 'Albert Edward', and his mother had made it clear that she expected him to keep both these names when he ascended the throne. 'It was beloved Papa's wish as well as mine,' she had written long ago, 'that you should be called by *both* when you became King, and it would be *impossible* for you to drop your Father's. It would be *monstrous*, and *Albert alone*, as you truly and amiably say, would *not do*, as there can be only *one* ALBERT!' The Prince had demurred at the time, saying, 'I quite understand your wishes about my bearing my two names, although no English Sovereign has ever done so yet, and you will agree with me that it would not be pleasant to be like "Louis Napoleon", "Victor Emmanuel", "Charles Albert", etc., although no doubt there is no absolute reason why it should not be so. . . .'[2]

But now he had made up his mind that, monstrous or

[1] *The Times*, January 23, 1901.

[2] *The Letters of Queen Victoria.*

not, he would follow his own inclinations. 'I have resolved,' he told the world, 'to be known by the name of Edward, which has been borne by six of my ancestors. In doing so I do not undervalue the name of Albert, which I inherit from my ever lamented, great and wise father, who by universal consent is, I think deservedly, known by the name of Albert the Good, and I desire that his name should stand alone.'

This was not the only matter in which the new King crossed Victoria's wishes. His mother had been very emphatic that Osborne must be kept as a family residence, and had repeated this wish in her will. But Edward regarded Osborne as a white elephant. Neither he nor his son had any wish to live in the ornate, inconveniently placed house which the dead Queen had valued so highly for its sentimental associations; besides, Buckingham Palace and Windsor Castle, Sandringham and Balmoral seemed costly enough to run as it was.[1] So, in spite of agonised cries and angry protests from his three sisters, he finally arranged that Osborne should be given to the nation for use as a convalescent home for officers. His mother's rooms were roped off and kept as a memorial.

In the meantime an army of carpenters and plumbers and painters moved into Buckingham Palace and Windsor and Balmoral. The kitchens were antiquated, the servants' quarters primitive and the plumbing almost non-existent. At Buckingham Palace most of the rooms had been disused for nearly forty years, and the darkened paint-work and endless dust sheets had prompted Bertie to name it 'the Sepulchre'. It had only come to life for Drawing Rooms or Garden Parties, and on the rare occasions when the Queen allowed some Royalty to spend a few days there. This honour was accorded

[1] Balmoral and Sandringham were private residences; Osborne would have made a third, which even Edward VII regarded as too much of a financial strain.

the Shah of Persia in 1873, but he caused considerable perturbation by sacrificing a sheep on one of the best carpets, and Victoria did not invite him again.

Besides the general alterations, there was a mass of sorting out to do. Victoria had never thrown anything away, there was a sixty-year-old collection of gifts and ornaments and bric-à-brac; of photograph albums and dresses and bronze statuettes; of dolls and miniatures and granite paper weights; of parasols and feathers and vases. Experts were called in to separate the valuable things from the trash and the possessions were distributed among the family. The ornaments no one seemed to want were the endless statuettes of John Brown, who had died in 1883. All these were destroyed, and so were the full-size statues in the gardens of Balmoral. Every reminder of this man, whom Edward had always detested, was relegated to the dustbin.

At both Buckingham Palace and Windsor Castle Edward chose to occupy his father's suite. These rooms, which had been kept exactly as the Prince had left them, with his clothes laid out afresh each evening and even his medicine bottle and spoon in place, were now given a shake-up and treated to the aroma of a good cigar. But although new paint was in evidence everywhere the sturdy Victorian carpets and fabrics showed no sign of wear, and many of them were left undisturbed. When the aged Empress Eugénie came to visit the new King at Windsor and was shown the bedroom she had occupied nearly a half a century before, she could only exclaim dejectedly, '*Toujours ces affreux rideaux!*'

As far as the works of art were concerned, Edward took a personal interest in supervising the rearrangement. The valuable paintings were separated from the lesser ones by Sir Lionel Cust, the Surveyor of the King's Pictures. But Edward insisted on giving instructions as to how and where they should be hung. He liked, wrote

Cust, to sit 'in a roomful of workmen giving directions. "Offer it up," he would say, "and I will come to see," and when he came he said Yes or No at once. It was no use asking him to suggest this or that, as he had little imagination, though a quick trained eye and instinct for what was right and what pleased him. "I do not know much about Arrt," he would say with the characteristic rolling of the r's, "but I think I know something about Arr-r-angement." '[1]

THE King seemed to thrive on his new independence. Lord Esher, a courtier in whom Edward placed great faith, wrote that he seemed to be revelling in his liberty; and Lord Redesdale, a life-long friend, was impressed by the zest with which he tackled the routine affairs of state. At the King's bidding, Redesdale dropped in to see him one evening. 'I found him in his private sitting-room all alone, and we sat smoking and talking over old times for a couple of hours. Towards midnight he got up and said, "Now I must bid you good-night, for I must set to work," pointing to a huge pile of familiar red boxes. "Surely," I said, "your Majesty is not going to tackle all that work tonight!" His answer was, "Yes! I must! Besides, it is all so interesting. . . ." '[2]

Many people found it difficult to accustom themselves to the changed atmosphere of the Court. Lord Esher regretted the disappearance of the mystery and awe which had surrounded the Queen. During the last twenty years of Victoria's reign, dinner parties had been conducted in almost complete silence; no one spoke unless addressed by the Queen, and even in a drawing-

[1] *King Edward VII and His Court:* Sir Lionel Cust.

[2] *King Edward VII:* Lord Redesdale.

room full of people, groups far away from the Sovereign conducted their conversation in whispers. With Edward, the fear vanished. There was politeness, but no more hushed, frightened voices. Besides, discipline was greatly relaxed. Courtiers were allowed to smoke in the King's presence, and no longer need ask permission to leave the room; they could bow and disappear. Apparently Lord Esher was apprehensive lest this new informality should detract from the dignity of the Crown, for he wrote to a friend that the King struck him as 'too human'.

He need not have worried. Edward had his own little tyrannies. Although the conversation was freer, he was far more of a martinet about the correct wearing of dress and decoration than his mother had been. Not the smallest slip escaped his vigilant eye. Once when the Duke of Teck, Queen Mary's father, wore his new Colonel's uniform for the first time, Edward's smile suddenly turned into a frown and he said in a forbidding voice, 'Francis has got the wrong buttons.' He advised a friend appointed to an important post to be careful not to wear too high a collar; he told Sir Henry Ponsonby he could not receive the German Emperor in 'that old coat'; he commented sadly on the antiquity of Lord Haldane's hat which, he said, looked as though it had belonged to Goethe; he rebuked Sir Felix Semon for pinning the star of the Victorian Order to his right breast instead of his left; and he told Sir John Fisher gravely, 'That is a very old suit you are wearing.' 'Yes, Sir,' replied the Admiral brightly, 'but you've always told me that nothing really matters but the cut.'[1]

It was not so easy to correct foreigners when they made mistakes. But once, when the Swedish Minister appeared at Court with his medals in the wrong place, the King waited until he was bidding him good-night, then added

[1] *Memories:* Lord Fisher.

confidentially, 'Hunt and Roskell, 148 Piccadilly.' The Minister looked surprised, but he took the hint and the Court jewellers put him right. Often, however, foreign diplomats consulted the King about the right dress to adopt; years previously, the Russian Ambassador, M. Benckendorff, had asked Bertie whether he thought it proper for him to attend the races since he was in mourning; and Bertie had promptly replied: 'To Newmarket, yes, because it means a bowler hat; but not to the Derby, because of the top hat.'[1]

The only foreigners whom the King had no control over were the Americans. He had given up worrying about them. They could never understand the difference between breeches and trousers, frock coats and morning coats. Once when Lord Rosebery arrived at Windsor Castle wearing plain trousers instead of the silk stockings and breeches he had been commanded to appear in, the King bowed to him and said acidly: 'I presume you have come in the suite of the American Ambassador.'

IF the King revelled in his independence, so did the new Queen. Although the coronation was not scheduled to take place for nearly eighteen months, plans were already being discussed. When Arthur Ellis, the Comptroller of the Household, made suggestions about her toilette she replied airily, 'I know better than all the milliners, and antiquaries. I shall wear exactly what I like, and so shall my ladies—Basta!'[2]

She was still astonishingly beautiful. In 1903, a French diplomat described her to President Loubet saying, 'Queen Alexandra will reach her sixtieth year next

[1] *King Edward and His Times:* André Maurois.

[2] *Journals and Letters of Reginald, Viscount Esher.*

December. She is surprising, and preserves her looks with meticulous care; she might be taken for a woman of thirty-five . . .'[1] Although she was now nearly stone deaf she refused to allow her wearisome affliction to spoil her fun. She carried on a stream of light-hearted chatter, and Lord Esher was astonished by the grace with which she could talk to a dozen people in a room, putting each at their ease, without hearing a word that was said. Esher saw a good deal of the King and Queen and makes frequent references to Alexandra during the first few months of the reign. 'She was in tearing spirits and will enjoy her new home . . .'; 'she was in excellent spirits and full of rag and mischief. . . .'[2]

A good illustration of what he meant by this 'rag and mischief' was shown when her sister, Marie, the widow of the Czar of Russia, was visiting her at Buckingham Palace, but was ill in bed with lumbago. Her nephew, Prince Christopher of Greece, was also one of the party, and he tells how he received a message from Alexandra to go to her room. 'On the bed,' he writes, 'was laid a miscellaneous collection of mantles, dresses, and bonnets of every description that had belonged to Queen Victoria. Queen Alexandra was examining them, her eyes dancing with merriment. "Now Christo," she said when I came in, "you've got to put this dress on and go down to Aunt Minnie's (the Empress's) room and make her laugh."

'We chose the dress Queen Victoria had worn in the days of her youth to open the Great Exhibition in Paris under Napoleon III, an alarming creation in tartan taffeta. I struggled into it, perched a befeathered bonnet on my head and added a lace parasol to my costume. Thus attired, I was led by the Queen through endless corridors, past scandalised servants, until we reached the

[1] *King Edward and His Times:* André Maurois.
[2] *Journals and Letters of Reginald, Viscount Esher.*

Empress's room, where I was solemnly announced as "Her Majesty Queen Victoria".'[1] Apparently the Empress's shock at the sight of the life-like apparition was followed by such fits of laughter that she had a serious relapse.

Queen Alexandra was not only loved by the British public, but she inspired affection in all those who knew her. Not in the least clever, she was so charming and kind no one ever had the heart to speak against her. She had a small circle of friends, the chief of whom was Lady de Grey, who shared her great love of the opera. But in the main her affections were reserved almost exclusively for her family—for her parents and brothers and sisters, for her children whom she adored, and Bertie whom she idolised. Her bedroom was always cluttered with pictures and souvenirs and mementoes marking sentimental associations. It was a sea of bric-à-brac ranging from old programmes and odd bits of ribbon to a brooch from a Maharajah and a fishing fly given her by a ghillie in Scotland. There was scarcely a free surface anywhere, and when she went aboard the royal yacht she insisted on taking her personal knick-knacks with her. More than once, in a rough sea, her cabin would be reduced to shambles, resembling the aftermath of a particularly hectic jumble sale.

She had been a remarkably patient wife, forgiving Bertie his 'pleasant little wickednesses' (as Wilfrid Blunt put it, but probably not so agreeable in Alexandra's eyes) and always trying to arrange amusing entertainments for him. Her husband appreciated her tolerance and gentleness, and now that he was King was determined that she should receive every honour in his power to bestow. He at once made her a Lady of the Garter.[2] The ladies at the Royal School of Needlework were given

[1] *My Fifty Years:* Prince Christopher of Greece.

[2] Queen Alexandra was the first non-sovereign lady to be given the Garter since 1488.

the task of making new banners to be hung in St. George's chapel; but they rebelled against embroidering the naked female figure on the Irish harp and substituted a plain stringed harp instead. The King immediately was deluged with inquiries asking whether he proposed to change the Royal Standard, and there even were rumours that the new emblem was a deliberate slight against Ireland. The King angrily rejected the banners, and insisted that the traditional design be followed.

Queen Alexandra had only one irritating fault. That was her unpunctuality. All her life she had been anything from ten minutes to an hour late. For forty years Bertie had expostulated with her, but it was to no avail. Now that she was Queen, the unpunctuality became really serious, for programmes were planned to the minute. On one occasion the King arranged for himself and the Queen to receive a series of deputations, each with an address to present, starting at noon and scheduled for a ten-minute audience. 'But when it came to twelve o'clock,' wrote the King's Assistant Secretary, Sir Frederick Ponsonby, 'there was no sign of the Queen. Meanwhile the second deputation arrived and then the third, fourth and fifth, which upset all the arrangements. In order that they should not get mixed up, a different room had been allotted to each, and so on until every room was filled with eminent men in uniform, but in spite of repeated messages there was no sign of the Queen. The King in full uniform sat in the Equerries' room drumming on the table and looking out of the window with the face of a Christian martyr. Finally at ten minutes to one the Queen came down looking lovely and quite unconcerned. All she said was, "Am I late?" The King swallowed and walked gravely out of the room.

'The Queen's unpunctuality,' continued Ponsonby,

'must have been very trying, but by then he had accepted it as inevitable and never attempted to remonstrate with her. Generally she was twenty to thirty minutes late for dinner, but I remember once at Windsor her being five minutes too soon. Pages and footmen were sent running to warn the guests and the members of the Household.'[1]

On one occasion, however, when the King was at Sandringham, and was particularly anxious for lunch to start punctually, so that he could have a long afternoon shooting, he decided to punish Alexandra for delaying him half an hour. There were thirty guests present, and the King and Queen were always served first, with the footmen then working their way down both sides of the long table. At the end of each course, it was the custom for the King to ring the bell for the plates to be cleared away. This time, he rang the bell as soon as he himself had finished, regardless of the fact that at the far end of the table the last people were only just being served. The startled guests had over ten exquisite dishes set before them, only to be whisked away before they had time to pick up their forks. The Queen was so miserable at what was happening, knowing that she was responsible, that she sat in silence, scarcely touching the food before her.

EDWARD VII's reign did not expand into its full opulence until nearly two years after his accession. The Boer War was dragging on and the casualties were distressing; Buckingham Palace was in the midst of its overhaul and could not be occupied; and news arrived from Germany that the Empress Frederick was suffering

[1] *Recollections of Three Reigns:* Sir Frederick Ponsonby.

agonising pain from the grip of cancer, the same deadly disease that had killed her husband.

In February 1901, only a month after the funeral of Queen Victoria, Edward was informed that his sister had very little longer to live. He cancelled his engagements and hurried to Germany, taking with him his Assistant Private Secretary, Sir Frederick Ponsonby, and his personal physician, Sir Francis Laking, who he thought would be more humane in giving the Empress morphia to quell her pain.

It was a dramatic trip. The Emperor William met his uncle at the station, and drove him to Friedrichshof; there he found gathered the Empress' three daughters and a number of German generals and diplomats who formed part of the royal entourage. Although in the last two years William's relations with his mother had improved, he was in a sociable mood and did not show any marked sign of distress. For nearly a decade the Empress' letters to Queen Victoria had been dominated by distraught and bitter references to her son. 'William ignores my existence in everything'; 'I am only a silent and much-distressed spectator'; 'William and Dona . . . do not want me'; 'William . . . has no heart'.[1] But by the turn of the century the bitterness seemed to have faded into a remote sadness and disquietude. The lonely, pathetic Vicky made only infrequent references to her son. 'Dear William has made a new speech with much fanfaronnade. I wish the German Government would give up the policy of constant fireworks. . . .'

However, despite the apparent *rapprochement* between mother and son, the Empress was far from trusting William to carry out her dying wishes. After King Edward and his equerries had been in the house three days, Sir Frederick Ponsonby suddenly received a message that the Empress wished to see him. He was taken

[1] *Letters of the Empress Frederick.*

upstairs to her sitting-room, and found her propped up with pillows, her face racked with pain. Despite her shocking appearance, her mind was quite alert. She plied him with political questions for half an hour, then said suddenly, 'There is something I want you to do for me. I want you to take charge of my letters and take them with you back to England.'

Sir Frederick replied that he would be glad to do so, and she went on, 'I will send them to you at one o'clock tonight and I know I can rely on your discretion. I don't want a soul to know that they have been taken away, and certainly Willie must not have them, nor must he know that you have got them.'

Sir Frederick Ponsonby worked late that night in his room. He heard the Castle clock strike one, and shortly afterwards a knock came on his door. Four men came in carrying huge boxes, the size of portmanteaux, and covered with black oil-cloth. 'The cords around them,' he wrote, 'were quite new and on each box was a plain white label with neither name nor address. I noticed that the men wore blue serge breeches and long riding boots and I came to the conclusion that they were not trusted retainers but stable-men quite ignorant of what the boxes contained. They put the two boxes down and retired without saying a word.

'It now dawned on me that I had undertaken no easy task and I began to wonder how I was to get such large boxes back to England without anyone suspecting their contents. I had assumed, perhaps not unnaturally, that the expression "letters" meant a packet of letters that I should have no difficulty in concealing in one of my portmanteaux. But these large corded boxes were quite another thing. . . . To adopt any method of concealment and to attempt to smuggle them away was to court disaster as the whole place was full of secret police, but on the other hand, to account for these boxes which apparently had dropped from the skies was no easy matter. I therefore wrote on the label of one "Books with care" and on the other "China with care" with my private address, and determined to place them in the passage with my empty boxes without any attempt at concealment . . .

'On March 1st we left Friedrichshof to return to London. That day a party of soldiers from the garrison was employed to carry all the luggage down. I was talking to the Emperor in the hall at the time and out of the corner of my eye I could see the procession of soldiers carrying portmanteaux, suit-cases, despatch boxes, etc.; when these two black boxes came past they looked so different from the rest of the luggage that I became nervous lest someone should inquire what they were, but no one appeared to notice them, and the Emperor went on talking. . . . He was holding forth on some subject that interested him, and naturally everyone, including myself, listened attentively. It was a great relief when I at last saw the tarpaulin cover drawn over the luggage and a few minutes later heard the wagon rumble away.'[1]

This story had a dramatic sequel, enacted many years later. The boxes contained the bulk of the Empress' correspondence with Queen Victoria stretching over a period of forty years. Apparently the Queen had returned the letters to her daughter, in order to enable her to read them over with a view to publication at some future date.

This was exactly what William II and his advisers were determined to prevent. They had taken great pains to depict the Empress as an enemy of Germany and they had no wish for her side of the story to reach the public.

She did not die until four and a half months after Edward's hurried visit. Once again the Palace was surrounded by police, and after her funeral it was

[1] *Letters of the Empress Frederick.*

thoroughly ransacked. None of her private papers was found. A few days later Count Eulenburg, the head of the Emperor's household, asked Sir Frederick Ponsonby confidentially if the Empress' letters were in the Windsor archives. Sir Frederick obligingly wrote to Lord Esher, the Keeper of the Archives, who replied truthfully that he had no idea of their whereabouts.

There the matter rested until 1929. Then Sir Frederick decided to publish the letters. Emil Ludwig had written a biography of the Kaiser in which he had painted a disparaging picture of the Empress; Sir Frederick felt that the time had come to let the records speak for themselves.

The Kaiser, who now was in exile in Holland, did everything in his power to prevent publication. He claimed that, as his mother's heir, he was the lawful owner of the copyright. But after a long legal argument the lawyers decided that the Empress had given the copyright to Sir Frederick and that he could dispose of the letters as he saw fit.

The Kaiser wrote a preface to the German edition of the book, in which he said that his mother 'always had a strong, passionate temper' and that after her husband's tragic death her nerves 'began to suffer severely'. 'Everywhere,' he continued, 'she saw enemies harbouring aversion for her, hate even. She was sensitive. Anything hurt her. She was used to quick words and she wrote them down. . . .' Historians must sift the truth for themselves.

Royalty, the world over, was at the height of its glory and splendour as the new century progressed. Thrones sparkled thickly in Europe and stretched across the Middle East and Asia to the far reaches of Japan. As preparations for the coronation of Edward VII rolled forward, scheduled for June 26, 1902, people declared that the event would be unparalleled in history for its brilliance. Although Edward had declared flatly that 'crowned heads should not come, only representatives, owing to the extreme difficulty of precedence', the reigning houses had agreed to send their sons and heirs. Crown Princes galore were due to arrive; from Russia, Italy, Denmark, Rumania, Portugal, Saxony, Greece, Sweden and Norway, Siam, Montenegro, and Belgium. Austria was to be represented by the ill-fated Archduke Franz Ferdinand; Spain by the Prince of the Asturias; China by Prince Tsai Chen; Japan by Prince Akihito Komatsu; and dozens of minor princes and princesses related by birth to the more important royalties had accepted invitations.

Only the Kaiser threw a spanner into the works. He refused to allow his son, the Crown Prince, to attend the ceremony because, he said, he disapproved of the unseemly frivolity into which the young man had been drawn during his last visit to England. The Kaiser's objections were not based on invention. The Crown Prince had discovered more than one English lady who was liberal with her favours; and on one occasion after a ball when his distracted hostess had searched for him in the small hours of the morning so that the other guests could take leave of His Royal Highness, she had found him in a bedroom, and not alone. The Crown Prince's behaviour had been recounted to the Kaiser by Count Eulenburg, who had been delegated to look after him, and returned to Germany in a state of exhaustion. No; although King Edward offered to give the German Crown Prince precedence over all the other Crown Princes, the Kaiser insisted that his son must remain at his studies.[1]

He was the only heir to a throne in all Europe not

[1] The Kaiser's brother went instead.

present. On Monday, June 21, trains rolled into Victoria Station almost every half-hour bearing royal visitors. The Buckingham Palace officials carried out a marvellous piece of organisation, for the visitors arrived with dozens of attendants and mountains of luggage. The driveway in front of the station was cleared of ordinary traffic and was crammed with wonderful carriages, grooms and footmen and outriders in superb livery and uniforms, special porters and messenger boys, and equerries whose job it was to get the right visitors into the right vehicles.

That night the King and Queen gave a dinner at Buckingham Palace which has never again been equalled for the magnificence of the foreign royalty. *The Times* carried a full list of guests the following day, that reads like the pages of a fairy tale. Besides the Crown Princes and Princesses there was His Imperial Highness the Hereditary Grand Duke Michael of Russia, the Hereditary Grand Duke of Mecklenburg-Strelitz, His Serene Highness the Hereditary Prince of Monaco, His Imperial Highness Yi Chai-Kak, Prince of Eui-Yang (Korea), Ras Makunan (Ethiopia), Said Ali (Zanzibar), His Highness Prince Mohamed Ali Pasha (Egypt). And so the list went on, for one solid, closely printed column.

However, the King was not looking his best that night. For over a week, there had been rumours that he was in poor health. He had been resting at Windsor, and although the doctors issued statements that he was 'much refreshed', some of the courtiers wore worried expressions.

Their fears were not groundless. On Tuesday morning, the day following the grand banquet, the House of Commons was deeply shocked to be informed that the King had just undergone an operation for appendicitis (in those days a major illness) and that the Coronation was 'indefinitely postponed'.

The consternation can be imagined. The royalties at

once began to make preparations to leave London; the wires were crowded with messages; the post office flooded with letters changing plans. Workmen who had not yet received contrary instructions went on hammering at the grandstands, and the flags and decorations floated gaily from windows and standards. 'It was impossible to spend the day in the streets of London . . . without saying to oneself over and over again "Oh the pity of it",' wrote a Special Correspondent of *The Times*. For not only was London filled with distinguished foreign visitors, but with thousands of loyal subjects who had come from all parts of the British Isles. 'The pavements seethed with unaccustomed faces, and passage to and fro far from easy upon them. Down the carriageway . . . poured (when it could) an endless flood of vehicles of every conceivable kind. There were private carriages, many of them Royal and containing the King's guests, omnibuses, chars-à-bancs, country-carts fitted with longitudinal planks for seats, spring carts, vans, costermongers' carts—and all were loaded, to say nothing of many that were overloaded. . . .'[1]

Even in the kitchens of Buckingham Palace consternation prevailed. What was to be done with the tons of food ordered for the Coronation Banquet? Much of it was already prepared. 'The caviar could be kept on ice,' wrote one of the royal chefs many years later, 'and it was possible to preserve the two thousand five hundred quails. But there were huge amounts of cooked chicken, partridge, sturgeon and cutlets, not to mention all the fruit and cream desserts which would not keep. A little could be put aside for the staff, but the rest, it was decided, would have to be given to charitable organisations dealing with the poor.

'We were in touch with a good many of these charities, who had literally hundreds of hungry and homeless fami-

[1] *The Times*, June 26, 1902.

lies on their books, and the Buckingham Palace staff often passed on to them broken or spoilt food. In this case they would be receiving something a little different—six or seven courses from the coronation banquet of a King—and from all the many charities it was hard to choose one which could be relied on to handle the disposition of the food fairly and discreetly. Finally we stored the food in hampers for the Sisters of the Poor. . . . On June 26, the date the banquet was to have been held, it was the poor of Whitechapel and not the foreign kings, princes and diplomats who had the *Consommé de faisan aux quenelles*, *Cotelettes de bécassines à la Souvaroff* and many of the other dishes created by the royal chef. . . .'[1]

The Coronation took place in August, seven weeks after the date originally set. The foreign princes, with the exception of those related to the British Royal Family, did not return to England. Only the members of the Abyssinian Special Mission were present, for the simple reason that they had never dared to go home. They would lose face, they explained, if they returned to Abyssinia without having seen the crowning of the great white potentate.

Despite the lack of foreign visitors, the Empire was magnificently represented, and London was a blaze of colour. The King seemed well, but this time there were other worries. Dr. Temple, the tall, octogenarian Archbishop of Canterbury, looked so feeble, there were whispers that he would never survive the ceremony. The Bishop of Winchester was so alarmed at his tottering gait that he offered him a meat lozenge to give him strength. But the Archbishop rasped, 'What's the good of that? My trouble's in my *legs*, not in my stomach!'[2]

Somehow the old man got through the ceremony. But when he was anointing the Queen his hand shook, and

[1] *Royal Chef:* Gabriel Tschumi.

[2] *Men, Women and Things:* Memories of the Duke of Portland.

some of the oil trickled down her nose. He leaned heavily against the convalescent King throughout a long portion of the service; and after kneeling down to pray he found he could not rise again, and once more the King came to the rescue by stepping forward and helping him to his feet. After the ceremony was over, someone asked the King if he was tired. With a wry smile he answered, 'Wonderfully enough, I am not!'

But the incident that delighted the *haut monde* was the fall of the imperious Duchess of Devonshire, generally known as 'The Double Duchess'. This haughty lady, who did not like taking 'no' for an answer, was eager to leave the Abbey in the wake of the Royal procession. However, a line of Grenadier Guards had been drawn across the steps at the end of the choir to prevent anyone leaving until the royal party and other minor processions were well out of the way. The angry Duchess began to berate the officer in charge, then started to push her way forward regardless of his protestations; she missed her footing and plunged down the stairs. 'She fell heavily forward,' wrote an eye-witness, Sir Almeric Fitzroy, 'and rolled over on her back at the feet of Sir Michael Hicks-Beach, who was just leaving his stall; her coronet fell off and struck the stalls at some distance from the spot. The Chancellor of the Exchequer was too paralysed by the suddenness of the apparition to offer any assistance; but willing hands, directed by the indefatigable Soveral, at last restored the illustrious lady to her legs, Mrs. Asquith secured her coronet and placed it on her head, and after some little attention to her ruffled hair she was permitted to proceed, not apparently much the worse for the accident.'[1]

By present-day standards the Coronation was an unrehearsed shambles, but everyone seemed satisfied that it had 'gone off well'.

[1] *Memoirs:* Sir Almeric Fitzroy.

CHAPTER TWELVE

THE ENTENTE

THE Kaiser made a deep impression on the British public by his attitude at the time of Queen Victoria's funeral. The sincerity of his affection for his grandmother could not be doubted and Englishmen warmed to his evident devotion. The Royal Family was also deeply touched by his long, tireless vigil at the death-bed, and his almost pathetic eagerness to help by taking charge of tiresome details. 'His tenderness and firmness were extraordinary,' wrote Lord Esher, 'so unlike what was expected of him. He refused to allow Banting's man to measure the Queen for her shell. He turned them all out of the room. He sent for Reid (the Queen's doctor), and took all the measurements himself. He and the King and the Duke of Connaught lifted the Queen into her coffin.'[1]

The Kaiser responded to the wave of affection he engendered with almost childish elation. He returned to Germany glowing with goodwill for the people who had treated him so well. 'I found him,' wrote his Chancellor, Count von Bülow, 'completely under the spell of his English impressions. As a rule he could not change his military uniform often enough, but now he wore civilian clothes as he had done in England. He wore a tie-pin with his deceased grandmother's initial on it. The officers, who were summoned from Frankfurt nearby to dine with him, were surprised to find their "Supreme War Lord", as they called him, wearing civilian clothes. They did not seem to be very pleased by his constant enthusiastic allusions to England and

[1] *Journals and Letters of Reginald, Viscount Esher.*

everything English that, in his own words "ranked far above German habits and customs".'[1]

But the Kaiser was not well-served. He was surrounded by violent Anglophobes, the chief of whom was Count Eulenburg, the Master of the Royal Household. The latter at once began to drop poison into his ears by telling him that the British were only trying to flatter him because they were in difficulties with their South African War.

Eulenburg was a malevolent pederast who had no loyalty to anyone. Although he paraded as the Kaiser's faithful servant, the following letter, which he wrote to the Chancellor, von Bülow, when the Kaiser was in England for Queen Victoria's funeral, gives some indication of his disagreeable character. 'I am anxious when I think of the beloved Kaiser in Osborne: I think of all the things he will say! He will be like a child amidst these people who are crude despite their mourning. Amongst them he forgets all his "shrewdness". A sort of trustful embarrassment takes possession of him and any one of them could easily get at the secrets of his soul (and our state secrets). And at the same time he is really in the way. The family scold him behind his back, and his own adjutants wring their hands and wish they could go home. . . . I hope the walks in Osborne and the visits to all the warships, whose crews are receiving him with the greatest indifference, will agree with him. . . .'[1]

A more distorted picture would be hard to devise, in view of Lord Esher's comments. But it shows the pressures and influences to which the Kaiser was subjected; and it is not surprising that a few weeks later the impetuous Emperor was again delivering tirades against the British, making curt demands for indemnities in South Africa, and unflattering references concerning the British handling of the Boxer uprising in China.

[1] *Memoirs:* Prince von Bülow.

In April, he sent a letter to King Edward in which he alluded to the disagreement in China and spoke of the British ministers as 'unmitigated noodles'. The King angrily sent for Baron von Eckardstein, his personal friend at the German Embassy, and read him part of the Emperor's letter. 'He commented on the Kaiser's assurances of friendship for England,' wrote Eckardstein, 'with a sarcastic, "I hope that is so". And when he came to where the Kaiser referred to British Ministers as "unmitigated noodles" he laid the letter down on the table and said to me, "There, what do you think of that?"

'After thinking a bit, I said, "Wouldn't it be best if your Majesty treated the whole thing as a joke?" He laughed at that and replied: "Yes, you are quite right. I must treat the thing as a joke. But unluckily I have already had to put up with many of these jokes of the Kaiser's, and even worse than this one too, and I suppose I shall have to put up with many more." Then he went on: "Whatever would the Kaiser say if I allowed myself to call his Ministers such nice names! . . . There is room in the world for both Great Britain and Germany. Only we can't keep pace with these perpetual vagaries of the Kaiser. Moreover, as you know, some of my Ministers have the greatest distrust for the Kaiser and Bülow, especially Lord Salisbury. I have always tried to dissipate this distrust, but after all one can't go on forever. And the abuse and threats that the German *Flottenverein* and its organs are perpetually pouring on us are not calculated to get rid of this distrust." '[1]

DURING these same weeks, the first months of 1901, Britain was approaching a turning-point in her history.

[1] *Ten Years at the Court of St. James:* Baron von Eckardstein.

Mr. Joseph Chamberlain, the Colonial Secretary and the most important member of Lord Salisbury's Conservative Government, was trying to reach an agreement with Germany which would result in an Anglo-German Alliance.

Mr. Chamberlain was now in his late sixties. Born the son of a London boot and shoe manufacturer,[1] he had begun his career as a radical, but had broken away from Gladstone over the Irish Home Rule policy and joined the Conservatives. Cold, poised and confident, he was a master of debate and mesmerised the House of Commons with his brilliant, caustic speeches. He was said to have no heart. As Lord Salisbury once remarked, 'Mr. Gladstone was hated, but he was also very much loved. Does anyone love Mr. Chamberlain?'

Yet, curiously enough despite his lack of warmth, despite his ironic mask, he had an astonishing power of compelling assent, and commanded a large following among the masses. Perhaps it was due to his independence of mind. He had become a Tory, but unlike most Tory converts he had no wish to build himself a country seat and ape the ways of the gentry. He was incorruptible and he went his own way. The only frivolity he allowed himself was an increasing interest in dress. He was immensely dapper. His clothes were perfect, he always wore an orchid in his button-hole and a gold-rimmed monocle in his eye. Disraeli once likened him to 'the cad of the omnibus', but had to admit that 'he wore his monocle like a gentleman'.

CHAMBERLAIN was an arch-imperialist. He was responsible, almost single-handed, for the shameful Boer War,

[1] Mr. Chamberlain did not move to Birmingham until he was eighteen.

which not only aroused the fury of the Liberals in the House of Commons, but brought more odium on Britain the world over than any other act of her imperial life. Instead of ending in three months, as Chamberlain had predicted, the war dragged on for three years, and was only half over when King Edward ascended the throne.

Chamberlain's reputation suffered surprisingly little, owing to the patriotic emotions raised by British reverses. He still remained the most formidable minister in Salisbury's Cabinet. However, the difficulties the Army was encountering in South Africa strengthened his conviction that the days of Splendid Isolation, the foundation-stone of Victoria's reign, were over. The Empire circled half the globe. To the hungry nations of Europe it seemed to have delectable plums to offer; and now that British arms were fully occupied with the Boer guerrillas those plums were becoming increasingly tantalising. No; isolation was growing into a positive danger. Britain must find a strong ally with a strong army to protect her interests; in return she would have to make concessions, of course, but the bargain would be worth while.

Chamberlain had sounded the Kaiser and his Foreign Minister, Count von Bülow, during their visit to Windsor in the early months of the Boer War. They had given him an encouraging reaction, and in November 1899 he had declared in a speech at Leicester, 'No far-seeing statesman could be content with England's permanent isolation on the continent of Europe. . . . The natural alliance is between ourselves and the German Empire. . . . Both interest and racial sentiment unite the two peoples.'[1]

But Chamberlain's gun misfired, owing to Bülow's weak, vacillating character. (His colleague, Tirpitz, once remarked that compared with Bülow, an eel was a leech.) When Bülow found that feeling in the Reichstag

[1] *The Times*, December 1, 1899.

against England had flared into a passionate new hostility on account of the Boer War, he threw Chamberlain over without a moment's hesitation, making an insulting and threatening speech in which he declared that the new century would determine whether Germany was to be 'the hammer or the anvil'.

Chamberlain was furious at this treachery; and Lord Salisbury, who was not only Prime Minister but Foreign Secretary as well, was equally furious that Chamberlain should have spoken with no support or authority from him.

Salisbury did not agree that the days of Isolation were over. He still viewed the two blocs which divided Europe with satisfaction. He still felt that the Triple Alliance, dominated by Germany with the largest army on the Continent, and composed of Italy and the feeble Austro-Hungarian Empire, served as a perfect balance to the Dual Alliance partnered by France, with the second largest army on the Continent, and Russia, the untried colossus. As Prime Minister and Foreign Secretary, Salisbury had been successful in throwing Britain's weight first on one side then on the other according to the problem of the moment. It had worked surprisingly well, and he was unconvinced that the time had come for a change in tactics.

Historically, of course, in times of real danger Britain had always given her support to whatever coalition opposed the strongest power on the Continent. She had fought Philip II of Spain, Louis XIV and Napoleon. But at the turn of the century it was not easy to decide which combination, the Triple or the Dual Alliance, constituted the greater threat. Was it France who was casting envious glances at North Africa; or Russia who was showing expansionist desires both in China and the Persian Gulf; or was it Germany who not only possessed the most formidable army, but was now increasing her navy as well, and talking about the glories of the coming century in a disturbingly belligerent way? The fact was that all three nations wished to expand at Britain's expense. For those, like Chamberlain, who were determined to find an ally, it was not a question of siding with the most peaceful, but with the least aggressive.

However, after von Bülow had repudiated Chamberlain, the British statesman was obliged to lie low for some time. He was rapped sharply over the knuckles by Lord Salisbury, and he wrote to Baron von Eckardstein, the German Chargé d'Affaires, a rather subdued note, 'I will say no more here about the way in which Bülow has treated me! But in any case I think we must drop all further negotiations on the question of the Alliance. Whether it will be possible to return to them after the end of the South African War that has raised so much dust—must be left for further consideration.'[1]

CHAMBERLAIN did nothing for thirteen months. Then in January 1901, a few days before Queen Victoria's death, he made another attempt to drive through an Anglo-German Alliance. Lord Salisbury was reaching the end of his career, and would resign soon; besides, the old man was going abroad for several months and Chamberlain was eager to grasp the opportunity of negotiating the main points of the agreement before he returned. Then, with the support of several influential Cabinet colleagues such as the Duke of Devonshire, Lord Lansdowne and Arthur Balfour, he felt sure he could push it through whether Salisbury liked it or not.

Chamberlain was more convinced than ever that Britain must waste no time in finding an ally. He re-

[1] *Ten Years at the Court of St. James:* Baron von Eckardstein.

garded Germany as the least dangerous of the three powers. Indeed, he felt that Germany's support was imperative to prevent Russia from expanding in China. During the Boxer uprising the previous year, the European powers had sent troops to China to protect their interests and uphold the policy of the 'Open Door'. Russia had seized the opportunity virtually to annex Manchuria. Chamberlain not only argued that Britain needed Germany to hold Russia in check, but that an Anglo-German Alliance would prevent the nightmare possibility of Germany and Russia patching up their differences and forming a coalition. A few months previously he had written a Cabinet paper in which he had said, 'Both in China and elsewhere it is our interest that Germany should throw herself across the path of Russia. An alliance between Germany and Russia . . . is the one thing we have to dread. . . .'[1]

Consequently, Baron von Eckardstein suddenly received a letter from the German-born Duchess of Devonshire asking him to come to Chatsworth to talk over affairs with her husband and Mr. Chamberlain. 'As we shall have a house-party of fifty or so for the theatricals you will easily get an opportunity of a quiet talk with the Duke and Joe. It is true Asquith and some other leading members of the Opposition will be with us too, but that will not matter, for there are in the "Schloss" plenty of rooms where you will be able to talk without anyone noticing it.'[2]

Chamberlain put his cards on the table with Eckardstein. He told him that England must find allies on the Continent; that if she could not work out an agreement with Germany and the Triple Alliance, she must turn to France and the Dual Alliance. Although China was uppermost in Chamberlain's mind he offered the bait

[1] *The Life of Joseph Chamberlain:* Julian Amery.

[2] *Ten Years at the Court of St. James:* Baron von Eckardstein.

first. If Britain and Germany could come to an agreement, Britain would be willing to make concessions in North Africa. . . .

The ball had started rolling. Then came Queen Victoria's death, and the Kaiser's visit to England. When he learned from Baron von Eckardstein of Chamberlain's proposition he wired von Bülow ecstatically. 'So "they come" it seems. This is what *we* have waited for.'[1]

Now let us turn for a moment to Germany's foreign policy. It was not in very wise hands. The reins were held by three men: the tempestuous Kaiser, the deceitful von Bülow (now the Chancellor), and the mysterious, cynical and pathetically stupid Holstein, who served as head of the Political Section of the Foreign Office. Holstein was the key figure. He seemed to have Bülow in his pocket. Some said this was because Bülow was a homosexual and Holstein possessed evidence of his relations with numerous male attendants. Whatever the reason, Holstein's words had a profound effect, not only on Bülow, but on the Kaiser as well.

The Kaiser's reaction to Chamberlain's proposal had been sound; Britain needed Germany's help, and here was Germany's opportunity to win concessions from Britain. Even more important, if Britain was determined to find Continental allies it was vital that she did not find them in the *bloc* opposing Germany. It was essential to Germany that England should at least remain neutral if Germany became involved in a war with the Dual Alliance. But what was Holstein's reaction to Chamberlain's plain statement that if he could not find allies in one camp he would turn to the other?

[1] *German Diplomatic Documents:* translated by E. T. S. Dugdale.

Holstein simply did not believe it. 'The threatened understanding with Russia and France is a patent fraud,' he wrote to Metternich, the senior diplomat in the Kaiser's suite. 'Time is on our side. As I see it, a rational agreement with England—that is to say, one where the almost certain risk of war, which we should have to assume, would be paid off by suitable concessions—will only come within reach when England feels the pinch more acutely than she does today.'[1]

Holstein was in the position of a gambler on the Stock Exchange. British shares had dropped and it was a profitable time to buy. But might they not drop still further? Might it not be even more profitable to buy in another year's time? This was the German Government's stupid, greedy, short-sighted answer to an opportunity which might in the long run have proved disastrous to England, but must have been profoundly beneficial to Germany.

So Chamberlain's attempt to reach an understanding once again came to nothing; and the Germans, who had already assured the Russians that they would not oppose the Czar's control over Manchuria, rubbed Britain's nose in it. 'What may become of Manchuria?' Bülow asked the Reichstag. 'Why, gentlemen, I cannot really conceive what could be a matter of more indifference to us. . . .'

Both Holstein and Bülow were supremely happy in their fool's paradise. Even the news that Britain was negotiating a military pact with Japan as a protection to both nations' Far Eastern interests did not open German eyes. Surely this was proof enough that Lord Salisbury's 'Isolation' was drawing to an end; that Britain was in earnest pursuit of allies. Bülow, however, remained confident in the judgment he had earlier expressed to the Kaiser. 'The understanding with the Dual Alliance is nothing but a scarecrow made up to intimidate us in the

[1] *German Diplomatic Documents:* translated by E. T. S. Dugdale.

way the English have already practised for years. . . .'[1]

There was one last flicker before the candle went out. This was largely due to poor Eckardstein, who, bitterly disappointed at the lack of co-operation from the Wilhelmstrasse, was determined to have one last fling himself. He sought an interview with Lord Lansdowne, the Foreign Secretary, and proposed an Anglo-German military pact. Lord Lansdowne was under the impression that the offer had come from Berlin, and Berlin was given to understand that the initiative had come from London. Negotiations were conducted by the Foreign Office, but there was never any real hope of success. The *casus foederis* suggested that Britain and Germany should come to each other's aid militarily, if either one found itself attacked by more than one power. Lord Salisbury commented acidly that 'the liability of having to defend the German and Austrian frontiers against Russia is heavier than that of having to defend the British Isles against France.'[2] And even Lord Lansdowne, who had been eager to reach an agreement with Germany, admitted that there was no hope of pushing such a document through Parliament.

The negotiations hung fire, and the Reichstag continued to pursue its favourite sport of abusing Britain. In the summer of 1901 there were many impassioned speeches about British 'atrocities' in South Africa. Count Bülow did nothing to mitigate the ill-will they aroused in England. Contentedly, he adhered to his waiting game. Then in October Chamberlain answered the charges; he not only struck at Germany but at all the other European countries who were criticising England. He said that British 'cruelty' had never rivalled the methods employed 'in Poland, in the Caucasus, in

[1] *German Diplomatic Documents:* translated by E. T. S. Dugdale.

[2] *British Documents on the Origin of the War:* edited by Gooch and Temperley.

Algeria, Tonkin and Bosnia, and in the Franco-Prussian War'.

A howl of rage broke out from Berlin. The newspapers vied with each other in abuse of Chamberlain, and the agitation spread to universities, professional associations and even church assemblies. In January, when the Reichstag reassembled, one of the members called Chamberlain 'the most accursed scoundrel on God's earth'. Then Count Bülow made an inflammatory speech, quoting from Frederick the Great who had once replied to an attack on the Prussian Army with the words, 'Pay no heed to the fellow and don't get excited; he is biting on granite!' There were prolonged cheers; and with them went the last, dim hope of an Anglo-German settlement.

The following month, in February 1902, the King gave a large dinner party at Marlborough House to which Baron von Eckardstein was invited. Among his fellow guests were M. Paul Cambon, the French Ambassador, and Mr. Joseph Chamberlain. 'While we were smoking and drinking coffee after dinner,' wrote the Baron, 'I suddenly saw Chamberlain and Cambon go off into the billiard-room. I watched them there and noted that they talked together for exactly 28 minutes in the most animated manner. I could not catch what they said and only heard two words "Morocco" and "Egypt".

'As soon as the French Ambassador had left Chamberlain I entered into conversation with the latter. He complained very much of the bad behaviour of the German press towards England and himself. He also referred to the Chancellor's speech in the Reichstag, and said, "It is not the first time that Count Bülow has thrown me over in the Reichstag. . . . Now I have had enough of such treatment and there can be no more question of an association between Great Britain and Germany." '[1]

[1] *Ten Years at the Court of St. James:* Baron von Eckardstein.

From that moment Eckardstein realised that Chamberlain was ready to adopt the alternative solution of negotiating with the Dual Alliance. If he had any lingering doubts they were dispelled before the evening ended. 'Just as I was leaving,' he wrote, 'I was intercepted by an equerry, who told me that the King wanted to see me later, in his study.' After the company had left, he was conducted to a private room, and a few minutes later the King came in, having changed into more comfortable clothes. He offered Eckardstein a fat cigar, and a whisky and soda which he poured himself.

He was friendly and gracious and thanked the Baron for all the efforts he had made to bring about an Anglo-German understanding. But he told him, bluntly, that there was no longer any possibility of reaching an agreement, because of the way Germany was reacting. 'If the Kaiser now writes me long letters assuring me of his friendship for England, I cannot, I am sorry to say, give much weight to what he says. The renewed abuse of England in the German press and the unfriendly and sarcastic remarks of Count Bülow in the Reichstag have aroused so much resentment among my Ministers and in public opinion that for a long time at least there can be no more any question of Great Britain and Germany working together in any conceivable matter. We are being urged more strongly than ever by France to come to an agreement with her in all Colonial disputes, and it will probably be best in the end to make such a settlement, because England only wants peace and quiet and to live on a friendly footing with all other countries. . . .'[1]

THE King was playing a curious rôle. He had always been fascinated by foreign affairs, and as Prince of Wales

[1] *Ten Years at the Court of St. James:* Baron von Eckardstein.

had not hesitated to seek information and express his views at private gatherings. He had travelled more widely than most diplomats, he was related by blood to half the sovereigns in Europe, and for more than forty years he had grasped the opportunity of meeting all the leading statesmen of the day. He was always interested in personalities and consequently he had a thorough understanding of the nuances of international politics, and of the pressures and influences that made men behave as they did.

He came to the throne, therefore, with the experience of a professional diplomat. He read the state papers avidly, and followed every move on the chess-board with critical attention. As a result the Foreign Office was inclined to defer to him. His ministers informed him of their plans not merely out of courtesy but because they were genuinely interested in his reactions. As a constitutional monarch he did not try to interfere directly with policy; although he had his own ideas which he had clung to throughout the years with remarkable consistency, his flair was not in the field of hard negotiation, but in smoothing the path for others.

When Chamberlain informed the King that he was eager to reach an agreement with Germany, Edward was dubious about the outcome. His own experience had taught him to be wary of the protestations of the Kaiser and von Bülow. Nevertheless he gave Chamberlain his full support; and when, in the summer of 1901, Anglo-German negotiations came to a standstill, he agreed to discuss the difficulties with the Kaiser. He went to Germany armed with a memorandum from Lord Lansdowne, the Foreign Secretary, which stated the government view on the subjects most likely to be raised.

This meeting between uncle and nephew was far from satisfactory. In the first place, Lord Lansdowne's instructions had been extraordinarily vague. The King was under the impression that he wished him to hand the memorandum to the Kaiser, which he did. He discovered later, that it had been intended for his private use alone. No harm was done aside from the fact that Lansdowne 'had been compelled' (in the words of his official biographer) 'to write in great haste and a *lapsus calami* in which the word "Transcaspian" was inadvertently substituted for "Anatolian" gave an excuse for a typical gibe at British ignorance. The memorandum had spoken of the "Transcaspian" Railway terminating at Koweit. "Good heavens!" exclaimed the Kaiser, in a marginal note in English: "How is that to come there? The British Foreign Office ought to learn geography!" '[1]

The King was at a serious disadvantage with the Kaiser. Although he was the only man who could meet the German Emperor as a social equal, he could not discuss diplomacy as a political equal. The Kaiser was an autocratic ruler and Edward was a constitutional monarch. As a result, the Kaiser dominated the conversation from beginning to end. He was better informed than the King, and he told him that the Czar of Russia was planning to visit Paris and insinuated that it was a deliberate move against England. He talked about 'perfidious Albion' and 'treachery'; but the vital question of Morocco was never raised. The King was not sorry to say good-bye, and he never again attempted to carry on any direct negotiations himself. From then on he employed his talents with more subtlety and far greater effect.

WHEN Mr. Chamberlain informed the King, in January 1902, that His Majesty's Government was now deter-

[1] *Lord Lansdowne:* Lord Newton.

mined to achieve a *rapprochement* with France, Edward was delighted. For forty years he had preached the advantages of an Anglo-French Entente. Instinctively he had always had qualms about striking a bargain with Germany for the simple reason that an autocracy is never subject to the safety-lever of public opinion, but solely at the mercy of the impulses of its rulers. It had always seemed to the King that France and England had a deeper and safer affinity of interests; they were both dependent on the wills of their people which prevented them from following rash and impetuous policies; they shared the same code of social behaviour, the same appreciation of the refinements of life, and the same fundamental wish to gain their objectives by peaceful means.

The King knew that the French Foreign Minister, Delcassé, was strongly in favour of a *rapprochement* with Britain. Indeed, he had sent his most accomplished diplomat, M. Paul Cambon, to London to achieve this very purpose. For a year the French had waited patiently for the outcome of the Anglo-German talks. Then, when Mr. Chamberlain informed M. Cambon that the negotiations had been broken off, the latter prepared a memorandum for the British Foreign Secretary outlining subjects that might be discussed. 'Next evening,' M. Cambon recalled many years later, 'there was a big dinner at Buckingham Palace. I was placed next to King Edward who said: "Lansdowne has shown me your letter. It is excellent. We must go on. I have told the Prince of Wales about it. You can discuss it also with him." '[1]

This was the beginning. But it soon became apparent that the path was not easy. In France public opinion was fiercely anti-British. The 'Fashoda' incident of 1898

[1] Interview given by M. Cambon to *The Times*, December 22, 1920.

was still a burning issue. This concerned a French officer by the name of Captain Marchand who had staked a claim in the Sudan, but was forced by Kitchener to relinquish it. As a natural sequel to this humiliation the French had become violently pro-Boer, and the Chambre des Députés rang with almost daily denunciations of English imperialism. Besides this, French and British interests seemed to clash all over the world; in North Africa, in Egypt, in Indo-China, in West Africa, even in Newfoundland. The difficulties appeared almost insurmountable. Even if the officials could work out compromises, it seemed unlikely that with public opinion at such white-heat the parliaments of the two countries could ever agree to ratify them. So for nearly a year the talks remained at a standstill. Then in the spring of 1903 King Edward decided to take matters into his own hands. And his action brought about the greatest diplomatic *coup* of his reign.

ON his own initiative, the King planned a Mediterranean cruise on board the royal yacht. He decided to visit the King of Portugal and the King of Italy; and before he returned home, to spend three days in Paris. Lord Lansdowne, the Foreign Secretary, received the news of his itinerary with alarm. Because of the anti-British feeling in France, the King had not visited Paris for four years. Lansdowne was doubtful whether the King would even be received 'respectfully'. But he reassured M. Cambon, who was also anxious, that the visit would be 'quite an informal affair'. And M. Cambon wrote to an equally worried M. Delcassé that he believed the King would be content with 'a private luncheon at the Elysée, with the President of the Council and yourself. . . . For my own part I believe this mode of reception preferable to any other.'[1]

But when Delcassé inquired officially 'as to how the King would like to be received', Edward replied firmly 'as officially as possible and that the more honours paid to him the better it would be'. Both the French and the British Foreign Ministers held their heads in their hands, but there was nothing to do but prepare for the visit.

Among the members of the King's suite were Sir Frederick Ponsonby, the Assistant Secretary, the Marquis de Soveral, friend and confidant, and Sir Charles Hardinge, a rising star at the Foreign Office. The visits to Lisbon, Gibraltar, Naples and Rome went off well, but as Paris drew closer, Prince von Radolin, the German Ambassador, wrote to von Bülow, 'The nearer we approach toward the day of the King of England's arrival, the more energetically do the nationalist papers oppose an Anglo-French Alliance. . . .'[2]

The royal party travelled from Rome to Paris by train. At the station in the Bois de Boulogne President Loubet and a large number of officials were waiting. There were six carriages, each drawn by four horses and postillions; and a large escort of cavalry. The King and the President rode in the first carriage, and the drive was an ordeal for both. There were cheers for the head of the French Republic but they were not loud enough to drown the angry reproaches flung at the British Sovereign. Above the subdued hurrahing came excited shouts of 'Vive Marchand!' and 'Vive Fashoda!' and 'Vivent les Boers!' The poor President tried to distract the monarch's attention by animated conversation, and seized every opportunity of pointing out the few fluttering handkerchiefs in the crowd. The British carriages in the

[1] *King Edward and His Times:* André Maurois.

[2] *German Diplomatic Documents:* translated by E. T. S. Dugdale.

rear of the procession had a fairly rough time, for by the time they approached the cheers were distinctly jeers.

One of the King's military aides afterwards remarked that he was the only Englishman to receive a warm reception; because of his brown uniform, he observed dryly, he had been mistaken for a Boer.

The hostile temper of the crowd did not escape the King but he behaved with brilliant dignity. Quite unperturbed, he saluted first to the right then to the left. One of the King's suite whispered to him that the French did not seem to like them. 'Why should they?' replied the King bluntly.

That night the King went to the Théâtre Français. The Comédie Française had suggested that he might like to see *Le Misanthrope* by Molière. 'Oh no!' said the King. 'I have seen *Le Misanthrope* there a dozen times; they really must not treat me like the Shah of Persia. Let them give me a new play.'[1] So he was given *L'autre Danger* by Maurice Donnay which he thoroughly enjoyed.

The feeling in the theatre, however, was distinctly cold. There were even hisses when he arrived. The King, however, paid no attention; and during the *entr'acte* he insisted on strolling through the foyer.

He spotted the actress Mlle Jeanne Granier talking to friends. He went up to her and stretching out his hand said, 'Mademoiselle, I remember applauding you in London. There you represented all the grace and spirit of France.'[2]

The remark was overheard and soon the lobby was buzzing with it; the audience was beginning to feel ashamed of its bad manners, particularly since they were achieving no effect. The King absolutely refused

[1] *King Edward and His Times:* André Maurois.

[2] Letter to *The Times*, May 10, 1922.

to be put out. When the chief of protocol asked him anxiously what his impressions were of his reception at the theatre he replied blandly, 'I thought I heard a few hisses. . . . But no, I heard nothing . . . I heard nothing.'

The King's conduct never altered. Warm and smiling and courteous he expressed his immense enjoyment at everything that was done for him. But although he was exercising all his charm and tact to win over his sullen audience he never made the mistake of sacrificing, even to the smallest degree, his dignity as King. For example, when he first arrived the *Chef de Protocole* sent the King a programme which went into great detail and even prescribed what dress the Sovereign would wear on each occasion. Edward promptly erased all reference to himself, and Sir Frederick Ponsonby was instructed to inform the *Chef* that the King 'was not accustomed to be guided by foreign authorities when he paid a State visit'. 'I reminded him,' wrote Ponsonby, 'that no one had a larger experience of State visits than the King and that it was therefore only natural that His Majesty should know what was fitting. He again expostulated, but I ended up by saying more or less *Le roi le veult*, and that ended the discussion. I was amused to see later that the *Protocole*, so far from resenting the King's attitude, always sent to ask what he wished before attempting to issue more programmes.'[1]

The following morning the French press reported the speech the King had made the previous afternoon to a deputation from the British Chamber of Commerce. It was a speech from the heart, given without notes. 'A Divine Providence has designed that France should be our near neighbour, and, I hope, always a dear friend. There are no two countries in the world whose mutual prosperity is more dependent on each other. There may have been misunderstandings and causes of dissension

[1] *Recollections of Three Reigns:* Sir Frederick Ponsonby.

in the past, but all such differences are, I believe, happily removed and forgotten, and I trust that the friendship and admiration which we all feel for the French nation and their glorious traditions may in the near future develop into a sentiment of the warmest affection and attachment between the peoples of the two countries. . . .'

The King's words made a deep impression. That morning when he drove through the poorer section of Paris to attend a review at Vincennes the atmosphere was noticeably warmer. Afterwards, at the reception given in his honour at the Hôtel de Ville he had another opportunity to express his feelings, which he did with almost touching simplicity. 'I shall never forget my visit to your charming city, and I can assure you that it is with the greatest pleasure that I return each time to Paris, where I am treated exactly as if I were home.'

In the afternoon there was a race-meeting at Longchamps, and in the evening a state banquet at the Elysée. At the end of dinner the President made a speech. He was ill at ease and dared not depart from a written text which he propped up on the table in front of him. He leaned forward to read the words, and as a result the guests had difficulty in hearing him. When the King rose to reply, he offered a refreshing contrast. He spoke confidently and without notes; and he delighted his audience by speaking in perfect French. 'I am glad of this occasion which will contribute to the friendship of our two countries in their common interest,' he said firmly. 'Our great desire is that we may march together in the path of civilisation and peace.'

The next day there was a luncheon at the Quai d'Orsay, a dinner at the British Embassy, and a gala performance at the Opera. One could feel the warmth increasing hour by hour. And when the King left Paris the following morning, the route was once again lined with crowds, but this time they had not come to jeer;

instead they shouted themselves hoarse with the cry, '*Vive notre Roi!*'

The King had captivated the people. His visit had become a thrilling personal triumph. It was as though his whole life had been lived for this single effect. His sociability, his sophistication, his delight in Paris, his charm, his tact, his common sense, even his frivolity, seemed to have combined to make this one moment possible. Within three days he had completely altered the feeling of an entire country; and from that date to this there has been no enmity between France and England. One of the secretaries at the British Embassy wrote to Lord Lansdowne triumphantly that a violent Anglophobe had remarked to him sourly, 'I can't think what has come over the population of Paris. The first day they behaved well, the second day they merely displayed interest, but the third day it was heartbreaking—*ils ont acclamé le Roi.*'[1]

Four months later the French President and his wife returned the royal visit, and were delighted by the enthusiasm of the London crowds. This was the final signal for the Foreign Ministers to go full steam ahead with the work of thrashing out the details of the Entente. The agreement was not signed until the following year. There were no military clauses of any kind. It covered, instead, every part of the globe where the national and commercial interests of the two countries were in rivalry with one another. The main clauses acknowledged French claims in North Africa and British claims in Egypt. It was a matter of compromise the whole way through and, astonishingly enough, both nations were enthusiastic about the final result.

The public gave King Edward the credit for the Entente. He had not initiated the talks, but without the friendship and trust inspired by this visit to Paris, it is more than doubtful if the agreement could have been

[1] *Lord Lansdowne:* Lord Newton.

carried through. The Foreign Secretary, Lord Lansdowne, resented the fact that his own labours were overshadowed. Many years later his official biographer wrote, 'It not infrequently happens that when a distinct success has been obtained, credit is given to the wrong person, and in the case of the Anglo-French Agreement the public has been led to believe that it was brought about by the visit of King Edward to Paris in 1903.' [1]

It is not difficult to appreciate Lord Lansdowne's chagrin when he found that his triumph at signing the treaty, after a year of laborious effort, was received with perfunctory congratulations, while a whirlwind of praise still centred on the King. Nevertheless the French never had any doubt to whom the credit belonged. Many years later, M. Paul Cambon remarked to a friend, 'Any clerk at the Foreign Office could draw up a treaty, but there was no one else who could have succeeded in producing the right atmosphere for a *rapprochement* with France.'[2] And M. Poincaré, in a speech delivered in Cannes two years after the King's death, declared, 'We cannot forget that it was King Edward VII who first encouraged, initiated, and pursued this friendly co-operation between France and the United Kingdom.'[3]

Historically, the Entente was the most important event of the King's reign.

[1] *Lord Lansdowne:* Lord Newton.

[2] *Recollections of Three Reigns:* Sir Frederick Ponsonby.

[3] *The Times*, April 15, 1912.

CHAPTER THIRTEEN

THE PURSUIT OF PLEASURE

EDWARD VII excited more interest than any other figure of the decade. The Kaiser was spectacular, and the Czar was all-powerful, but the King of England was the leader of high society. The glittering world of wealth and privilege, from one end of Europe to the other, took its cue from London and accepted without question the dicta of the British sovereign.

Edward was the picture of opulence. With his heavy-lidded protruding eyes, his sensual mouth, his air of geniality, his enormous cigars, and his huge, over-fed body, always superbly attired, he was the symbol of the good life. He had never made any pretence of deriving pleasure from intellectual pursuits. His pleasures were the pleasures of the senses—food, women, magnificence, and above all else, comfort. He had indulged his tastes for forty years, but his appetite was still unsatiated. As a result the Edwardian era sprang into being.

Edwardian society modelled itself to suit the King's personal demands. Everything was larger than life-size. There was an avalanche of balls and dinners and country house parties. More money was spent on clothes, more food was consumed, more horses were raced, more infidelities were committed, more birds were shot, more yachts were commissioned, more late hours were kept, than ever before. It was, in short, the most ostentatious and extravagant decade that England had known.

The Edwardian era had other distinguishing features about it. It was vibrant and adventurous. The fact that the King liked City millionaires and Jewish jokes and American heiresses and pretty women (regardless of their origin) meant that the doors were open to anyone who succeeded in titillating the monarch's fancy. To the outsiders Society became a grim and exciting business; to the aristocracy it became an opportunity for profitable matrimonial alliances which resulted in a general refurbishing of the family coffers. The three men closest to the King were the Duke of Devonshire, the Marquis de Soveral and Mr. Ernest Cassel. They perfectly represented the new social order. The aristocracy with its immense estates was still predominant; but foreign diplomats and modern Jewish Crœsuses also had their place.

Oddly enough, Edward VII was immensely popular with the working classes. They liked a King who lived in magnificent style, yet constantly showed himself to his people. Scarcely an important social event took place without the Sovereign being present. They warmed to the fact that for all his royal grandeur he possessed the human appetites; that he liked to bet on the races and eat Gargantuan meals and surround himself with beautiful women. Wherever he went cries of 'Good old Teddy!' greeted him, and the chorus swelled as the reign progressed.

It would be wrong, however, to give the impression that everyone was enthusiastic about Edward's succession. Walburga, Lady Paget, the beautiful 'Wally' of long ago, who in her youth had served as a maid of honour to the Princess Royal, could only muster up mixed praise. 'The King as King,' she wrote in her diary in 1904, 'is much more useful than he was as Prince of Wales. He has a great deal of ability, but is always surrounded by a bevy of Jews and a ring of racing people. He has the same luxurious tastes as the Semites, the same love of pleasure and comfort. Still, he is a *charmeur* and very able.'[1]

[1] *In my Tower:* Walburga, Lady Paget.

The squirearchy, and a section of the aristocracy, were openly disgruntled. Society had become so lavish that the gentry with their relatively modest means could no longer take part in the Court life. They were horrified by the 'common' women who found their way to Buckingham Palace, and did not hesitate to brand the new King as 'unspeakably vulgar'. The writers and poets were not much better pleased. There was no place for them in the elaborate drawing-rooms of rank and wealth. The King smiled on the celebrities of the stage, but he had little use for intellectuals. Rudyard Kipling sourly described his monarch to a friend as 'a corpulent voluptuary'.

IT might be said that the Edwardian era officially began when the King and Queen moved into Buckingham Palace. The first season of the new occupancy was that of 1903, and it was suitably spectacular. The tedious 'Drawing Rooms' of Queen Victoria's day were abolished, and instead King Edward gave a series of splendid Court Balls. He entertained profusely, and on many evenings of the summer months carriages rolled into the Palace yard with the handsome men and women who had been bidden to dine with their Sovereign.

The King played his part unstintingly, but in return he insisted on being amused. By the time of his accession this had become an increasingly difficult task. Although his appetite was still sharp it was temperamental and selective. When he was enjoying himself he was the picture of affability; but when he was bored his mouth turned down at the corners and a sullen look appeared in his eyes. He began to drum on the table, and say 'Yes, yes . . . quite so', which was the signal to his unfortunate hostess that he wished to be rescued at once.

The King did not like discussing abstract subjects. At dinner he preferred a light, bantering conversation and amusing bits of gossip. At country house parties this provided something of a problem, for the *placement* was arranged according to rank, which meant that the same lady often found herself next to the King at every meal. Once Lady de Grey whispered to Sir Frederick Ponsonby in desperation, 'For heaven's sake, suggest a topic for me to discuss with the King as I have sat next to him for three nights.' Ponsonby replied, 'Give away your relations and friends and repeat any secrets about them.' 'But I did that the first night,' she laughed![1]

However, despite his restlessness, the King had a larger number of personal friends than any monarch who has sat on the British throne. His enormous acquaintance cut through the sporting world, the theatrical world, the political world, and the social world, of most of the capitals of Europe. He took an intense interest in the private lives of his friends, particularly in their peccadilloes. He loved to receive their confidences, and went to great trouble to help them out of scrapes and difficulties. For example, when young George Cornwallis-West, the son of the King's old friend, decided to marry the widowed Lady Randolph Churchill, who was old enough to be his mother, the colonel of Mr. West's battalion told him he must leave his regiment. Mr. West at once took his troubles to King Edward (then Prince of Wales), who calmed him down and gave him sensible advice. ' "Is it your intention to make soldiering your profession for the rest of your life?" he said. "If it is, then I advise you to sit tight. If, however, it is not, why make enemies of men who have been your friends and who probably will continue to be your friends after all this has blown over? My advice to you is to go on half-pay

[1] *Under Three Reigns:* Sir Frederick Ponsonby.

for six months or a year, look around and see if you can find something else to do, and then make up your mind at the expiration of the time." '[1]

Although the King encouraged his friends to approach him on an equal footing, their relations with him were never entirely free from anxiety. Fundamentally, Edward VII was immensely royal, almost to the point of eccentricity. Unlike Queen Victoria he did not concern himself with the moral character of those whose company amused him. So long as people did not become involved in open scandals, so long as they outwardly obeyed the conventions of the day and took trouble to observe the niceties of Society, they were acceptable to him. Thus he set the tone of Edwardian England which worshipped 'form' above all else.

But 'form', to the King, covered a very wide range. He had a passion for detail and nothing escaped his notice. It really pained and angered him when his subjects were careless about arranging their medals, or appeared in what he considered unsuitable attire. Once when he and the Queen were cruising in the Mediterranean, the daughter of the British Consul in Algiers was bidden, five minutes before lunch, to join the royal party and make up the right number. The poor girl hurriedly arrived in a grey flannel suit and a squash hat to find all the other ladies much more elaborately dressed. The King was furious at her 'sports clothes'; even when it was explained to him that she had only been asked at the last minute, he found it hard to forgive her.

On another occasion Lord Rosebery came aboard the royal yacht in a Yacht Squadron mess jacket and a white tie, which no one else thought amiss, but the King eyed him furiously through the whole dinner. And on still another occasion, when Sir Frederick Ponsonby was

[1] *Edwardian Hey-Days:* George Cornwallis-West.

required to wear a blue frock-coat, and appeared in one that had turned a bit green under the Indian sun, the King's eyes nearly shut in repugnance. That night Sir Frederick received a message from the Sovereign never to wear the coat again.

The King was even stricter as far as royal etiquette was concerned. Anyone who made a *faux pas* at Buckingham Palace or Windsor would never be bidden again. One poor matron attended a ball in a dress that was too tight, and a train that was too clumsy to manage. She fell flat on her face in front of the King and Queen. Edward was furious and never forgave her. Though it was an accident, it simply should not have happened; her name was struck off the Court list.

Even at Sandringham, where the King took pains to create an informal atmosphere, friends knew better than to take any liberties which might reflect on the royal dignity. For instance, no lady was allowed to go to bed before the Queen, and no gentleman before the King. Even though the King sometimes sat up until two or three in the morning he was unrelenting about this rule. One night, when Queen Alexandra left the drawing-room at midnight the King went around counting the heads to make sure that no gentleman had slipped away at the same time. He found himself one head short. Immediately he sent for a page and told him that one of the gentlemen was missing, to find out who it was and to go and fetch him. It turned out to be the seventy-five-year-old Sir Dighton Probyn, the Keeper of the Privy Purse, who had not felt well and had gone to bed. The page, however, woke him up and told him the King wanted him. 'King Edward, who had imagined it was one of the younger guests,' wrote Sir Frederick Ponsonby, 'was very much amused at this, but Sir Dighton was not.'

THE King left no one in any doubt as to the seriousness with which he regarded kingship. In 1903, when King Alexander and Queen Draga were brutally assassinated, and England broke off diplomatic relations with Serbia, much pressure was exerted to restore harmony between the two countries. Russia and Italy sent Envoys to make a special appeal to King Edward, but he informed them that public opinion was too outraged by the atrocity for his government to meet their wishes. 'I have another, and, so to say, a personal reason,' he added. '*Mon métier à moi est d'être Roi*. King Alexander was also by his *métier* "*un Roi*". I cannot be indifferent to the assassination of a member of my profession. . . . We should be obliged to shut up our businesses if we, the kings, were to consider assassination of kings as of no consequence at all. I regret, but you see that I cannot do what you wish me to do.'[1]

As King, Edward VII expected to be perfectly served, and could not bear to have arrangements go wrong. He had a violent temper that often flashed out without warning, and the equerry unfortunate enough to make a slip resulting in inconvenience to His Majesty, occasionally found the King roaring at him like a bull. However, he was fundamentally kind-hearted. Half an hour later he invariably went out of his way to bestow a gracious remark and a charming smile to show that all was forgiven.

Occasionally mishaps of the King's own making provoked the same sort of royal storm. Prince Christopher of Greece tells of a large dinner party before a ball, when the King spilled some spinach on his immaculate white shirt. His face went red with fury and he plunged both hands into the spinach dish and smeared it over his front. 'Then seeing the expressions of polite consternation stamped on the faces of his guests,' wrote Prince Christopher, 'he laughed in his infectious way, "Well, I

[1] *King Edward in his True Colours:* Edward Legge.

had to change anyway, hadn't I? I might as well make a complete mess of it." '[1]

However, the King's temper seemed to be a form of indulgence of which he had perfect mastery. He never lost control of himself when foreign visitors were present; indeed, he was a model of long-suffering patience and gave striking examples of courtesy. On one occasion in 1907 he held a dinner at Buckingham Palace in honour of an Indian Prince who was visiting England for the first time. Asparagus was served, and the King looked up from his plate to see the footman staring at the distinguished guest in amazement. The Prince was eating the asparagus but throwing the stalks over his shoulder on to the carpet. There was a moment of nervous silence, then the King began to do the same thing. The rest of the party took their cue and soon everyone was tossing away the stalks as though it was normal procedure.

The King was always extremely good-tempered with children. He adored his own family, and now he took an intense interest in his grandchildren. During the first year of his reign his eldest son, the Duke of York,[2] left England on a tour of the Empire, accompanied by his wife. They were away nearly eight months, and during their absence the four children were left in the charge of their grandparents. With a governess and a battery of nurses and under-nurses they trailed after the King and Queen, from London to Sandringham, from Osborne to Balmoral. 'If the superimposition of four noisy children upon the Royal Household,' wrote the Duke of Windsor many years later, 'was ever a nuisance, my grandparents never let us know it. On the contrary, they encouraged our innate boisterousness to such an extent that the quiet routine of York Cottage suffered a brief but harmless

[1] *Memoirs:* Prince Christopher of Greece.

[2] The Duke of York was not created Prince of Wales until November 1901.

set-back. For a little less than a year our lessons had been in charge of an Alsatian lady, Mlle Helen Bricka, who had taught my mother as a girl. By now plump and elderly, Mlle Bricka had undoubtedly been an ideal governess for a girl of finishing-school age, but she was to find that the teaching of small and restless boys presented problems outside her previous experience. Nor were her conscientious efforts furthered by the fact that I had passed temporarily under the sunny auspices of a grandfather who remembered how dull his own lessons had been, and of a grandmother who believed that lessons were less important to children than their own happiness. If my grandparents were not entertaining distinguished company at lunch, they liked to have us romping around in the dining-room. In this congenial atmosphere it was easy to forget that Mlle Bricka was waiting for us upstairs with her French and German primers. If we were too long in going, she would enter the dining-room timidly to warn us that we were already late for our afternoon lessons. Usually my grandmother would wave her away, and my grandfather, puffing at his cigar, might add reassuringly to the governess, "It's all right. Let the children stay with us a little longer. We shall send them upstairs presently." So unconcerned were my grandparents over the lapses from the schoolroom routine that on taking us to Sandringham for a two-weeks' stay, they left poor Mlle Bricka behind in London lest she spoil the fun.'[1]

Prince Christopher of Greece was present at one of these uproarious family luncheons, when the small Duke of Windsor, who was standing behind the King's chair, began tugging at the latter's sleeve. The King was in the middle of an anecdote and bade the child be quiet until he had finished his story. Finally he turned to him and asked him what he wanted. 'It doesn't matter now,

[1] *A King's Story:* H.R.H. The Duke of Windsor.

grandfather. I was going to tell you there was a slug in your salad, but you've eaten it.'

It is not recorded how amusing the King found little David on that particular occasion, but as a rule he was delighted by everything the child said or did. In order to please the King, distinguished clerics and diplomats often turned themselves into elephants (an animal for which the child had an unconcealed passion) and gave him rides on their backs. One day the Bishop of London, Dr. Creighton, joined the family games.[1] Wouldn't little David like a ride on his back, too? The boy eyed the immensely tall, immensely thin Bishop and replied firmly, 'I don't like riding on giraffes.'

This remark delighted the royal grandfather.

The King's energy was prodigious. He had an enormous number of official duties which ranged from laying foundation stones and attending public dinners to visiting hospitals and opening cathedrals. He also had many routine obligations which included the daily reading of the Cabinet papers. Nevertheless, he managed to continue the same overflowing social round that he had followed as Prince of Wales. After opening Parliament at the end of January, he would spend a week or so in Biarritz, with stops in Paris both ways. Then, like as not, he would go for a short Mediterranean cruise, or travel to Copenhagen for a brief reunion with the Queen's family. He was always present at Ascot and Epsom and Goodwood. He went to Cowes in August, then to Marienbad for the 'cure', to Balmoral in October and to Sandringham for a few weeks in November and December. When his presence was required in London he divided his time between Buckingham Palace and

[1] This incident took place shortly before Edward VII became King.

Windsor Castle. Yet he always found time to pay at least a dozen visits to private friends each year. He liked to stay with the Duke and Duchess of Devonshire at Chatsworth in January, and he often visited the Sassoons at Brighton, the James at West Dean Park, Lord Rosebery at Mentmore, Lord Crewe at Crewe Hall, Lord Carrington at Daws Hill, and many other friends. When one considers the tedium of travel fifty years ago, and the length of the journeys by boat and train and carriage, one can only marvel at the physical energy of the sixty-year-old monarch. Queen Alexandra often begged the King to curtail his activities, but the quiet family life that his son, the future George V, found so agreeable had no fascination for King Edward.

He adored people and was exhilarated by a constantly changing scene. If he found himself confronted with an idle day he was as restless as a caged animal; as a result every hour was mapped out in advance. Even so, if the company provided for him fell below his expectations he seemed unable to hide his boredom. To keep the King amused became the chief preoccupation of the most important hostesses of the era. Many of them came to the conclusion that the Hon. Mrs. George Keppel was the only answer.

This charming lady, who was married to a younger son of the Earl of Albemarle, succeeded in captivating the King shortly before his accession. Winston Churchill's aunt later claimed that her husband was responsible for the introduction. According to this account, Mr. Jack Leslie was strolling about with Mrs. Keppel at the Sandown races when he met the Prince of Wales 'and dear Jacksy introduced his fair companion. The Prince immediately asked her to accompany him and his face lit up with such a smile that Jacksy knew he would not see her again for a long time!' [1]

[1] *The Fabulous Leonard Jerome:* Anita Leslie.

The King's attachment for Mrs. Keppel lasted throughout his reign. She was a very remarkable woman. Discreet without being dull, witty without being malicious, she was so engaging and unaffected that she not only managed to win the admiration of the great hostesses of the day, but of the Queen herself. It soon became obvious to even the most obtuse onlookers that the King was in a far better humour when Alice Keppel was present than when she was not; and since the great preoccupation of the day was to divert the King, Mrs. Keppel soon found herself invited to all the same country house parties as the Sovereign. And when the generous-minded Alexandra nodded her approval Mrs. Keppel's position became almost that of a second wife.

No one could soothe the King's ruffled temper so easily as this accomplished lady. She shared many of his interests, particularly his liking for bridge. Although Edward VII was a keen player, he was not particularly proficient. Every night, directly after dinner, he liked to sit down to a few rubbers. He was childishly pleased when he won, and very critical of his partner if he lost. Consequently many people were afraid to play with him. Once, when he invited a pretty young lady at Marienbad to be his partner, she refused with a charming smile saying, 'I am afraid, Sir, I can't even tell a King from a Knave.'

Most hostesses were relieved when Mrs. Keppel was present to cope with the King. One evening when he was grumbling about bad cards and showing disconcerting signs of temper he suddenly put Mrs. Keppel into a high no-trump bid. He was dummy and when he laid down his hand there was scarcely a trick in it. Mrs. Keppel had poor cards as well. She glanced at her hand ruefully, then remarked in a doleful voice, 'All I can say, Sire, is: God Save The King and preserve Mrs. Keppel!' The King roared with laughter, and when the game was over paid his losses without complaint.

Queen Alexandra herself often found Mrs. Keppel useful in calming the irate King, and began to invite her with increasing regularity to Sandringham and Windsor. Mrs. Asquith told of an occasion when she spent several days at Windsor with her husband, the Prime Minister. One afternoon they were due to leave with Their Majesties at four o'clock to take tea at Virginia Water.

'On my arrival in the courtyard the King came up to me,' wrote Mrs. Asquith, 'and said, "Where is the Prime Minister?" Curtseying to the ground, I answered: "I am sorry, sir, but I have not seen him since lunch: I fear he cannot have got your command and may have gone for a walk with Sir Edward Grey." His Majesty (angrily turning to his gentlemen-in-waiting, Harry Stonor and Seymour Fortescue): "What have you done? Where have you looked for him? Did you not give him my command?" The distracted gentlemen flew about, but I could see in a moment that Henry was not likely to turn up, so I begged the King to go into his motor. He answered with indignation: "Certainly not: I cannot start without the Prime Minister."

'He looked first at his watch and then at the Castle clock, and fumed crossly about the yard. Seeing affairs at a standstill, I went up to the Queen and said I feared there had been a scandal at Court, and that Henry must have eloped with one of the maids of honour. I begged her to save my blushes by commanding the King to proceed, at which she walked up to him with her amazing grace and, in her charming way, tapping him firmly on the arm, pointing with a sweeping gesture to his motor and invited Gracie Raincliffe and Alice Keppel to accompany him: at which they all drove off.'[1]

As usual Mrs. Keppel placated the royal wrath. And when it later transpired that the Prime Minister really

[1] *The Autobiography of Margot Asquith.*

had gone for a long walk with one of the Queen's charming ladies, King Edward was highly amused.

ONE of the King's chief pleasures was food. Like many of his contemporaries he had a huge appetite, but he was extremely particular about the dishes set before him and nothing short of perfection would do. Although the Palace staff was reorganised by Lord Esher, and the three hundred and fifty indoor servants cut to three hundred, the kitchen staff of forty-five was left intact. But whereas under Queen Victoria the entertaining had been limited to a few official functions a year, now the kitchens buzzed with activity. All morning long vans and carts clattered into the Palace courtyard delivering literally hundreds of pounds of meat and groceries and fish and vegetables.

King Edward retained the same French chef that his mother had employed, and many elaborate dishes were served, some of them taking several days to prepare. For instance, a dish which the German royal family particularly fancied was a turkey stuffed with a chicken, inside the chicken a pheasant and inside the pheasant a woodcock, made into a pie and served cold.

M. Ménager was a perfectionist and would not pass any dish unless it was a complete triumph. At Queen Victoria's diamond jubilee in 1897 he had decided to give the guests *Rosettes de saumon au rubis*, a salmon dish served cold with claret jelly. It had to be made three times with all new materials before M. Ménager was satisfied. To be a success the dish must be a rich transparent pink, and if the salmon is over-cooked, the colour is not right. The first time M. Ménager shook his head; then he instructed one of the Paris chefs, imported especially for the occasion, to make a second attempt. This time the claret jelly did not clear sufficiently. The chef tried to disguise it by a skilful blending of the claret, but he could not fool M. Ménager. 'A good jelly,' announced M. Ménager in thunderous tones, 'should be like a drop of whisky, quite clear, without the slightest cloud in it. Whisky. You know what that is, eh? Then *make* the claret jelly as clear as whisky.'

One of M. Ménager's young Swiss apprentices, M. Gabriel Tschumi, tells about his first day at Windsor Castle. 'I had risen about 7 a.m., washed and dressed, and come to the kitchens expecting that, as lunch and dinner were meals of about eight or ten courses, breakfast would be a very light meal indeed. I found, instead, that the coal ranges were red-hot and the spits packed with chops, cutlets, steaks, bloaters, sausages, chickens and woodcock. The roast chefs were deftly removing them and piling them on to huge platters. In other parts of the kitchen cooks were trimming rashers of streaky bacon, a quarter of an inch thick, for grilling, and preparing egg dishes. . . . I asked how many different dishes were served to the Royal family for breakfast. "Five," came the reply. . . . Any servant could have the same number of courses at breakfast. Quite a number of them managed it daily without trouble.'[1]

Although King Edward ate a Continental breakfast when he was abroad, he always liked 'an English breakfast' consisting of haddock, poached eggs, bacon, chicken and woodcock, before setting out on a day's shooting or racing. Luncheon and dinner, of course, were meals that stretched from ten to fourteen courses, and tea was an elaborate affair with every sort of scone and crumpet, tart and roll and cake. Besides this, snacks consisting of lobster salads and cold chicken were often served at eleven in the morning to appease the King's hunger, and even after dinner a plate of sandwiches, and sometimes a quail or a cutlet, was sent to the Royal apartments.

The 'picnic' luncheon that the Royal party took to

[1] *Royal Chef:* Gabriel Tschumi.

Ascot and Goodwood, and the 'shooting' luncheons that were packed in hampers at Sandringham, were fantastically elaborate. And when the King attended the Opera, and had dinner served in the room behind the Royal box, he expected the meal, prepared by his own chef, to be every bit as plentiful and delectable as though he were at home. 'Six footmen went down early in the afternoon of the day,' wrote M. Tschumi, 'with hampers packed with cloths, silver, the finest gold plate and everything which might add to the comfort of the thirty or so guests usually entertained. I accompanied them in the old Horse Brake, which bore the King's coat of arms, with about a dozen hampers of food based on the menu which had been passed for supper of the previous day. Sometimes there were nine or ten courses, all served cold, and sometimes up to a dozen; and as each guest had to be given a clean plate for each course, the footmen had a strenuous time of it carrying in the hampers which often contained three hundred and sixty or four hundred plates alone, to say nothing of all the other silver used during the meal.'[1]

The King's scale of living was expensive. Parliament had voted him an annual income of £450,000 which included £60,000 for the Privy Purse. He also had an annual income of £60,000 a year from the Duchy of Lancaster. This made a total of over half a million pounds a year, and did not include the annual grant of £60,000 for the Queen's private use. Even so it was not enough. The King soon found that his expenditure was outstripping his income. So he turned to Mr. Ernest Cassel for advice, and soon Cassel was controlling all the King's investments.

The first public proof that the King gave of his friendship for this shrewd, blunt, unsmiling, financial genius, who in appearance was almost his double, was in 1901 when he attended the wedding of Cassel's only daughter to

[1] *Royal Chef:* Gabriel Tschumi.

Mr. Wilfrid Ashley. The following year he created Cassel a Privy Councillor and made him a Knight of the Order of St. Michael and St. George. And a short while later he stood as godfather to the Ashley child, named Edwina in his honour, and known today as Lady Mountbatten.

Rumours began to spread that Cassel had been given his knighthood in return for a large gift of money. These stories continued throughout the King's reign. Repeatedly it was said that Cassel 'settled up' whenever the monarch found himself in financial difficulties. This was putting an unpleasant twist on the facts. Cassel invested the King's money, and industrial shares were steadily rising. There is no doubt that Cassel made large profits for the King, but it was not the same thing as bestowing large gifts on him.

Despite these ill-natured tales, which were widely quoted abroad, the King's friendship with the financier continued to grow. He liked to be kept informed about the great financial deals that were taking place, and he always found the stock market a fascinating topic of conversation. He placed implicit faith in Cassel's judgment and loyalty, and by the end of his reign he was seeing more of Sir Ernest than any other single person.

Another friend whom the King grew increasingly dependent upon as his years advanced was the Marquis de Soveral. This clever Portuguese diplomat was equally well-liked by both the King and the Queen. He was the complete reverse of Cassel; charming, urbane, polished and witty. He adored women and was said to be the best dancer in Europe. 'He was universally popular in England,' wrote Sir Frederick Ponsonby, 'where he made love to all the most beautiful women and all the nicest men were his friends.' Soveral was not only witty, but extremely shrewd. When the King asked him if he had seen *The Importance of Being Earnest*, he replied quickly, 'No, Sire. But I have seen the importance of being Ernest Cassel.'

CHAPTER FOURTEEN

THE KING'S TRAVELS

EVERY spring the King and Queen went for a cruise on board the royal yacht, the *Victoria and Albert*. This huge vessel was the last word in luxury. It was a blaze of flowers and gold plate and footmen in scarlet livery. A Marine band, stationed on the deck, played music during meals. The Queen's cabin, painted in white and gold with built-in book-cases, was large enough to have a grand piano in one corner. The King had a private sitting-room, and a special room filled with dozens of uniforms, hats, medals and clothes of every weight and description which he deemed necessary to have on hand. He always stepped ashore, whether it was Portugal or Denmark, Italy or Greece, immaculately attired in whatever costume was most likely to please the population. The same care was taken, of course, in home waters. Once when his yacht was nearing the coast of Scotland, Austen Chamberlain heard His Majesty say to his Swiss valet, '*Un costume un peu plus écossais demain.*'

The crew consisted of three hundred, and there were thirty royal servants aboard. The King's chief *chef*, M. Ménager, usually went on these trips and was assisted by three master cooks. The cuisine was the finest on any ship afloat, although the galley left much to be desired. It was a large room, but it was equipped with coal ranges that altered greatly in temperature whenever the wind changed. Sometimes they went out altogether, at other times they blazed furiously. Therefore it was necessary to keep the room as airtight as possible, and the cooks had instructions not to leave the galley for more than a few minutes at a time. 'You had only to turn your back for the wind to change,' wrote M. Tschumi, 'and unless you were very quick a soufflé or a lark pudding was soon ruined in a cold oven. We got into the habit of standing by the stoves the whole time until every dish was ready. . . .'[1]

Most of the time the galley was like an inferno. Every Sunday King Edward made an inspection tour and he invariably remarked on the heat and the lack of ventilation. 'After a very perfunctory glance round at the pantry and larders, the King's face would be as red and shining as the faces of the kitchen staff,' wrote Tschumi, 'and he was only too glad to beat a retreat from such an over-heated atmosphere. Once I overheard him remark to the equerry who accompanied him on these rounds of inspection, "Phew! I'm glad that's over." '[1]

Whenever the King stepped ashore he was received with great ceremony. When the yacht dropped anchor off Lisbon, the King of Portugal came out to greet him in a centuries-old gold barge rowed by eighty men in red. At Rome the King of Italy and his two sons waited at the station for the royal train with a glittering guard of honour. At Athens the Sovereign's brother-in-law, the King of Greece, led him to the Palace behind a wonderful white-uniformed cavalry escort. Everywhere cannons boomed and flags fluttered. When the King left Malta for Naples, the Royal Navy provided an escort. The King instructed Sir Frederick Ponsonby to wire ahead and say that he would be arriving incognito, 'which seemed rather absurd,' wrote Ponsonby, 'as no other human being in the world could come with eight battleships, four cruisers, four destroyers, and a dispatch vessel.'[2]

These trips to the Mediterranean were by no means the King's principal sojourns abroad. During his reign

[1] *Royal Chef:* Gabriel Tschumi.

[2] *Recollections of Three Reigns:* Sir Frederick Ponsonby.

he made half a dozen trips to Germany, and he frequently went to Copenhagen with Queen Alexandra to celebrate the birthdays of his octogenarian father-in-law, King Christian IX of Denmark. Every year with clock-like precision he went to Biarritz for a week in the early spring, and to Marienbad in August for the 'cure'. And of course he visited Paris *en route*, for several days at a time.

On many of these trips the King was besieged for decorations. In Edwardian days form and appearance were everything, and even the most exalted of men seemed to have a mania for medals. The Shah of Persia, for instance, asked bluntly for the Order of the Garter and said no other honour would do.[1] This caused a fearful commotion, for Lord Lansdowne, the Foreign Secretary, weakly told him he might have it which enraged the King. Edward VII did not approve of giving the Garter to non-Christian rulers and claimed angrily that if his wishes in this matter were to be ignored, surely the Emperor of Japan, Britain's ally, should be the first to receive it. When the Foreign Office Box containing the Order arrived on board the yacht, he picked it up and hurled it across the cabin. But because of Lansdowne's promise, in the end the King was forced to give in. The Shah came aboard the yacht especially to receive the Garter, and the monarch, inwardly fuming, bestowed it with as much grace as possible.

The Germans, however, were the worst decoration-hunters of all. They literally showered their own decorations about, giving as many as 30,000 a year, and they expected the same treatment in return. By British standards this was impossible. In the first place there were only three orders that the sovereign might distribute entirely as he liked. One was the Royal Victorian Order founded by Queen Victoria in 1896; the other two were orders instituted by the King himself in

[1] His father, Nasr ed Din, had been given the Garter by Queen Victoria in 1873.

1902. The first was the Order of Merit, given for outstanding achievement, and the second the Royal Victorian Chain given to persons of high rank for services to the Sovereign.

In Edwardian days a maximum of 800 decorations were distributed each year. This was a good deal more than Queen Victoria had allowed, but even so, to the Germans it seemed a mere pittance. When the royal yacht went to Kiel, Count Eulenburg, the sinister head of the Kaiser's household, and von Bülow, the Chancellor, both compiled lists containing two hundred names to whom they wished honours accorded.

The King was astonished that they could have so little understanding of British customs, and replied that he could give a decoration to each minister to be passed on to whatever person the latter designated. The Germans could not believe that this edict was final. They bombarded members of the King's retinue with arguments and pleas, and finally sent one of their ambassadors, Count Metternich, to the royal yacht to plead with the King's secretary. But Edward VII remained firm, and finally the matter was dropped.

The King, however, was much more lenient in allowing British subjects to accept foreign decorations than any sovereign before him. This had been a matter of controversy for several centuries. Although Queen Elizabeth occasionally permitted her favourites to receive foreign honours she was not enthusiastic about it, and once remarked that she 'did not like her dogs to wear any collar but her own'. King Edward allowed his subjects to accept medals from abroad, but he made it clear that they should be worn 'only on the occasions when they are to meet His Majesty, members of the Royal Family, or Foreign Royalties'.

The constant fuss about decorations provided Sir Frederick Ponsonby with a good deal of extra work. He had quite enough to do, as it was. For no matter whether the King was at Biarritz or Marienbad, or cruising in the Mediterranean, the royal routine continued as though he were at home. Shoals of official telegrams arrived each day, and Ponsonby had to make arrangements for the King's Messengers, entrusted with Cabinet papers and dispatches, to be met at every port. Besides this, he had innumerable other duties. 'At Malta,' he wrote from Naples on April 24, 'I was with the King after breakfast till 10.30, during which time he gave me about fifteen letters to write and a list of decorations to be prepared. Also two copies of letters to do. I then went to a Review, then to luncheon with the Artillery, then to a Levée and back on board at 5.30. The King sent for copies of letters to show the Queen at tea. Answer, not yet done. Afterwards he sent for me to discuss decorations and asked for *typed* list. Answer, not done. Had I written yet to so and so; answer, no. Then the King said, "My dear man, you must try and get something done." So I got a list of decorations typed by a Petty Officer on board. He spelt two names wrong and left out a third, all of which the King found out. . . . Although I sat up until 1.30 to get straight, the King is left with the impression that nothing is done.'[1]

Of all his journeys, the King apparently enjoyed his annual trip to Marienbad the most. Although the object of the visit was to take the 'cure', which consisted of drinking the mineral waters and observing a stringent diet, the King refused to follow the prescribed routine too closely. He arose at seven in the morning and took a two-hour walk before breakfast, but he insisted on

[1] *King Edward VII:* Sir Sidney Lee.

lunch being the same substantial meal that it was at home.

The King enjoyed the rough, wild countryside and frequently went shooting with Prince Trauttmansdorff, who lived on a nearby estate, and with the Abbot of Tepl, a great dignitary of the Roman Catholic Church, who owned the mineral waters of Marienbad. The Abbot was the head of the Tepl Monastery. The monks of this Order spent two years behind their walls, followed by two years in the world. Consequently they wore long white cassocks and black top hats which nicely represented their alternating roles. Although shooting with the Abbot was rather primitive, he always gave the King a magnificent luncheon, and provided wonderful wines which those taking the 'cure' were supposed to forgo, but found it impossible to resist.

In the afternoon the King usually went for a drive or a walk, then he played croquet. He had almost as much of a passion for this game as for bridge, and he did not try to hide the fact that he disliked being beaten. Once when the pretty Duchess of Sermoneta was a guest at Sir Ernest Cassel's country house in England she was several times invited to play croquet with the King. She was not good at the game and missed the easiest hoops, which put him in a good temper. But one evening she lost patience and gave the ball a mighty smack. 'It flew right across the ground,' she wrote, 'straight through the right hoop (I didn't even know it was the right one) and continuing its glorious career hit the King's ball straight into the rose bushes. But by the icy stillness that prevailed I realized that never, never was such a thing to happen again.'[1]

Sir Frederick Ponsonby had the same sort of experience with the King at Marienbad, but his was not accidental. He disliked croquet, and when the King

[1] *Things Past:* Duchess of Sermoneta.

insisted on his making up a foursome he was determined to make sure that it would not happen a second time. His partner was old Harry Chaplin, and the King's was Madame Letellier. Whenever Ponsonby got an opportunity he sent the King's ball to the other end of the ground. 'This made him quite furious,' wrote Sir Frederick, 'and the beautiful Madame Letellier, who was quite a good player, begged me with tears in her eyes not to make him so angry, adding that she understood that courtiers always allowed monarchs to win. I replied that this was out of date and that personally I always made a point of beating the Royal Family at every game I could.'[1]

However, the result was not what Ponsonby expected. Madame Letellier's emotions were aroused and she flung herself into the game with all her might. Her opponents looked as though they were winning but at the crucial moment she made things awkward for them; then the King did several hoops successfully, with the result that he and his partner won at the post. Flushed with triumph, His Majesty announced that it was the best game he had ever had, and said he would like to play with the same foursome again the following day. In the end he relented and let Ponsonby off.

However, it was not the croquet or the shooting or even the mineral waters that drew the King back to Marienbad every year. This little resort with its cluster of hotels, its forests, its cafés, and its famous cure attracted some of the richest men in Europe; consequently, it also attracted dozens of beautiful adventuresses of every nationality. There were American *divorcées*, Russian demi-mondaines, and fascinating Austrian widows of doubtful origin.

Since the King always visited the resort *en garçon*, accompanied only by two equerries, it was not difficult

[1] *Recollections of Three Reigns:* Sir Frederick Ponsonby.

for him to arrange a good many assignations. Despite his years, he was still extremely virile. His amours were never dramatic or even serious, but he continued to crave the stimulation of female company, and he preferred it to be varied and plentiful. Sometimes the King invited these ladies to his hotel to take supper with him; sometimes he took them for drives in his carriage; sometimes he asked them to stroll with him through the forests. 'The thickly wooded district which surrounds the Bohemian watering-places,' wrote Sigmund Münz, an *habitué* of Marienbad, 'had already afforded Goethe an opportunity to pursue his wonted occupations, the *ars scribendi* and the *ars amandi.* And now on many an afternoon during those seven summers, it provided secluded retreats to which Edward VII could retire, for his zest for life endured to the end, and the waters of Marienbad seemed not only to help restore his health but also to renew his perennial youth.'[1]

Sir Frederick Ponsonby often accompanied the King to the resort, and occasionally was landed with surprising problems. He was startled to find himself pursued by a 'beautiful lady from the half-world in Vienna who wanted to have the honour of sleeping with the King. On being told this was out of the question, she said if it came to the worst she would sleep with me, so that she should not waste the money spent on her ticket; but I told her to look elsewhere for a bed.'[2]

Of course the King's patronage of Marienbad attracted a flow of visitors from all over the world. One summer the King of Greece appeared; another the future King of Bulgaria. English notables flocked into the resort, but not all of them represented the fashionable world. Sir John Fisher was a regular visitor; so was Sir Henry Campbell-Bannerman; so was the radical M.P., John

[1] *King Edward VII at Marienbad:* Sigmund Münz.

[2] *Recollections of Three Reigns:* Sir Frederick Ponsonby.

Burns. As well as attracting visitors, the King's presence attracted a stream of theatrical companies and music-hall artists. His Majesty's reputation for being a *bon vivant* sometimes prompted the singers to put on skits that were considered very shocking. When a young man dressed as a priest tried to resist the blandishments of a beautiful woman by singing mournfully, 'Were it not for my holy robes. . .' and the lady trilled back merrily 'Then take off your holy robes. . .' the King felt obliged to leave the theatre; after all, he frequently was the guest of the Abbot of Tepl, and this song seemed to be going a bit too far.

On another occasion he also left the theatre, but this time it was because he thought he was going to see a melodrama and found himself at a variety show, which was sung in German and interminably boring. Apparently, it was very *risqué* as well, for the King's abrupt departure was interpreted as disapproval. A few days later he received a letter from the Bishop of Ripon, thanking him on behalf of the Church of England for his firm stand in the cause of morality. But King Edward was not a hypocrite and he refused to take credit falsely. 'Tell the Bishop the exact truth,' he instructed Ponsonby. 'I have no wish to pose as a protector of morals, especially abroad.'

When the King quitted his luxurious suite at the Hotel Weimar every stick of furniture in his suite was sold at twice its value. However, this hero-worship did not prevent the tradespeople from making preposterous charges, and his staff had to check all the accounts with great care to try and prevent their master being robbed. Sir Frederick Ponsonby made heated protests when the garage from which he had rented a motor car, on the King's behalf, sent a bill for £1,500 for spare parts.

The King did not have the same freedom of movement at Biarritz as at Marienbad. However, he made up for it by taking a party with him which usually contained Mrs. Keppel. The life in this Atlantic resort centred around delicious food, bracing walks, bridge games, and motor-car drives. The King was an enthusiastic motorist and took many trips to neighbouring villages in the Pyrenees, or across the frontier into Spain. These trips were always fraught with adventure, for the motor cars of 1902 were far from perfect. The King owned two Mercédès and a Renault, and the Queen was the possessor of a Wolseley. In England the royal cars did not carry any number plates, but abroad they bore a special marking assigned to them by the various countries they travelled through.

The King usually had the Mercédès sent ahead when he went to Marienbad or Biarritz. Although he suffered many inconveniences in the shape of minor breakdowns, his enthusiasm did not cool, and finally, in 1905, he solved the problem by engaging his own 'motor engineer', a Mr. Stamper, who sat on the front seat with the chauffeur ready to leap out if anything went wrong. Whenever the King successfully completed a journey, no matter how short, he always stepped out saying, 'A very good r-run, Stamper, a very good r-run, indeed!'

On one trip to Newmarket, however, he found little to praise. He was proud of the fact that the Mercédès did the 'run' in two hours and a quarter, but on this particular day the chauffeur did not see a culvert in the road and went over it at a speed of fifty miles an hour. There was an appalling jolt, the car swerved, then righted itself and continued on its way. 'Stop, stop! Do you want to kill me?' cried the King. 'Just look at my hat!'

'With this', wrote Mr. Stamper, 'the king leaned forward and held out his brown bowler hat for me to see. The outward curve of its crown was gone.'[1]

In Paris the King's movements were somewhat cur-

[1] *What I Know:* C. W. Stamper.

tailed because of the vigilance of the French police. He loathed being followed about by detectives and did everything he could to dodge them. However, M. Lepine, the head of the police, took his duties very seriously, and finally devised a scheme by which all his men were required to disguise themselves so that His Majesty would not know he was being guarded. No matter where he went, whether it was to the opera or a *bistro* on the left bank, the police were always there suitably attired in evening clothes, or in the working man's blue denim. Once, Lepine's men slipped up. The King had gone off to meet a noted beauty in the Jardin des Plantes. Ponsonby learned of his plan from the courier, and informed Lepine who sent two detectives the King did not know by sight. But one of them was taken ill, and on his own initiative asked a detective to take his place who was well known to the King, having often accompanied him before. 'The King was walking with the lady,' wrote Sir Frederick Ponsonby, 'when he caught sight of the detective he knew and this completely spoiled the romance of the assignation. When he got back to the hotel he asked me how I knew where he was going and why I had warned the police. . . . He contented himself by remarking that he would take good care another time I did not know his movements, and after blowing off steam about the absurdity of the police shadowing him in Paris of all places, he never alluded to the incident again. But after that he not only tried to dodge the police but also to dodge me. He would order the motor at four and then change his mind suddenly and send for it at three, when he would slip out before anyone else was ready. But these tricks were useless with the French police, and although they were caught napping the first time, afterwards they always had motors ready and had no difficulty in following him.'[1]

[1] *Recollections of Three Reigns:* Sir Frederick Ponsonby.

The King's private life could only function at odd intervals. No matter where he was his diary was studded with engagements with the most powerful and eminent men of the times. When he was at Marienbad, he motored to Vienna to call on the Emperor Francis Joseph; when he was at Biarritz he drove to San Sebastian to have lunch with his nephew-in-law the King of Spain. Besides his visits to his father-in-law, the King of Denmark, his brother-in-law the King of Greece, and his nephew, the Emperor of Germany, there were innumerable meetings with lesser royalties who were related to him by birth or marriage. He was the sun around which the other royal planets revolved. With his myriad connections, it is small wonder the Parisians nicknamed him *L'Oncle de l'Europe*; and with his many journeys from one end of the Continent to the other it is not surprising that the English began to hum,

The King goes touring about, about
With his comely face and his jovial smile,
You hear the foreigners soulful shout,
'Oh linger with us awhile, awhile,
If only a little while!
A King of warrant, a King, a King!
We'll give him a welcome if he'll but come
For he's the monarch to make things hum—
The King, the runabout King!'

EDWARD VII was out of England from three to four months every year; yet no one complained. The fact was, that ever since his brilliantly successful trip to Paris in 1903, the English public had entertained a growing conviction that he was a master diplomat. They saw him as the inspiration and guiding force behind the Foreign Office. He had been everywhere and met everyone. He was tri-lingual, he was worldly, he understood Foreign Affairs. They began to interpret each trip, each social engagement, almost each conversation as a carefully planned move to serve British interests. In short, they believed that he was the real Foreign Secretary, and Lansdowne and Grey were only figureheads. In 1907 even the cynical Wilfrid Blunt was writing in his diary, 'Horace Rumbold has been staying with me . . . He gave me an interesting account of the King's influence in foreign affairs. His Majesty insists now on making all important diplomatic appointments himself, and busies himself much more than ever the Old Queen did in the foreign policy adopted.'[1]

This was not a very accurate picture. Edward VII seldom interfered in diplomatic appointments. Nor did he have any wish to take the responsibility of initiating policy. He disliked details and he was incapable of putting forward closely reasoned arguments. He did not possess the kind of mind that could study or ponder, or for that matter, even read much. Nevertheless, it would be wrong to minimise the contribution he made. Although the public underestimated his frivolity, and overestimated his capacity for work, it was not mistaken in recognising him as a genuinely powerful force.

The role the King took upon himself was not that of master, but of mistress. He cajoled and ameliorated and charmed. He smoothed the path of his ministers in whatever direction they desired. Although he possessed limited intellectual attributes, he had a deep understanding of human nature, which made him shrewd. He operated on instinct and impulse; and these feminine qualities, combined with unerring tact, rarely let him down.

[1] *My Diaries:* Wilfrid Blunt.

Never have a Sovereign and his Foreign Office worked together so closely or so successfully. Instead of following the custom of taking a cabinet minister on the royal tours, the King asked for a diplomat in the person of Sir Charles Hardinge, one of the ablest men in the service. It was a perfect combination. The experts planned the moves and carried out the negotiations while the King created the favourable climate for their success. One has only to contemplate the rôle of a constitutional monarch to realise the power his crown gives him. He can see anyone he wishes at a moment's notice; he can bring any combination of people together at any time; he can say the friendly word with the warm assurance that unfriendly actions cannot be directly ascribed to him. And since a King's attentions are always bound to be flattering, he possesses a magic which invariably places the odds in his favour.

King Edward used his influence in the field of foreign affairs to a greater degree than any constitutional monarch before or after him. For forty years he had believed in an Entente with France; and for fifteen years he had talked about a *rapprochement* with Russia. When he ascended the throne he did not try to impose his views on his ministers. Indeed, he fell in with Chamberlain's attempt to reach an agreement with Germany. But once his Government abandoned this idea, and decided on its own accord to court France and Russia, the King was able to be of incalculable service.

He had very little aptitude for the written word and, unlike his mother, expressed himself on paper with economy. Most of the minutes he inscribed on dispatches were brief and mundane. 'A very good dispatch'; 'The information is important'; 'A very satisfactory communication'; 'This is more satisfactory than could be expected'. However, whenever Germany entered the picture a revealing note of acidity crept into the King's comments. On Germany's attitude toward Spain, 'A case of bullying as usual!'; on von Bülow's observations, 'How badly informed he is'; on negotiations with Russia, 'Germany is certain to act against us—behind our back'; on Holstein's views, 'This is nearly as absurd as it is false'.[1]

The King's contributions did not lie in the written word. They lay in personal contacts and a superb sense of showmanship. In 1905 he helped to stage a dramatic display of friendship between England and France that played a large part in saving the young Entente from destruction.

THE crisis of 1905 was engineered by Germany and brought Europe to the brink of war. It was part of a carefully contrived plot to smash up the agreement between England and France. When the Entente was signed in 1904 Germany had made no protest. She accepted it with surprising *sang froid*, and Prince von Bülow even commented favourably upon it in the Reichstag. Nevertheless, beneath the surface, he was deeply disturbed. He had not believed it possible for Britain and France to patch up their differences, and to the very last had felt that ultimately France would join the German orbit.

As the months progressed he viewed the Entente with increasing anxiety and his ire against England swelled in proportion. He finally came to the conclusion that, late in the day though it was, the situation would have to be altered. Anglo-French unity must be destroyed. But how was it to be done?

Prince von Bülow and Herr Holstein believed the

[1] *British Documents on the Origins of the War:* edited by Gooch and Temperley.

way to achieve their purpose was to demonstrate to France that Germany, and not Britain, was the master of Europe. All they had to do was to threaten France with war, and show her that Britain had no intention of giving her military support. This, alone, would sow such dissension between the two Powers that the accord could not survive. Of course it was absolutely essential to secure the resignation of M. Delcassé, Germany's arch-enemy, but that would follow as a natural consequence.

The Moroccan situation seemed to offer the perfect opportunity for the German scheme to be brought into operation. Great Britain, under the terms of the Entente, had given France the right to expand in Morocco. This had been done with Spain's acquiescence. But what right had Britain to make this generous offer? It was perfectly true that Britain, the ruler of Gibraltar, France, the owner of Algeria, and Spain, the possessor of a settlement at Melilla, were the three European powers most concerned with North Africa. But after all Germany had commerical interests and a number of colonists in Morocco; and had not many of the great powers, including Russia and Italy, signed the Treaty of 1880 which established an open door policy in North Africa? It was true that Bismarck had declared at the time that Germany had no substantial interest in Morocco; it was also true that Prince von Bülow had told the Reichstag only the year before that 'the affairs of Morocco were outside the field of German interest'. These words must be forgotten; it was important that an issue should be created.

So on February 22, under von Bülow's guidance, the Kaiser made a bombastic speech at Bremen declaring that the future would bring 'a world-wide dominion of the Hohenzollerns'. Then he boarded his yacht and sailed to Tangier. When he arrived he made a speech to the German colony that reverberated around the world. He was determined to uphold 'the interests of the Fatherland in a free country. The German Empire has great and growing interests in Morocco. Commerce can only progress if all the powers are considered to have equal rights under the sovereignty of the Sultan and respect the independence of the country. My visit is the recognition of the influence.'[1]

King Edward was cruising in the Mediterranean when the speech was relayed to him. He was shocked and angered by it, but came to the conclusion that it was only another of the Kaiser's infuriating gestures to attract attention. 'The Tangier incident,' he wrote to Lord Lansdowne, 'was the most mischievous and uncalled-for event which the German Emperor has ever been engaged in since he came to the Throne. It was also a political theatrical fiasco, and if he thinks he has done himself good in the eyes of the world he is very much mistaken. He is no more nor less than a political "enfant terrible" and one can have no faith in any of his assurances. His own pleasure seems to be to wish to set every country by the ears.'[2]

The King had failed to appreciate the damage to French morale. He grew less sanguine when he learned, a few days later, that M. Delcassé's colleagues had immediately urged him to show a more conciliatory attitude toward Germany, and that the Foreign Minister's reply had been to hand in his resignation. The King, who had just landed at Algiers, requested the Governor-General to send the following telegram to Delcassé. 'I am charged by His Majesty King Edward VII to inform you that he personally would greatly regret your departure. He said in conversation that the news left him in consternation, and asked me to press you very strongly to retain your portfolio, in view of his confident

[1] *The Times*, April 1905. [2] *King Edward VII:* Sir Sidney Lee.

and steadfast relations with yourself, and of the great authority you possess today for the settlement of outstanding questions.'[1]

The King drew a breath of relief when he heard that Delcassé had withdrawn his resignation. He hurried to Paris to confer with the French leaders. But he still failed to grasp the significance of Germany's actions and wrote to Lord Lansdowne optimistically, 'President Loubet was most amiable . . . but I could see from his manner that he considers the German conduct at Tangier, if not a direct menace to France, at any rate a covert insult. However, no further notice will be taken of it.'[2]

The full implications of the German plan did not become obvious until the end of May and the first week in June. During those days the Sultan of Morocco, acting under German instructions, made two statements. First of all he turned down France's civil and economic proposals for reorganising Morocco; secondly, he called for a conference of all the powers which had signed the Treaty of 1880 (among them Germany) to decide the future of his country.

This invitation was promptly rejected by Britain with the proviso that His Majesty's Government would reconsider if France decided to assent. Russia and many of the smaller powers followed the British lead. Now all that remained to be seen was what France would do. In spite of opposition from his colleagues, Delcassé declined to attend.

Now the Germans were ready to play their trump card. The German Ambassador, Prince von Radolin, called at the Quai d'Orsay and made it clear that Germany was behind the Morocco Conference. If France persisted in refusing to acquiesce, Germany might be forced to use the coercion of war!

[1] *King Edward and His Times:* André Maurois.

[2] *King Edward VII:* Sir Sidney Lee.

The result was everything that Germany had hoped. The French Government panicked. Despite stiffening assurances from London, including a pledge from Lord Lansdowne that Britain was ready to discuss what joint steps might be taken in the event of German aggression, the French Cabinet was paralysed with fear. It was too frightened even to reply to the English offers; intimacy with England might provoke reprisals. Even M. Cambon, the French Ambassador in London, advised M. Delcassé to remain non-committal as far as British help was concerned. 'I think it more prudent to reply in terms cordial enough not to discourage Lord Lansdowne's goodwill, and vague enough to set on one side any suggestion of immediate concert. . . .'[1]

M. Rouvier, the Prime Minister, was more rattled than anyone. 'No concerted action' became his battle-cry. He called to see President Loubet in a fearful state of alarm. The President's secretary described the scene in his diary. 'This morning M. Rouvier came to the President's study gravely upset. He has received the most startling news of the state of mind of William II. War is hanging over our heads; the Emperor can invade France in twenty-four hours; the worst eventualities are to be feared; if war breaks out, it will mean, within a couple of days, the outbreak of revolution in Paris and the great cities.

' "Where did you receive this information?" I asked him when he left the President.

' "From trustworthy emissaries, and primarily from a communication made to me by Bülow. Have you not been struck by the Emperor's silence? He alone amongst the European rulers did not send the President the customary telegram of congratulation and sympathy after the attempt on his life in the Rue de Rohan."

' "Then what solution do you envisage?"

' "Delcassé must tender his resignation. Otherwise the

Chamber will overturn him and we shall fall into an indescribable mess." '[1]

On June 7th Delcassé was forced to hand in his resignation. And a few weeks later France humbly expressed her willingness to attend the Morocco Conference. Her humiliation was complete.

GERMANY was elated. Her plan had worked brilliantly. M. Delcassé, the author of the Anglo-French alliance, had been thrown out of office; France had caught a glimpse of the real master of Europe and had bowed to Germany's will; and there were signs of dissension between London and Paris. True, the dissensions had not sprung up exactly as Germany had expected. Britain had stood by France with amazing vigour, and had not given her any chance for complaint. On the other hand, the English were plainly shaken by the complete collapse of their partner.

Here the King stepped in. His faith in France had not altered, he was determined to do everything in his power to prevent the Entente from disintegrating. The tone of his Prime Minister, Mr. Balfour, was not altogether encouraging. The latter pointed out to the Sovereign that 'Delcassé's dismissal or resignation under pressure from the German Government displayed a weakness on the part of France which indicated that she could not at present be counted as an effective force in international politics. She could no longer be trusted not to yield to threats at the critical moment of a negotiation. . . .'[2] And Lord Lansdowne wrote frankly to the British Ambassador in Paris, 'Delcassé's resignation has, as you may well suppose, produced a very painful impression

[1] *King Edward and His Times:* André Maurois.

[2] *King Edward VII:* Sir Sidney Lee.

here. What people say is that if one of our Ministers had had a dead set made at him by a Foreign Power, the country and the Government would not only have stood by him, but probably have supported him more vigorously than ever. . . . Of course the result is that the Entente is quoted at a much lower price than it was a fortnight ago.'[1]

The King was perturbed by the way things were going and realised that it was essential that the two nations should make an immediate and public demonstration of goodwill. It was decided that the two fleets should exchange hospitality. The British fleet would visit Brest in July, and the French fleet would call at Portsmouth in August.

King Edward understood human nature well enough to appreciate the benefits that might ensue. But the idea proved to be even more successful than he had envisaged. When the British Atlantic Fleet came steaming into Brest, the French population went wild with excitement. Emotions that had been deeply stirred by the German threats now spilled over and the people shouted, cheered and wept as they greeted the sailors, whose nation had stood behind them firmly in time of need.

The reception of the French Fleet at Portsmouth was no less moving. The King and Queen received the French Admiral and his officers on board the royal yacht: then for the next three days they entertained them at a magnificent series of luncheons, dinners and receptions, ranging from Windsor Castle to the Guildhall, from the Admiralty to Westminster Hall. But it was the popular demonstration that made the deepest impression. The Entente had been an agreement between the statesmen of the two countries; now the public was making it clear that it was not just a paper transaction; that genuine bonds of friendship united the two peoples.

[1] *King Edward VII:* Sir Sidney Lee.

This surprising display on both sides of the channel infused a new resolve into both French and British leaders. For it showed them that far from languishing, the Entente was breathing more vigorously than ever before. The successes Germany had been gloating over now seemed to be receding. It was plain that she had not accomplished all that she had intended. Furthermore she was faced with the Morocco Conference scheduled to take place in Algeciras in January. In order to thwart France she had posed as a champion of Moroccan independence, yet she was not at all clear as to what line to follow.

As a result, she made a complete mess of it. In the first place she sent as her chief representatives the cold and arrogant Herr von Radowitz, and Count Tattenbach, whom the British delegate, Sir Arthur Nicolson, described as 'a really horrid fellow, blustering, rude and mendacious. The worst type of German I have ever met.'[1] In the second place she could not make up her mind to pursue any single course. 'Germany is playing a double game,' wrote Sir Arthur to his wife, 'false, and contradictory. She says one thing at Berlin, another at Washington, another at St. Petersburg, another at Rome and Madrid. And Radowitz says different things from all these and different things to every person he talks to. The reason is that Germany does not know what she wants.'[1]

The only thing that Germany was sure about was that she must prevent France from gaining control of the Moroccan police, for that would give her control of the country. This resulted in weeks of prolonged and fruitless discussion, with Germany putting obstacles in the way of most of the solutions that were proposed. These tactics, combined with her officiousness and double-dealing and indecision, gradually lost her the favour of the Conference.

[1] *Lord Carnock:* Harold Nicolson.

Sir Arthur Nicolson was one of Britain's ablest diplomats. He had been patiently biding his time. As soon as he sensed the changed atmosphere he was ready to strike. His opportunity came when Germany suggested that the thorny problem of the police should be temporarily shelved. Nicolson voiced his disagreement, and boldly asked that the matter be put to a vote. The delegates decided in his favour 10 to 3.

This vote may seem harmless enough, but it completely routed the Germans. They saw that they could no longer command a majority among the delegates, and their morale completely collapsed.

As a result the Conference ended with very few sacrifices on the part of France. She emerged as the dominating power in Morocco. But it was Britain who left Algeciras with the highest prestige. She had outwitted Germany all along the line. The Kaiser was so angry that he sacked Holstein from the Foreign Office; and when he received a dispatch from one of his ambassadors, quoting the American delegate as saying that Algeciras was a victory for Britain, he minuted the paper angrily with the single word, 'Correct!'

The Kaiser's Tangier gesture was now regarded as a dismal diplomatic failure. The Entente had not only survived, but it had been strengthened; for the affair had convinced Britain and France of the value of exchanging military information, and conversations were now taking place between the two chiefs of staff. Tangier was destined to take its place in the history books, in the words of Winston Churchill, as 'the first milestone to Armageddon'.

CHAPTER FIFTEEN

AT HOME

THE King was bored by home affairs. Underneath the glittering façade of Edwardian splendour there was serious social unrest. Keir Hardie, a miner, had been elected to Parliament in 1892, the first working man to take his seat in that august assembly since its inception. It did not escape His Majesty's notice that he went down to the House of Commons in a ridiculous cloth cap and made speeches about social equality. Even Lady Warwick had become so tedious on the subject of socialism that one of the King's advisers, Lord Esher, had to write and tell her it would be better if she discontinued her correspondence with Buckingham Palace.

As for Mr. Balfour, the Prime Minister, he was altogether uncongenial to His Majesty. He had taken over the premiership from his uncle, Lord Salisbury, in 1902, and although no one could accuse him of having radical tendencies, in the eyes of the King he had an even more serious failing; he was a highbrow. Many people found him charming, but it was not the sort of charm the Sovereign appreciated. He was apt to discuss philosophy or to produce Latin tags; and he was the inspiration of the Souls. No, Arthur Balfour was not at all to the liking of the King. He was vague and indolent and superior. He stayed in bed all the morning, he hated racing, and even his love affairs were said to be on a spiritual plane.

Perhaps it was his disdain for public opinion that most distressed the King. He seemed to walk on Olympian heights which rendered him totally indifferent to what people said about him. He refused to read the newspapers, and when Winston Churchill told him that he subscribed to a press-cutting agency he replied blandly, 'I have never put myself to the trouble of rummaging through an immense rubbish-heap on the problematical chance of discovering a cigar-end.'

The King's lack of enthusiasm for his Prime Minister turned into resentment in 1904. This was due to the fact that Mr. Balfour stripped His Majesty of one of his last important royal powers. Authority to cede territories had always been vested in the Sovereign, and did not require the assent of Parliament. The signing of the Entente with France involved a certain number of territorial exchanges, and the King made it clear that his signature was sufficient to settle the matter. But Balfour insisted on taking the matter to Parliament on the grounds that some of the clauses required financial backing. The King protested angrily, but the Prime Minister refused to give way, and the age-old prerogative of the monarch became the newest privilege of the Lords and Commons.

From then on the King's tone to his first minister was cold and formal. He even took pleasure in the spectacle of young Winston Churchill attacking his leader on the floor of the House. Of course Winston was outrageous. Everyone knew that, and the King himself had not forgotten the time when the young subaltern had kept him waiting twenty minutes for dinner. But he liked his spirit. Several years previously when his mother, Lady Randolph Churchill, had sent him a copy of her son's book, *The Malakand Field Force*, which told of the fighting on the North-West Frontier of India, he had taken the trouble to write him a letter in his own hand.

'My dear Winston,

'I cannot resist writing a few lines to congratulate you on the success of your book! I have read it with the greatest possible interest and I think the descriptions and the language generally excellent. Everybody is reading it, and I only hear it spoken of with praise. Having now seen active service you will wish to see more, and have as great a chance I am sure of winning the V.C. as Fincastle had; and I hope you will not follow the example of the latter, who I regret to say intends leaving the Army in order to go into Parliament.

'You have plenty of time before you, and should certainly stick to the Army before adding M.P. to your name.

'Hoping that you are flourishing,

'I am,

'Yours very sincerely,

'A.E.'[1]

ALTHOUGH Winston had not followed his Sovereign's advice about Parliament, the King could not fail to follow his career with interest. On May 31, 1904, the young man crossed the floor of the House and joined the Liberals. The issue was Chamberlain's tariff policy, but some people believed that the real reason was because Mr. Balfour had not given him office. Whatever the true motive, for the next eighteen months he subjected his ex-leader to many biting attacks. He jeered at him for his 'miserable and disreputable shifts' and for his 'gross and flagrant ignorance'. 'We have been told *ad nauseum*,' he said, 'of the sacrifices which the Prime Minister makes. I do not deny that there have been sacrifices. The House ought not to underrate or deny those sacrifices. Some of them must be very galling to a proud man. There were first sacrifices of leisure and then sacrifices of dignity.... Then there was the sacrifice of reputation....'[2]

The Prime Minister struck back disdainfully, but

[1] *My Early Life:* Winston S. Churchill.
[2] *Hansard*, March 28, 1905.

Winston Churchill always seemed to emerge triumphant; and the King did not find Mr. Balfour's discomfiture altogether unpleasing.

PERSONALLY His Majesty was not sorry when the seventy-year-old Sir Henry Campbell-Bannerman took over the reins of government in January 1905. This was followed by the great electoral landslide which gave the Liberals 401 seats and reduced the Conservatives to 157.

For a number of years the King had avoided meeting 'C.-B.' at private gatherings. He had disapproved strongly of the Liberal leader's pro-Boer sentiments, and had always thought of him as a priggish and parochial reformer. However, when the King's old friend, Lord Carrington, brought the two men together in Marienbad in 1904, the monarch was enchanted by the genial Scot. He discovered that he was not only witty and worldly, but shared two important tastes with his Sovereign: a love of France and a delight in good food. Sir Henry could not help being flattered by the King's cordiality and wrote to Captain Sinclair, 'I have seen a great deal of him and found him most friendly; I avoid him mostly on the promenade, but meet him at dinner and supper, and he asked me ten days ago to come and see him and have a talk, when he expressed his satisfaction at having the chance of a frank conversation on things abroad and at home, as I must soon be in office and very high office. Thereupon he discoursed with the greatest fullness on the state of Europe (Germany and France and ourselves; very apprehensive, to put it mildly), Japan and Russia (not the new treaty); India, Army; and, among other domestic things, Ireland. . . .'[1]

[1] *The Life of the Rt. Hon. Sir Henry Campbell-Bannerman:* J. A. Spender.

The following summer, five months before Sir Henry was bidden to take over the premiership, he was drawn even more vigorously into the King's circle. 'About half my meals have been taken in H.M.'s company,' he reported. 'H.M. has been uniformly and openly friendly beyond anything one could expect. I think my countrymen (and women much more) were astounded to find with what confidence, consideration, and intimacy he treated me.'[1]

However, there were certain drawbacks to becoming a member of the King's entourage. Sir Henry took his 'cure' seriously and liked to follow his doctor's prescriptions to the letter. He had never before regarded Marienbad as a social resort. Now he found himself going ou almost every evening. 'Dinner,' he wrote, 'begins at 7.30, eating plain food, but far too much, a mixture of Court restraint and jollity; then while the dismal mysteries of bridge are being performed, sitting making dismal conversation with one's fellow non-players, and at 10 getting home to bed.'[1]

When the King and Sir Henry met in public the press invariably jumped to the conclusion that they were conferring on great events. An illustrated magazine printed a sketch of King Edward talking very seriously and striking his hand in his palm while Campbell-Bannerman listened with an anxious face. Underneath the caption read 'Is It Peace or War?' When the magazine was shown to C.-B. he said solemnly, 'Would you like to know what the King was saying to me? He wanted to have my opinion whether halibut is better baked or boiled!'

The friendly relations which the King established with Campbell-Bannerman continued throughout the two years of the latter's premiership. The King was relieved to find that the new Foreign Secretary, Sir

[1] *The Life of the Rt. Hon. Sir Henry Campbell-Bannerman:* J. A. Spender.

Edward Grey, was ready to carry out Lord Lansdowne's policy of firm support to France. Indeed, it was under the Liberal Government that the exchange of military information between the two countries first took place.

The only complaint the King had against his agreeable First Minister was the latter's laziness in fully reporting the deliberations of the Cabinet to him. The King was insistent on this for two reasons: first, because a concise summary from his Prime Minister saved him a good deal of trouble in wading through the lengthy papers; secondly, and even more important, because the monarch had the right to be informed. The King was jealous of his royal dignity and his royal due, and refused to countenance any slighting of them. Repeatedly, he complained of the sparseness of the information he was receiving, and on the bottom of one of Sir Henry's reports, just seven lines long, he wrote sarcastically, 'What valuable information! E.R.'

King Edward was particularly annoyed at the sparseness of details when he felt that the subject directly concerned him. This was the case with the controversy over the Government's Education Bill of 1906. The Bill was passed by the Commons but mutilated past recognition by the Lords, who were determined to prevent its passage. And this began the bitter quarrel between the two chambers which raged with increasing ferocity throughout the King's reign.

Edward VII's views on the subject were clear. He was a passionate supporter of the monarchical principle, and he was convinced that this principle was bound up inextricably with the hereditary principle. Therefore he was a fervent believer in the sanctity of the House of Lords. He advised the peers to move with restraint, but he did not feel that the wrong was on their side alone. He felt that the Commons should also try to be more conciliatory, and did his best to promote a spirit of compromise. But the Liberals were in no mood for compromise. They had waited a long time for office, and they determined to push through a whole series of reforms, which the Lords appeared equally determined to thwart.

As a result the Government's radical members began to make fiery speeches, which shocked and angered the King. The House of Lords might be behaving stupidly, but a threat to the existence of that House seemed to him practically treason. When on December 1, Mr. Lloyd George told an audience at Oxford that 'whether dissolution comes sooner or later, it will be a much bigger issue than the Education Bill. It will come to this issue: whether the country is to be governed by the King and his Peers or by the King and his People.'[1]

Today, this hardly strikes one as a disrespectful reference to the monarchy, but the King saw it in a very different light. Angrily he instructed Lord Knollys to write to Campbell-Bannerman. 'The King desires me to point out to you that Mr. Lloyd George brought in His Majesty's name in the speech which he made against the House of Lords at Oxford on Saturday.

'The King sees that it is useless to attempt to prevent Mr. Lloyd George from attacking, as a Cabinet Minister, that branch of the Legislature, though His Majesty has more than once protested to you against it. He believes that at his request you remonstrated with Mr. Lloyd George as to these attacks, and it is difficult for the King to understand why he has paid no attention either to the wish of the Sovereign or to the warning addressed to him by the Head of the Government.

'But His Majesty feels he has a right, and it is one on which he intends to insist, that Mr. Lloyd George shall not introduce the Sovereign's name into those violent tirades of his, and he asks you, as Prime Minister, to be

[1] *The Times*, December 2, 1906.

so good as to take the necessary steps to prevent a repetition of this violation of constitutional practice and of good taste.

'The King says he has no doubt he will be told that it was only "a phrase", but he must really make a point of his name being omitted even from "a phrase" in Mr. Lloyd George's invectives against the House of Lords.'[1]

But Mr. Lloyd George had a more ingenious reply than that; when Sir Henry took up the matter with him he said 'he would have considered it disrespectful to speak of "the Peers" and "the People" alone, omitting the reference to the supreme head of the State.'

The King was not satisfied but he was forced to accept the explanation.

To the King it was difficult to understand how his Parliament could be so passionately concerned with domestic issues when Europe hung in the balance between war and peace. Apart from his interest in protecting the hereditary principle of the House of Lords, the only 'home' matter that really gripped his attention was the battle taking place inside the Admiralty.

The principal adversaries in this bitter and dramatic feud were the volcanic Admiral Sir John Fisher who was determined to streamline the Navy by introducing radical reforms; and the reactionary but fiercely patriotic Admiral Lord Charles Beresford who referred contemptuously to his opponent's innovations as 'Fisher's toys'.

The quarrel split the Admiralty and the Fleet into two camps and raged during the whole nine years of King

[1] *The Life of the Rt. Hon. Sir Henry Campbell-Bannerman:* J. A. Spender.

Edward's reign. High-ranking officers were known either as 'Fisher's men' or 'Beresford's men'. Lord Charles wielded great power as the Commander-in-Chief of the principal Fleet, but 'Jackie' Fisher got the upper hand when, in 1904, he was appointed First Sea Lord.

Fisher was a stormy, voluble creature with a rugged face and burning black eyes. He had joined the service in 1854 when the Navy's ships still carried sails, when many had no auxiliary steam, and none had armour. He was fascinated by the amazing developments of the times and was dedicated to the task of keeping the British Navy the most modern fleet in the world.

He was no respecter of persons and was not at all particular as to what means he employed to achieve his ends. Proudly he described himself as 'ruthless, relentless and remorseless'. He branded as traitors those who opposed him either secretly or openly and boasted childishly that their 'wives should be widows, their children fatherless, and their homes a dung-hill'. This threat was not altogether meaningless, for he ruined the professional career of more than one officer who criticised his policies. Those in Fisher's favour were described as being 'in the Fish-pond', and woe betide those who were not.

However, Fisher's lack of sentiment brought changes fast and furiously. Soon the British Fleet outstripped every other in scientific design. He scrapped dozens of ships which he declared could 'neither fight nor run away'. He reorganised the Navy's educational system, introduced the submarine, and replaced the Battle Fleet's twelve-inch guns with thirteen-point-fives, the biggest ever tried.

Fisher could not have carried out these drastic changes without the support of King Edward. The rough-shod Admiral had too many enemies to rally the necessary backing. But the King was convinced that Fisher was a genius in naval matters and worked behind the scenes to mobilise opinion for him. 'He gave me his unfaltering support right through unswervingly,' wrote Fisher many years later; and the result was wholly satisfactory.

Apart from his faith in Fisher's projects, the King was amused by the Admiral's tempestuous and outspoken nature. No doubt he found his wild indiscretions a relief from the guarded tongues that usually surrounded him; and Fisher, for his part, returned the Sovereign's friendship with an ecstatic schoolboy worship. This, however, did not involve sycophancy; on the contrary his manner was almost breath-taking in its breeziness. Considering the King's emphasis on etiquette this might have proved dangerous, yet curiously enough the monarch never took offence. Once Fisher suggested rolling back the carpets at Buckingham Palace and having an impromptu dance and King Edward smiled and nodded his assent. Another time, at a tedious lunch party, the irrepressible Admiral turned to the King and said, 'Pretty dull, Sir, this, hadn't I better give them a song?' Apparently the monarch was highly amused, and Fisher sang in unmusical tones the ditty about the tramps that begins, 'We lives in Trafalgar Square, four lions they guard us there.'

When Fisher was a guest at Sandringham, the King occasionally walked into his room unannounced to have a talk. At a particularly grand weekend party, in honour of Queen Alexandra's birthday, the Admiral had 'slunk off' to his room to unpack, and had a boot in each hand, when he heard somebody fumbling with the door handle. 'Thinking it was the footman,' wrote Fisher, 'whom Hawkins had allocated to me, I said, "Come in; don't go humbugging with that door handle!" and in walked King Edward, with a cigar about a yard long in his mouth. He said (I with a boot in each hand):

' "What on earth are you doing?"

'"Unpacking, sir."

'"Where's your servant?"

'"Haven't got one, sir."

'"Where is he?"

'"Never had one, sir; couldn't afford it."

'"Put those boots down and sit in that armchair."

'And he went and sat at the other side of the fire. I thought to myself, "This is a rum state of affairs. Here's the King of England sitting in my bedroom on one side of the fire, and I'm in my shirt-sleeves sitting in an armchair on the other side!"

'"Well," said His Majesty, "why didn't you come and say 'How d'you do?' when you arrived?"

'I said: "I had a letter to write and with so many great people you were receiving I thought I had better go to my room." Then he went on with a long conversation, until it was only about a quarter of an hour to dinner-time and I had not unpacked. So I said to the King: "Sir, you'll be angry if I am late to dinner, and no doubt Your Majesty has two or three gentlemen to dress you, but I have no one." And he gave me a sweet smile and went off.'[1]

THE friendship of the King and Admiral Fisher was galling to Lord Charles Beresford. In the old days Beresford had been the life and soul of the Marlborough House Set, but since the royal quarrel in 1891 over Lady Brooke he had not again been admitted to the inner circle. The Sovereign exchanged civilities with him but no intimacy was encouraged.

Even more galling was the knowledge that many of his rival's triumphs were due to the King's support. In

[1] *Recollections:* Sir John Fisher.

1906 Fisher began to press strenuously for the incorporation of the Channel Fleet and the Atlantic Fleet into one 'Home' Fleet which, he said, should be kept in the North Sea. 'Our only probable enemy,' he wrote to the King's sailor son, the future George V, 'is Germany. Germany keeps her *whole* fleet always concentrated within a few hours of England. We must, therefore, keep a fleet twice as powerful concentrated within a few hours of Germany.'[1]

Lord Charles, as the Commander-in-Chief of the Channel Fleet, opposed this suggestion violently; and so did the King's friend and diplomatic adviser, Sir Charles Hardinge. The latter reminded King Edward that British territory was far-flung, and that it was important to have ships within easy access of all the trouble spots. But Fisher replied airily, 'The absolute fact is that the Admiralty always knows better than the Foreign Office.'

In the meanwhile the Liberal Government was far more concerned with its domestic problems than the tensions in Europe. It was eager to reduce naval expenditure by half a million pounds to provide more money for social reform. In order to get his own way on naval reorganisation, the volcanic Admiral accepted the cuts unprotestingly. He insisted that if the navy were streamlined it could afford to cut down on both ships and men and still increase its striking power. 'Reduced naval estimates are no sign of reduced naval efficiency,' he wrote to the Prince of Wales in 1906. 'On the contrary, swollen estimates engender parasites both in men and ships which hamper the fighting qualities of the Fleet. The pruning knife ain't pleasant for fossils and ineffectives but it has to be used, and the tree is more vigorous for the loss of excrescences.'[1] As a champion both of economy and a strengthened navy, the admiral was unbeatable, and in the end he won.

[1] *King Edward VII:* Sir Sidney Lee.

ALTHOUGH the King had implicit faith in Fisher's naval views, he often was sceptical about his political judgment. 'That we have eventually to fight Germany,' the Admiral wrote to him in 1908, 'is just as sure as anything can be, solely because she can't expand commercially without it.'[1]

The King did not share this opinion. He did not believe that Germany was following a carefully thought out plan of aggression; at the same time he realised that with his unpredictable nephew at the head of affairs war could not be ruled out. In 1905, when the Danish diplomat, Count Frijs, discussed the danger of a European conflagration, King Edward replied, 'I think you take too gloomy a view of the future. . . . But I will admit this, that with a man of so impulsive a temperament as the German Emperor at the head of the greatest military power in Europe, anything may happen.'[2]

The uneasy relations between the two monarchs had deteriorated still further since the Tangier incident. The Kaiser's jealousy of his sociable uncle seemed to be growing out of all proportion; and the uncle resented the scathing remarks that were repeated back to him. Those who worked closely with King Edward were left in no doubt about his feelings toward his nephew. 'The King talks and writes about his Royal Brother,' wrote Lord Lansdowne, 'in terms which make one's flesh creep, and the official papers which go to him, whenever they refer to H.I.M., come back with all sorts of annotations of a most incendiary character.'[3]

The Kaiser, on the other hand, did not confine his acid remarks to the secrecy of Foreign Office papers. In letters to the Czar he referred to King Edward as 'the arch mischief-maker of Europe', and at a public banquet

[1] *Memories:* Lord Fisher.
[2] *King Edward VII:* Sir Sidney Lee.
[3] *Lord Lansdowne:* Lord Newton.

in Berlin, in 1907, he blurted out hysterically to 300 people, 'He's a Satan, you can hardly believe what a Satan he is.'[1]

The bad blood between the two monarchs was worrying, and more than one attempt was made to improve the relationship. In 1906 and 1907 the King travelled to Germany to pay the Kaiser a visit; and in 1907 the Kaiser and Kaiserin were invited to Windsor. On the surface, uncle and nephew appeared to get on well. When they were together they seemed to come under the spell of each other's charm and affability. 'In the main,' wrote von Bülow, 'the King impressed the Kaiser. . . .' Compliments were exchanged, gifts were bestowed, and warm and effusive letters were written. Yet it was always the same story; once they were apart suspicion flared up and devoured goodwill, leaving behind it a new trail of animosities.

Some of the trouble was caused by the gossip which irresponsible tongues took delight in repeating. For instance, it was not only the Tangier incident which strained relations between the two monarchs in 1905. Count Metternich, the German Ambassador in London, wrote to Prince von Bülow, 'King Edward's displeasure with His Majesty can be attributed to more than politics. . . . It is said that the Emperor talked freely in yachting circles about the "looseness" of English Society, and in particular about King Edward's relationship with Mrs. Keppel. King Edward is very touchy on this subject and this seems to have annoyed him especially. . . .'[2]

The King had no illusions about the Kaiser's pretence of affection. And although his own dislike was often softened by a naturally tolerant nature, Queen Alexandra's attitude had considerable influence on him. Alexandra detested William II. She saw him as the

[1] *Twelve Years at the German Court:* Count Zedlitz-Trutzschler.

[2] *Memoirs:* Prince von Bülow.

incarnation of Frederick the Great, and worse still, of his grandfather, William I, who had brutally attacked poor Denmark. She had a steady and implacable hatred of all Germans from which she never deviated. She made no secret of her opinions and in 1903 told Daisy, Princess of Pless, how annoyed she was that the German Emperor was coming to Copenhagen 'to spoil their family party'. 'The Queen also spoke about the old old story of Schleswig-Holstein,' wrote the Princess in her diary, 'and how terribly the poor Danes there are treated. She takes in a little Danish paper published in Jutland giving particulars of all their miseries: forced selling of their old homes to Germans; burning of their Bibles written in Danish; school children torn from their mothers' arms and forced to learn German, and similar atrocities!'[1]

The bad blood between the monarchs was unfortunate, nevertheless it had little to do with the worsening relations between the two countries. The real point at issue was the alarming increase in Germany's naval programme. The Kaiser had always been fascinated by sea power. As early as 1897 he had declared in a flamboyant speech, 'The trident is in German hands . . . our future lies on the water.' In 1900 Germany's new Navy Law marked the earnest increase of her fleet, and as the years passed she periodically announced large extensions to her original plans.

It was not surprising that England began to grow nervous. Since Britain possessed only a small army and relied solely upon her navy for defence, she could not afford to sit back and allow the greatest military force in Europe to outstrip her in naval strength. This was pointed out to the Kaiser more than once, but the reply usually was an imperious retort that Germany was only building the necessary ships to protect her commercial

[1] *What I Left Unsaid:* Daisy, Princess of Pless.

interests. Indeed, in 1908 the Kaiser took the unprecedented step of writing a private letter to the First Lord of the Admiralty, Lord Tweedmouth. The immediate purpose was to deny a statement made by Lord Esher to the effect that every man in Germany would rejoice in the downfall of Sir John Fisher. This pretext gave the Emperor an opportunity to insist that it was 'nonsensical and untrue that the new German Navy Bill is to provide a navy meant as a challenge to British naval supremacy'.

Nevertheless the large increases authorised in 1908 had come as a shock to the British Government. The Foreign Secretary, Sir Edward Grey, came to the sanguine conclusion that only the King could ease the situation. He urged His Majesty to make another trip to Cronberg, and try to persuade the Kaiser to agree to a mutual limitation of shipbuilding, which would allow Britain the naval superiority so necessary to her defence.

Considering the fact that the King's personality irritated the Kaiser, it seems curious that the Foreign Office should have deemed this the best way to handle the matter. Sir Edward Grey's memorandum pointed out with foolish optimism: 'If it could be shown that, as a result of the interview between the two sovereigns, a slackening of activity in the building programmes of the two navies had ensued . . . the King and the Emperor would be rightly hailed together as the Peacemakers of Europe.'[1]

Reluctantly, the King agreed to go to Cronberg. He took Sir Charles Hardinge with him, but the trip was far from satisfactory. The Kaiser was excessively cordial until his uncle referred to naval expenditure and mentioned the fact that he had a memorandum from Sir Edward Grey. Immediately the German Emperor's expression hardened and he changed the subject in a deliberate manner.

[1] *King Edward VII:* Sir Sidney Lee.

Hardinge raised the matter that same afternoon. The Kaiser began by taking the line that Anglo-German relations were entirely satisfactory, but Sir Charles put the British view forcibly, claiming that whereas Britain's fleet did not constitute a threat to Germany, because of its small army, a large German fleet was bound to constitute a standing menace to Britain. The Kaiser replied that talk of Germany invading England was 'sheer nonsense'. 'Can't you put a stop to your building?' asked Hardinge. 'Or build less ships? An arrangement ought to be arrived at to restrict building. You must stop or build slower.' The 'must' was fatal. Furiously the Kaiser replied, 'Then we shall fight for it. It is a question of national honour and dignity.'[1] Naval reductions were not mentioned again, and the royal party gloomily quitted German soil.

THE King's cares were increasing. In 1908 Mr. Asquith succeeded Sir Henry Campbell-Bannerman as Prime Minister, and a month later Sir Henry died. Mr. Asquith was 'sound' on both home policy and foreign affairs, but personally the King found him much less congenial than 'C.-B.'. Margot Asquith was not worried by the strained conversations between the Sovereign and her scholarly husband and merely scribbled in her diary, 'He is personally fond of Henry, but he is not really interested in men.'

One of the first things Mr. Asquith did was to replace Lord Tweedmouth at the Admiralty by Mr. Reginald McKenna. As Sir Edward Grey had postulated, if Germany refused to curtail her shipbuilding, Britain had no alternative but to increase her own. McKenna in-

[1] *British Documents on the Origin of the War:* Gooch and Temperley.

formed the Sea Lords that he would agree to the lay-down of six new dreadnoughts in the coming eighteen months, but soon ran into violent opposition from two members of the Cabinet. They were the Chancellor of the Exchequer, Mr. Lloyd George, and the President of the Board of Trade, Mr. Winston Churchill. Lloyd George was determined to secure more money for Old Age Pensions and he ridiculed 'building ships against nightmares'. Faithfully following his lead was Winston Churchill who assured large gatherings that the war-scare was a Tory hallucination and that Germany had 'nothing to fight about, no prize to fight for, and no place to fight in'; and we rejoiced as a nation 'in everything bringing good to that strong, patient, industrious people'.

The King was furious at what he termed these 'irresponsible speeches', and asked Mr. Asquith to let his two Cabinet colleagues know that in his opinion ministers should not make speeches about Foreign Affairs without consulting the Foreign Secretary. In the end McKenna had his way, and the Admiralty was allowed to lay down six new ships.

Originally the King had not viewed the Entente with France as a move against Germany, but now he saw it as a defensive alliance. And he believed that Britain should form other alliances wherever she could. He did not regard war as inevitable, but he had come to the conclusion that the only hope of averting it was to possess a strong navy and plenty of friends.

CHAPTER SIXTEEN

ROYAL SPORT

CHATSWORTH opened its doors to the King and Queen more effortlessly than any other great house of the day. Although it was the ambition of every Edwardian hostess to entertain the King and Queen at a country house party, the strain on both purse and nerves was considerable. The King fancied ortolans so they were imported from France at fabulous cost; the Queen liked Strauss waltzes so an orchestra was brought from London to play during meals; the King liked bridge in quiet surroundings so a single table was placed in one of the grandest rooms for his use after dinner; the Queen liked amateur theatricals so guests who could sing or dance or recite were specially bidden to entertain her.

The Duchess of Devonshire took these royal visits in her stride. Now in her seventies, be-rouged and be-wigged and be-diamonded 'like the half ruinous shell of some castellated keep, with flower boxes in full bloom on the crumbling sills',[1] she still possessed amazing energy. She liked nothing better than to have fifty guests under her roof, which meant all told about two hundred mouths to feed because nobody dreamed of arriving without their servants. She loved power, and the fact that the King and Queen came to Chatsworth every January—the King for the shooting, the Queen for the fun—provided her with the dominating influence she desired. She revelled in being known as 'The Double Duchess' and gave her autocratic nature full vent. Once a rumour went about that Devonshire House was to be sold, and a friend unwisely asked the Duchess if it was

[1] *As We Were:* E. F. Benson.

true. 'Yes, perfectly true,' replied the great lady acidly. 'We are proposing to live at Clapham Junction instead. So convenient a train service.'

The Duke was a complete foil to the Duchess. He wandered around his vast house like a very detached and very indifferent guest. He always looked slightly scruffy, and made no effort to supply polite talk. Since he long ago had established himself as an eccentric, people did not expect the usual civilities from him and took pleasure in repeating the latest example of his vagaries. One morning he refused to get out of bed, complaining of the weather. His valet came to wake him three times, the last time well past noon, reminding him that the Duchess had arranged a large luncheon party. The Duke announced flatly that he was not going to rise in such a filthy fog. 'But there's no fog, your Grace,' the valet protested. 'It's only the tent that has been erected for Her Grace's garden party.'

Sometimes the Duke's vagaries threatened to go too far. Once, in London, he forgot he had invited the King and Queen to lunch and had to be dug out of his club at the last moment. At Chatsworth, he occasionally offended guests because he was too lazy to make arrangements for the shooting until the last moment. Since it was only possible for a limited number of guns to take part in the day's sport, no one knew until breakfast time whether or not he was on the list. Lord Rosebery was furious to arrive downstairs, suitably attired, to find that his name was not included.

Nevertheless the King and Queen were never disappointed with Chatsworth hospitality. The great parties were built entirely around them, and the Duchess saw to it that they wanted for nothing. One of the most popular guests was the sister of George Cornwallis-West, the beautiful, golden-haired Daisy, who had married a German, Prince Henry of Pless. The Princess was always called upon to sing and dance for the amusement of the guests. 'The Queen is charming and beautiful as always,' she wrote in her diary in January 1904, 'and the King very well and in good spirits. . . . The King has his bridge with Mrs. Keppel who is here—with lovely clothes and diamonds—in a separate room, and in the other rooms people are massed together, also of course playing bridge. Generally, to amuse the Queen, I am made to go and sing and dance in the corridor where the band is. . . .' Two days later she made another entry. 'The Queen danced a waltz with Soveral, and then we each took off our shoes to see what difference it made in our height. The Queen took, or rather kicked hers off, and then got into everyone else's, even into Willie Grenfell's old pumps. I never saw her so free and cheerful—but always graceful in everything she does. Everyone except myself left for London in the King's special train. . . .'[1]

The Princess of Pless was very outspoken in her comments. She complained that the King indulged in too much 'chaff', and she took umbrage at the fact that he called her a humbug. 'Probably because he imagines—goodness knows what,' she wrote, 'and because I would not be "nice" to him. . . .' And as for that famous lady-killer, the favourite of the King and Queen, the Marquis de Soveral, her comments were equally pungent. 'He imagines himself to be a great intellectual and political force and the wise adviser of all the heads of the Government and, of course, the greatest danger to women! I amuse myself with him as it makes the other women furious, and he is sometimes very useful. He is so swarthy that he is nicknamed the "blue monkey" and I imagine that even those stupid people who believe that every man who talks to a woman must be her lover, could not take his Don Juanesque pretensions seriously. Yet

[1] *What I Left Unsaid:* Daisy, Princess of Pless.

I am told that all women do not judge him so severely and some even find him *très séduisant*. How disgusting!'

Those who suspected that the pursuit of love played a large part in the design of Edwardian country house parties were not far wrong. The King set the fashion for everything, whether it was a command that dinner should be served within the hour or a smile of approval for a *ménage à trois*. The daughters of Edwardian hostesses, today women in their sixties, remember their mothers struggling over the *placement* in the delicate matter of bedrooms. Their sharp eyes noticed every nuance in the progression of their friends' love affairs, so they rarely made mistakes. They knew when it was right to assign a gentleman a bedroom some way off from the lady he admired; and when the time had come to move him nearer. And they delighted in the gossip that surrounded these affairs. A favourite Chatsworth story concerned the countess who told her lover she would leave a plate of sandwiches outside her bedroom door as a sign that the way was clear for him. Unfortunately the greedy Baron von Eckardstein was also a house guest and seeing the inviting sandwiches in the corridor, promptly gobbled them up. The lover waited anxiously half the night for the signal that never came.

Some of the ladies protested at the loose tone of Edwardian Society. Lady de Grey thought morals were deteriorating at an alarming rate. 'In my day we used to hide the pictures of our lovers, and put our husbands' on the mantelpiece,' she protested. 'Now it is the other way around.' The Princess of Pless was also taken aback by the boldness of the new *régime*. 'I lunched with Alice Keppel before leaving for Berlin,' she wrote in her diary. 'Three or four of the women present had had several lovers and did not mind saying so. . . .'[1]

Love affairs required careful planning; and so did

[1] *What I Left Unsaid:* Daisy, Princess of Pless.

clothes. For Ascot, or a royal week-end, a complete new wardrobe was a necessity. Those who could afford it bought their dresses from the House of Worth in Paris. And these clothes were not cheap. A ball-gown was about a hundred pounds. Of course they were magnificent creations; each one was designed exclusively for its wearer. When a *grande dame* flounced into the famous salon on the Rue de la Paix and announced that she must have a sensational ball-dress for the following night, M. Jean Worth did not fling up his arms and say it was impossible, but sat studying his subject, perhaps for half an hour, then clapped his hands and started to work. 'This', he would murmur, 'is the colour. This the outline—this—and this——'[1] The dress was always ready.

Although ladies spent a fortune on their clothes, the most expensive and spectacular creation of all was designed for a man. It was an order from the Duke of Marlborough for a costume for the Devonshire fancy dress ball. 'Although the shop in the Rue de la Paix had seen a number of freak orders taken,' wrote M. Jean Worth, 'this request from the Duke . . . was something new under the sun that shone on the Worth establishment. However we acceded to his demand after a few scandalised protestations, and we got to work on a Louis XV costume of straw-coloured velvet embroidered in silver, pearls and diamonds. The waistcoat was made of a magnificent white and gold damask that was an exact copy of a rare old pattern. Each pearl and diamond was sewn on by hand, and it took several girls almost a month to complete this embroidery of jewels. Had the Duke not insisted that his costume be perfection, we should never have dared put such costly work in it. But at last when I got it totalled it came to 5,000 francs. . . .'[2] Which was nearly three hundred pounds!

However, as far as cost was concerned, Daisy, Princess

[1] *Afterthoughts:* Lady Warwick. [2] *A Century of Fashion:* J. P. Worth.

of Pless went one better. At a ball at Buckingham Palace she wore a gold tissue dress, with a gold train that alone was worth four hundred pounds. When she confessed this to Queen Alexandra, the latter was scandalised. The Princess explained that the material had been a gift from an Indian Prince, nevertheless the Queen was horrified that anyone would wear such an expensive garment. 'I could not possibly afford such a sum,' she said firmly. And the Princess wrote in her memoirs, 'Dear Queen Alexandra, bless her, was the only person who ever took the trouble to make me understand that it would be a very wicked thing to pay such a sum for a court train.'[1]

Queen Alexandra remembered making her own clothes as a girl. Consequently, she was far more thrifty than most of her ladies. She patronised the shops in Regent Street, of which Liberty's and Jay's were the leaders. Her beauty was so striking, and her prestige as Queen so dazzling, that she had no need of Paris creations to make her the centre of all eyes. Besides, it would never do for the Queen of England to buy her clothes abroad. Apparently her indifference to the Paris dressmakers was resented by M. Jean Worth, for he acidly described the one and only occasion when she visited his establishment. 'We made only one dress for the Queen of England. . . . She came for the fittings herself . . . and three ladies-in-waiting accompanied her. Alexandra had scarcely stepped on the tiny stage to be fitted before these gadflies began: "Don't tire her Majesty." "Be careful of that pin." "Don't stick her Majesty." "Watch out now!" "Don't touch her Majesty." The poor fitter dripped with perspiration and trembled with nervousness, and in the end hardly knew whether she dared use a pin, let alone where to put it. Alexandra herself was pleasantly pliant and agreeable

[1] *Daisy, Princess of Pless:* by Herself.

to all suggestions, and, being rather deaf, missed all the uproar of solicitude going on about her.'[1]

FOR the highly placed ladies of Society the Edwardian era has often been cited as the apex of feminine influence and enjoyment. Yet a curious melancholy runs through the memoirs of the day. The Countess of Warwick writes, 'I cannot remember one friend of mine that was happy.' The Duchess of Marlborough confesses, 'A purely social life had no appeal'; and the Princess of Pless gloomily enters in her diary, 'I thought of them all in London—at a ball probably—the glare, the lights and the jewels; yet I did not envy them or wish to be back in a crowd where there is so much artificiality. I think London society is becoming stupid—there is no conversation; no "bon mots"; no repartee; after dinner it is always bridge, or one is obliged to sit *tête-à-tête* with a man (never three or four together) so there can be no arguments or discussions; you sit with your man, *c'est bien*; if he is an ordinary man his conversation is about friendship, then love. . . . Or another sort of man will tell you all about his hunting, polo ponies, golf or shooting. You will seldom find anyone to sit down with you and have a sensible conversation about current topics, the politics of the different countries, what they tend to, socialism, even religion.'[2]

It is obvious that some of the great ladies of the day tired of arranging the *placement* for dinner and carrying tins of food to the poor; that they rebelled against the restrictions that made it impossible for a lady to travel without a maid, or to be seen in a restaurant; conventions that forced her to spend hours a day at her toilette; to

[1] *A Century of Fashion:* J. P. Worth.
[2] *What I Left Unsaid:* Daisy, Princess of Pless.

pay innumerable calls; and forbade her from taking part in intellectual pursuits. The lady of birth was supposed to content herself with feminine talk, and like every age Edwardian Society had its own set of fashionable adjectives which dominated her conversation. 'Cheery' and 'ripping' were in vogue, and 'up-to-date' was just making its début. A royal personage was known as a 'man-man' and the tea-gown as the 'teagie'. 'Expie' meant expensive, 'deevie' divine, 'indy' indigestion, and 'fittums' was used to imply, 'What a perfect fit!' The 'g' at the end of a word was always dropped, and an 'r' was affixed to words ending with 'w', so that 'paw' had the same sound as 'pore'.

It was essential for the fashionable lady to master these complexities, to know how to curtsey and back out of the ball-room at Buckingham Palace, to know how to organise her week-end parties. But the fact that she was beginning to rebel was shown by Lady Warwick's crusade for socialism; by Lady Randolph Churchill's attempts to edit a monthly review; by the Duchess of Marlborough's absorption in welfare work; by the Princess of Pless' wails that there was no such thing as conversation.

The rebellion at the top was a reflection of the fierce surge for freedom that was gripping the women of the middle ranks. The suffragette movement was gaining an impetus each day. By 1908 it was occupying a good deal of the King's attention. The militant supporters were organising monster processions through the streets of London, they were screaming 'Votes for Women' from the galleries of the House of Commons, they were breaking up political meetings by ringing thunderous dinner bells. Worse still, they were smashing windows and assaulting policemen and pulling down statues. They gloried in going to prison, and refused to eat, and finally had to be forcibly fed.

In the King's view it was all very stupid and nasty.

He felt strongly that women should remain what he believed they were intended to be. Nothing was more repellent than an intellectual female. It was tragic that such a beauty as Lady Warwick should have become so repulsively serious-minded. And as for Margot Tennant, he originally had been struck by her appeal but—in her own words—'I liked talking and he hated listening,' so he ceased to seek her company.

Soon the Suffragette movement was causing the King as much concern as the Lords and Commons quarrel. 'The conduct of the so-called Suffragettes', he wrote to Sir Henry Campbell-Bannerman, 'has really been so outrageous and does their cause (for which I have no sympathy) much harm.' And once again, the King was disgusted at the part Lloyd George was playing. In 1908 he was furious to read in *The Times* that the Chancellor of the Exchequer was to preside at a Women's Suffrage meeting at the Albert Hall. He wrote to the Prime Minister that the Chancellor's presence as chairman at such a gathering showed 'an entire absence of good judgment, good taste, and propriety,' and he added, 'I shall have no more to do with him than what is absolutely necessary.'[1]

ONE of the reasons the King liked to go to Chatsworth was because he enjoyed talking shop with the Duke of Devonshire. Both men had begun their racing stables about the same time, nearly forty years earlier. However, the Duke of Devonshire had never had the same success as the King. Indeed, not an owner in England could surpass the sovereign's record, set up in 1900 during his last year as Prince of Wales, when his Sandringham-bred horses had won the Derby, the Grand National, the St.

[1] *King Edward VII:* Sir Sidney Lee.

Leger, the Eclipse Stakes, and the Two Thousand Guineas, all in the same year.

Since that time his horses had done badly. The Duke of Devonshire had leased the King's string for the twelve months of mourning following Queen Victoria's death, but instead of improving his luck the transaction seemed to have worsened it. When the King resumed racing in 1902, he fared no better than the Duke. For the next five years the results continued to be disappointing. He was anxious to have one really good win as King of England, and increased the number of horses in training. No improvement took place and people began to advise him to change his trainer, Richard Marsh. The King, however, was a fairly good judge of horse-flesh and did not believe Marsh was to blame. 'We have a number of very bad horses,' he told his trainer in 1906. 'I consider it my duty to get rid of these horses in order to save your reputation. . . .' He then instructed Marsh to lease half a dozen colts from Colonel Walker, who was known to have a good stable.

Two years later he again was scoring victories, and in 1909 his horse, Minoru, was the favourite for the Derby—that is, up until the day of the race itself. An American-bred colt owned by Mr. Louis Winans was believed to be a dangerous rival; just before the race began he had surpassed Minoru as the absolute favourite.

The crowd was immense. The King and Queen, accompanied by the Prince and Princess of Wales, were in the royal box. No reigning sovereign had ever won the Derby, and there was an electric feeling that history might be made.

The race was one of the most exciting on record. The challenge to Minoru did not come from the American colt, which fell early in the race, but from a horse called Louviers. Louviers and Minoru came down the home stretch neck and neck, while the enthusiastic and swelling cheers of the crowd became a thunderous and frenzied roar of excitement. Neck and neck the two horses shot past the winning post. There was an agonising moment of suspense. Then up went the numbers proclaiming a royal victory.

Never has such a scene taken place on Epsom Downs. The crowds went mad with joy. The King followed the tradition of going down to meet his horse. Instantly the police and the ropes were swept aside and he was in the middle of a mass of swaying humanity, patting him, calling to him, seizing his hands, and crying 'Good old Teddy'. 'Make way for the King,' he said evenly in his guttural voice, as he moved forward one step at a time toward the enclosure.

Marsh tried in vain to force his way to Minoru, but it was nearly ten minutes before he could reach the horse and take it to the King. Eventually he succeeded; King Edward led in his Derby winner; the band struck up *God Save the King*; people wept with pleasure.

AFTER racing, the King regarded shooting as the most exciting sport and his annual parties at Sandringham in November and December were almost a ritual. He always filled the house with people, although only a few crack shots were invited to participate. The rest of the guests had to amuse themselves as best they could. Those with enterprise could always try their hand at a new game called golf.

The King had taken a liking to this amusement at Marienbad, and had ordered a nine-hole course to be built in Sandringham Park. In order to ensure against mistakes, His Majesty had instructed his agent to erect wicker hurdles at the places where the bunkers eventually would be dug. Unfortunately, every time the King hit a long ball he drove it into a hurdle. Finally, panting with exertion and indignation, he asked who had been so stupid as to place the barriers in such idiotic positions, and ordered them to be altered in the morning.

But the same performance was repeated the second day; and on the third day the distracted agent brought two men with him to move the hurdles anywhere His Majesty commanded. At this point the game began to resemble an obstacle race, and still expostulating with indignation, the King commanded the agent to remove the offensive objects from his sight for good and to see that proper bunkers were dug.

Sport played a large part in the Christmas festivities, but Christmas itself was conducted in the traditional manner, and was always a spectacular occasion. The King was a fervent present-giver. All his life he had distributed gold cigarette-cases, brooches, and silver-handled paper cutters with the royal monogram on them, in appreciation of hospitality or kindnesses of one kind or another. But at Christmas he exceeded himself. The Sandringham ballroom was transformed into a riot of wreaths and garlands, with a tree in the centre, and a trestle-table running the entire length of the room groaning with largesse. Each person received a shower of gifts ranging from prints, water-colours and books to studs and silver ink-stands.

Not only were the guests of the household looked after. As soon as they had received their presents and removed them, quantities more arrived, this time for the staff. More than eight hundred gifts were given to servants and tenants. Besides this, on Christmas Eve, a joint of beef was distributed to each one of the families on the estate. The King and Queen sat near the door of the coach-house where the ceremony took place, wishing everyone a Merry Christmas. Awaiting their turn outside were the gamekeepers, gardeners, foresters, stable-hands, constituting three hundred people. To the Duke of Windsor, who attended these Christmases as a small boy, the wonderful decorations and the simple Christmas carols against the opulent background seemed to him in later life like 'Dickens in a Cartier setting'.

Christmas was not an exception. All the entertainments provided by the King and Queen the year round were on the same dazzling scale. Very few foreign royalties came to England without being impressed by the hospitality. When the Kaiser and the Kaiserin paid a visit to Windsor in 1907 the King entertained them at a gathering at which twenty-four royalties were present, not to mention many imposing members of the British aristocracy.

On these occasions there was always a renewed spurt of present-giving. Not only did the visitors bestow presents on their royal hosts, but the servants had to be rewarded as well. However, some of the royal guests were inclined to fall back on the substitute of decorations. Although decorations had originally been invented to save royalty the expense of costly gifts, when the King of Spain began distributing ribbons to the Buckingham Palace staff, Edward VII took him aside kindly and explained that five-shilling pieces would be a more satisfactory offering.

The King of Siam, on the other hand, was so pleased with the services rendered him by the King's butler that he tried to lure him back to Bangkok with him. The servant refused politely and the King complimented him good-naturedly on his integrity. Nevertheless, he insisted on giving him a present. 'You will receive the White Elephant,' he beamed.

The butler hurried from the room trying to conceal his anxiety. That afternoon he made inquiries as to whether the London Zoo would be willing to handle a white elephant. It was not until a ribbon arrived with a little ivory elephant attached to it that his mind was set at rest.

CHAPTER SEVENTEEN

TRIP TO RUSSIA

THE King's prestige was immense; abroad there was a mounting belief that his affable countenance hid one of the shrewdest and most profound political brains of the century. Every move in British diplomacy was attributed to him personally. The Germans, who had amused themselves for years by attacking him in the press as a libertine and a man of pleasure *par excellence*, now began to accuse him of travelling about in the masquerade of a *bon vivant* in order to conceal his Machiavellian schemes. In 1907 he visited the Kings of Spain and Italy; and that same year there were rumours that negotiations with Russia were nearing completion. Britain seemed to be settling her differences all around the clock, and Edward VII was the villain of the piece.

The German press began to comment on the situation with a nervous admiration which almost suggested panic. 'King Edward is the twentieth-century Napoleon with this difference—that he is working quietly behind the scenes, employing skilful diplomatic methods instead of brute force. Much as, in Germany's interests, we deplore King Edward's success, we are forced to admire the statesmanlike qualities which have characterised his kingship. King Edward is a cunning gentleman, but too much cunning spoils the game at times.'[1]

The visits to Spain and Italy were not of great consequence, but the talks with Russia were important. Ever since England had signed the Entente with France she had felt the necessity of securing a *rapprochement* with France's ally, Russia. Otherwise it was feared that the

[1] *King Edward in His True Colours:* Edward Legge.

weak-minded Czar Nicholas II might allow himself to drift into the German camp, which would completely nullify the effect of the Anglo-French accord.

On several occasions feelers were put out but nothing came of them until the spring of 1906. Then the British Ambassador at St. Petersburg wrote that the Russian Prime Minister was anxious to bring about a visit from King Edward. 'He says he will guarantee an arrangement with England if the King will come.'[1]

The reason for this sudden appeal was evident. Russia's disastrous war with Japan had ended only a few months previously. The country was not merely in a precarious economic state, but torn by internal violence. A well-organised group of revolutionaries were carrying on a savage civil war: all the great cities were in the grip of a wave of strikes, assassinations, bomb plots, mutinies and uprisings.

The disturbances had been taking place throughout the whole of 1905, and many people feared that the terror might spread into a general conflagration before the end of 1906. In order to restore discipline Russia needed to stabilise her finances, and that meant borrowing money. The Prime Minister, Count Witte, believed that if the King of England openly showed his friendship it would encourage the international banks to extend financial help. But the King did not warm to this idea. 'Witte's object,' he wrote, 'is that by my going I should enable him to float a Loan. What an extraordinary idea! and one that does not appeal to me in any way. . . .'[1]

The King regretted that he could not visit Russia at this particular time; nevertheless the British Government sent Sir Arthur Nicolson to St. Petersburg as ambassador to try and negotiate an agreement. Sir Arthur was fresh from his triumph at Algeciras and great faith was placed in his tact and skill.

[1] *King Edward VII:* Sir Sidney Lee.

He was faced with an unenviable task. The terrorist activities had forced the Czar to give way to popular clamour and a Duma with elected representatives had been set up two months before Nicolson's arrival. But although the Czar granted this concession, he immediately rendered it impotent by appointing the reactionary Goremykin to take Count Witte's place as Prime Minister. When the Duma demanded freedom of expression, a new electoral system, universal primary education, and, above all, agricultural reform, the answer was a point-blank refusal.

This aroused a tremendous storm of protest, but the only outcome was an order from the Czar to dissolve the Duma. Sir Arthur Nicolson called on Goremykin somewhat nervously, expecting to be received by a harassed and overworked man. Instead he was appalled to find the Prime Minister reclining on a sofa surrounded by French novels. 'An elderly man,' he recorded in his diary, 'with a sleepy face and Piccadilly whiskers. He treated the Duma with the greatest disdain: "Let them babble," he said, "the Government alone knows what is best." He was very indignant with the tone of *The Times* and *Daily Telegraph* in regard to the Jews, whom he characterised as the vilest people, anarchists, extortioners and usurers. I went away with a sad heart: the Russian bureacracy is incorrigible.'[1]

The main trouble, of course, was not the bureaucracy. It was the Czar. This thirty-nine-year-old ruler of all the Russias was a gentle, charming, uncertain little man. In his private life he was simple and unprepossessing. He seemed to have none of the normal greeds or vanities. He was indifferent about food and drink, he disliked pomp and ceremony, he shrank from the bright lights of society. His greatest pleasure was to spend long evenings alone with his wife talking or reading aloud.

[1] *Lord Carnock:* Harold Nicolson.

He was strong on only one point; unfortunately this was a passionate belief in the sanctity of his own autocracy. From his earliest childhood he had been taught that his mission as Emperor emanated from God. Any concessions which limited his own authority almost made him physically sick, for he felt that he was betraying God's will. He was not interested in using his power to rule Russia, but to prevent others from destroying the trust which the Divine Maker had reposed in him. And in this view he was vigorously supported by the Empress.

This lady was a disastrous influence on her husband. In the nineties, when Nicholas II had expressed the desire to marry the golden-haired Princess Alix of Hesse, his mother, the Empress Marie, a sister of Queen Alexandra, had done everything to thwart it. Like the Queen of England she had a loathing of all things German; and although Princess Alix was the daughter of King Edward's sister, Princess Alice, the Empress felt that she had fully imbibed the outlook and characteristics of her Hessian father. She was serious-minded, intolerant and deeply religious. Her tastes were excessively bourgeois and she had no use for the gaieties of society.

Nevertheless Nicholas was obdurate. He was deeply in love, and he announced that if he could not marry Princess Alix he would marry no one. This finally moved his parents to give their consent; but the Empress Marie was proved right in her fears. The royal bride found it impossible to fit into Russian court life. She had no gift for friendship; she was cold, tactless and contemptuous. Soon she had alienated all the most powerful elements of society, and began to withdraw into a narrow, vapid little circle of her own.

She drew her husband into her protected and illusory world. He was not a clever man. A grasp of history might have given him perspective and understanding; but he was badly educated. He was afraid of argument.

and so suspicious of the people around him that he even refused to have a private secretary and wrote most of his communications with his own hands. This made him increasingly dependent on his wife's devotion, and on her strong and tragically misguided outlook.

If possible, she was even more passionate than Nicholas in her belief in the Divine Right of Russia's ruler. And this belief gave her an arrogance and an *hauteur* which made her hated by the population. On one occasion, when she was pregnant, she travelled with her husband from St. Petersburg to the Crimea. Because of her condition she informed her Minister of the Court, Freedericksz, that she did not want any receptions on the journey or any watching crowds in the towns through which they passed. This message was passed on to the Minister of the Interior; nevertheless, in spite of the precautions of the police, a crowd of people dressed in their best Sunday clothes gathered at one of the stops.

The provincial governor was at the station and urged that His Majesty should show himself for a moment. 'The Czar made a move toward the window,' wrote Mossolov, the head of the Court Chancellery, 'but the Empress said to him at once that he had no right to encourage even indirectly "those who were not carrying out his orders". Freedericksz felt it necessary once more to press the matter. The Czar gave way, and went to one of the windows. The enthusiasm of the crowd was indescribable. But the Empress would not move her curtain an inch. The children pressed their faces against the slits on either side between curtain and window frame. They too had received a strict injunction not to let themselves be seen.

'The Dowager Empress learned . . . of Freederickzs' happy intervention. Her comment was, "If *she* was not there Nicky would be twice as popular. She is a regular

German. She thinks the Imperial family should be 'above that sort of thing.' " '[1]

ALTHOUGH Sir Arthur Nicolson was well aware that the Czar was weak on every point except his own autocracy, he found that he had many amiable and virtuous qualities, and considered him 'quite incapable of duplicity'. But perhaps the Kaiser summed him up more adroitly when he wrote a marginal minute on a dispatch. 'The Czar is not treacherous but he is weak. Weakness is not treachery, but it fulfils all its functions.'[2]

The Kaiser spoke with some bitterness for he had been nettled more than once by the Czar's indecisions and reversals in foreign policy. William, of course, had only himself to blame for the alienation of Russia from the German orbit. It was he alone who refused to renew the 'Treaty of Reinsurance' with Russia, which for years had been the cornerstone of Bismarck's policy. But ever since, he had made great efforts to rectify his mistake. He had wooed the Czar vigorously. He besieged him with long and flattering letters; he showered honours and decorations on him; he paid him innumerable visits.

The Czar received him with misgivings. He was no match for the Kaiser's brilliant and overpowering personality, and often felt like a schoolboy in his presence. Besides he did not know how to react to his strange jokes, his tactless and embarrassing speeches, and his sudden bursts of exhibitionism.

The Czar's entourage shared his nervousness. 'For members of the suite, interviews with the German Emperor were a thorough martyrdom,' wrote M.

[1] *At the Court of the Last Czar:* A. A. Mossolov.

[2] *German Diplomatic Documents:* translated by E. T. S. Dugdale.

Mossolov. 'All the time one had to be on one's guard; William II was sure to burst out with some astonishing and particularly embarrassing question. When he was in a good humour it was worse still. He permitted himself to play schoolboy tricks with the most aged and venerable of his Generals A.D.C. I myself saw him give friendly smacks to Generals like Schliefflin on the back—and elsewhere.

'One day, at lunch during a hunting expedition, William II had me placed next to him: he explained that he wanted to ask me about the Imperial ballets. But I had only time to reply to one or two questions; William II suddenly took charge and set to work to teach me the whole art of choreography. . . . Then there was the sermon that he gave us on board the *Hohenzollern*! The Czar had been invited to lunch; his suite had been convened an hour earlier, and found themselves in front of an altar, with William II as the officiating priest. The Kaiser had thrown over his uniform a Protestant pastor's surplice, and kept us standing for an hour while he expounded to us from every point of view a Biblical text which he had chosen for our edification.'[1]

The Kaiser was quick to sense the Russian Emperor's lack of decision. He knew that, like all weak men, he invariably expressed the opinion of the last person with whom he talked. This gave the German Emperor the idea of arranging a secret meeting with the Czar. If he could get him away from his advisers he might persuade him to sign a defensive treaty with Germany on the spot.

The Kaiser chose his time well. He gave the Czar sympathy and encouragement during the opening months of the Russo-Japanese War, then telegraphed that he would meet him anyhere that suited his convenience. The Russian Emperor, warmed by the Kaiser's

[1] *At the Court of the Last Czar:* A. A. Mossolov.

solicitude and concern, suggested Bjorko near Viborg. And since the Kaiser had written that he was travelling 'as a simple tourist, without any ceremony', he made the trip unaccompanied by political advisers.

The Kaiser's plan worked brilliantly. With the Secretary to the German Foreign Office at his side, he produced a treaty whereby both Germany and Russia pledged themselves to come to the other's assistance in the event of an attack by a third power. The Czar was induced to sign then and there, and the Kaiser departed, exulting over his victory.

But when the Czar showed the treaty to his Prime Minister and his Foreign Secretary they were horrified. They said it was a breach of the agreement with France and utterly impossible. The Czar did not remonstrate. He could be strangely apathetic. He quietly acquiesced to the objections and the treaty was annulled.

SIR Arthur Nicolson did not arrive at St. Petersburg until May, 1906, nearly a year after this incident. Strangely enough, he found the atmosphere very pro-German. In Government circles there were whispered regrets that the Kaiser's treaty had been torn up.

Certainly Britain was not popular. As Japan's ally, she was accused of having helped to promote the war against Russia. Even France was not viewed with much favour. She had shown herself so weak in the face of Germany's threats it did not seem as though her friendship would prove of much value in time of crisis. 'My own opinion,' wrote Nicolson to the British Foreign Office, 'is that if the Emperor and the Russian Government were free from any other political ties they would gladly form an intimate alliance with Germany . . . German influence today is predominant both in the Court and Government circles. . . .'[1]

What prevented the Russians from entering into a pact with Germany? Only one simple factor. Fundamentally, they did not trust her. They felt that even though they allied themselves with Germany, Germany might still turn round and attack them. If this happened, they would have no friends to help them. But if they sided with the alternative *bloc* they at least would possess allies.

This and this alone finally convinced the Russians that the time had come to settle their differences with Great Britain. The convention that Sir Arthur put forward had nothing to do with Europe; it concerned disputes in Persia, Afghanistan and China. Nevertheless it was a *rapprochement*; and when Russia put her signature to it in the summer of 1907, it was a sign to Europe that she was moving forward under the Anglo-French banner.

THE Russians still clamoured for King Edward to pay the Czar a visit. Finally, in the spring of 1908, the King agreed to travel to Reval. When this plan became known there was a furious outcry from the left-wing element in the House of Commons. The Radical and Labour M.P.s protested violently, saying that the visit would condone the brutalities of the Czar's reactionary Government. Ramsay MacDonald wrote an article for the *Labour Leader* entitled 'An Insult to Our Country'. He described the Czar as a common murderer and objected to the King 'hobnobbing with a blood-stained creature'. Keir Hardie claimed that the visit would

[1] *British Documents on the Origin of the War:* Gooch and Temperley.

condone the 'atrocities' of the Czar, and one of his colleagues, Mr. O'Grady, moved a reduction in the Foreign Office vote.

Sir Edward Grey defended the proposed visit by pointing out that the King's visits were of great benefit to the state, and assuring the House that rumours of a contemplated 'triple alliance' were unfounded; in the end only 59 M.P.s used their votes to register disapproval.

Nevertheless, the King was angry at the outcry. He was completely uninterested in Russian internal affairs, other than occasionally to express sympathy for 'poor Nicky'. And to show his displeasure he struck off the names of three M.P.s from the Buckingham Palace garden party list. Each represented a party or a group who had voted against the Foreign Office. One was Keir Hardie, the leader of the Labour Party, another, Victor Grayson, an independent member, and the third, Mr. Arthur Ponsonby, a Liberal.

This unwise action caused an even louder outcry. The Labour Party denounced the omissions as an 'attempt by the Court to influence Members of Parliament', and the Lord Chamberlain received a request to remove all Labour names from the royal list until Mr. Keir Hardie's name was restored. These methods worked, and the King found himself obliged to reinstate Hardie and Grayson. But he stubbornly refused to issue an invitation to Arthur Ponsonby.

Ponsonby was a brother of Sir Frederick Ponsonby; he had been born and bred in the purple and he should have known better. Although the King deplored the left-wing element in Parliament, he could understand the extremism of working men; but he found it impossible to forgive 'a gentleman' for lending himself to the cause. It was not until Ponsonby wrote a handsome apology, insisting that he had no intention of throwing criticism on the King personally, that the monarch relented.

THE trip to Reval was the oddest State visit that King Edward ever paid. The situation inside Russia was too dangerous for the monarchs to meet on *terra firma*, so they decided to meet in the Baltic Sea on board their yachts. Among the members of the King's suite were Admiral Sir John Fisher, Sir Charles Hardinge, Sir Arthur Nicolson, and Sir Frederick Ponsonby.

The royal yacht was escorted by a suitable number of cruisers and torpedo-destroyers and the ships made a stately procession. When they moved into the North Sea, however, there was a terrible gale; tea on board the *Victoria and Albert* ended with the Queen of England being hurled across the cabin and landing in a heap in one corner with most of the contents of the table on top of her.

As the yacht neared Reval there was a heavy fog. The entourage could just make out the shadowy outline of the two Russian yachts and the small fleet which had anchored a few hours previously. In the distance were the houses of Reval, which were to remain tantalisingly obscure because no one was allowed to go ashore.

The Czar came aboard and greeted 'Uncle Bertie' and 'Aunt Alix' with genuine affection. He then promptly returned to his own ship, the *Polar Star*, so that the English King and Queen could observe the proper ceremony by returning his visit. The three-day stay consisted of the two monarchs' going back and forth to each other's yachts for a relentless exchange of hospitality. The Russian suite comprised the Emperor's wife and children, his sister the Grand Duchess Olga, his Prime Minister and Foreign Secretary, and countless courtiers and diplomats. Honours were conferred, presents were bestowed, and a great deal of caviar and kirsch was consumed.

The Czar went to elaborate lengths to provide entertainment for his guests. One evening the two monarchs and their respective suites stood on the deck of the Russian yacht while a steamer full of female choral singers came alongside and the air was filled with weird songs. The head of the Russian police proudly assured the British royal party that the strictest security measures were being maintained; that the ladies of the choral society had been stripped and searched before they had been allowed to board their steamer.

In spite of the lavish hospitality, the atmosphere was always restrained. The Russian Empress had no lightness of spirit and the King found the long meals heavy going. Only Admiral Fisher seemed to enjoy himself. He had met the Grand Duchess Olga at Carlsbad, and was pleased to renew her acquaintance. He prevailed upon the ship's orchestra to play the 'Merry Widow' waltz and whirled her about with such abandon that even the Russian Empress laughed. 'At the banquet preceding the dance,' wrote Fisher, 'the Grand Duchess and I, I regret to say, made such a disturbance in our mutual jokes that King Edward called out to me that I must try to remember that it was not the Midshipmen's Mess; and my dear Grand Duchess thought I should be sent to Siberia or somewhere. We sailed at daylight, and I got a letter from her when I arrived in England saying she had made a point of seeing Uncle Bertie and that it was all right, I was not going to be punished.'[1]

The Russians seem to have been deeply impressed by the informality of the British entourage. M. Mossolov was amazed that people were allowed to sit in the

[1] *Memories:* Lord Fisher.

presence of the King and Queen. 'Our princes,' he wrote, 'were accustomed from their earliest childhood to standing for hours and hours; after meals they formed a "circle" dead-tired. On board the *Victoria and Albert* things were done differently. After dinner the King and his august guests sat down in comfortable arm-chairs; coffee and liqueurs were served; an arm-chair was left vacant alongside each person of high rank, and the officers with whom the King wanted to talk were invited to sit down in one of these chairs; after a fairly long conversation the King would nod and his interlocutor would retire for somebody else to take his place.'[1]

Sir Charles Hardinge had a few vague conversations with the Russian Foreign Secretary on the subject of Macedonia and the Persian railway but the King himself did not discuss politics in any detail. Nevertheless the Czar and the Prime Minister were deeply impressed by the British Sovereign's wide knowledge. This knowledge had been hastily collected by the King only a few hours before arriving at Reval. He had sent for Sir Arthur Nicolson and bombarded him with questions ranging from Russian agriculture to the railways, from the names and records of the Czar's staff to the purpose of the Czar's internal policy, from the relation between Government and the Duma to the scope of the Anglo-Russian Convention.

That same afternoon he talked easily and affably to the Czar and the Prime Minister touching on all these complex matters with an assurance that suggested a profound understanding. On the last day of the visit the Prime Minister expressed his amazement to Sir Arthur Nicolson 'at the grasp King Edward had shown of Russian internal and external policy'. '*On voit bien*', he said, '*que c'est un homme d'état.*'[2]

[1] *At the Court of the Last Czar:* A. A. Mossolov.

[2] *Lord Carnock:* Harold Nicolson.

The next morning there were elaborate farewells and the *Victoria and Albert* hoisted anchor and began her homeward journey.

NOTHING of importance had been discussed at Reval. It was mainly a family affair, yet it threw the Germans into a panic. They had greeted the Anglo-Russian Convention of the year before with the same indifference that they had first displayed toward the Anglo-French Entente. Now they were suddenly insisting that far more serious arrangements were afoot.

Their suspicions were not surprising in view of the fact that each sovereign was accompanied by his leading ministers of state. Nevertheless, the plain truth was that Reval was a courtesy call. But no matter how many denials were sent from London the Germans refused to believe it. The press once more talked excitedly of British attempts to 'encircle' Germany, and the Kaiser once more talked indignantly of his uncle's 'machinations'. He claimed that the King's actions were motivated by 'spite and envy' toward his nephew. When the German Ambassador in London, Count Metternich, tried to reassure him by insisting that the great mass of the English people wanted peace, and that this was also King Edward's policy, he picked up a pen and scribbled on the margin, 'Untrue. He aims at war. I am to begin it, so that he does not get the odium.'[1]

[1] *German Diplomatic Documents:* translated by E. T. S. Dugdale.

CHAPTER EIGHTEEN

THE LAST PHASE

THE King was not looking well. By 1909 people were whispering that he suddenly had begun to age. He was enormously stout. He still ate huge meals and smoked countless cigars. Every winter since 1905 he had suffered from severe attacks of bronchitis, and had developed a chronic cough which often made breathing difficult, and seemed to be growing worse. Once when he was shooting duck, with a fashionable young matron, Mrs. Hwfa Williams, to keep him company, he had such a bad fit of coughing he nearly fainted; nevertheless he would not consider returning home.

He refused to accept the advice of his doctors who begged him to limit his engagements, and continued the same restless routine he had followed for so many years; Marienbad, Paris, Biarritz; balls, theatres, country house parties; and, of course, at least one royal tour a year. In 1909 the Foreign Office urged him to make a state visit to Berlin. In spite of all his trips to Germany, all his meetings with the Kaiser, he had not visited the German capital officially since his reign had begun. He no longer was optimistic enough to believe that a visit would improve relations between the two countries; all he could hope was that it might prevent further harm being done. So, sighing, he made his preparations.

For Queen Alexandra the trip was even more of an ordeal, for she not only felt an aversion to all Germans in general, but to the Kaiser and the Kaiserin in particular. However by the time she had boarded the royal train from Calais to Berlin her spirits had begun to rise, and at dinner she kept everyone amused by her jokes. 'When the train lurched,' wrote Sir Frederick Ponsonby, 'and a footman upset some quails on her, actually leaving a quail hanging on her hair, she kept us in roars of laughter describing how she would arrive in Berlin *coiffée de cailles*.'[1]

The visit followed the usual pattern. The royal route was lined by 20,000 troops, there were banquets, receptions, reviews, and, of course, a Gala Night at the opera. The Kaiser personally supervised the operatic arrangements, and chose the play *Sardanapalus*, which consisted of a series of stirring scenes interlarded with song. The King dozed off in the last scene, during which the flames underneath a funeral pyre were supposed to spread into a blaze devouring poor Sardanapalus and his entire household.

The Germans organised the spectacle realistically. The whole stage was a glowing furnace framed by billowing clouds of smoke. The King suddenly woke up and thought the theatre was on fire. In a startled voice he asked where the firemen were. This caused the Kaiser intense merriment; but as a member of the British suite afterwards remarked dryly, a general conflagration was just the sort of thing one might expect the German Emperor to produce.

Before the three-day visit had ended the King had developed a cold and a fever, but he insisted on attending all the functions. After luncheon at the British Embassy he was sitting on a sofa, talking to Daisy, Princess of Pless, when he suddenly began to cough. The cigar dropped out of his hand and he fell back against the sofa unable to breathe. 'My God, he is dying,' she thought, 'Oh! why not in his own country!'[2] She tried to undo the collar of his uniform but it was too tight,

[1] *Recollections of Three Reigns:* Sir Frederick Ponsonby.
[2] *Daisy, Princess of Pless:* by Herself.

then the Queen ran up to help. The paroxysm suddenly passed, and he recovered himself.

As usual the visit was regarded as a success; as usual the King and the Kaiser appeared to get on well together. But beneath the surface ran the same current of suspicion and dislike. After the royal families had bidden each other an over-warm farewell, the two monarchs returned home to put their minds on the grim and dangerous problems of the future.

THE year 1909 was the most tumultuous of the King's reign. Once again the threat of war hung over Europe. The dangerous new situation had been produced by the Austrian Emperor, who, in the last part of 1908, had annexed Bosnia and Herzegovina from Serbia.

His action was taken without warning and in complete defiance of the Treaty of Berlin. The Kaiser stood by Austria who was his ally, and so did Italy. Thus the Triple Alliance presented a firm front. The infuriated Slav world cried to an equally infuriated Russia for help, but the Czar, with his country still torn by dissension, was powerless to intervene. Neither France nor Britain had any intention of plunging Europe into a world war, so in the end the Austrian Emperor was left with nothing more lethal to combat than sulky protests and smouldering resentment.

Nevertheless, this incident made a profound impression on the chancelleries of Europe. Here was an open repudiation of a treaty, backed by Germany and Italy. Gentlemen's agreements did not seem to count any more. For the first time King Edward had to admit that war could come at any time. In April he asked his Prime Minister 'whether in framing the Budget the

Cabinet took into consideration the possible (but the King hopes improbable) event of a European war.'[1]

There was another point that was causing the King much concern. That was Mr. Arthur Balfour's assertion to the House of Commons in February 1909 that German shipbuilding was progressing far more rapidly than the Admiralty had admitted; and that unless the British Government accelerated its naval programme, by April 1912 Germany might possess twenty-one dreadnought battleships to England's twenty.

Mr. Balfour's facts seemed unassailable and the King immediately sent his friend, Admiral Fisher, a severe rebuke. He instructed his secretary to write and say that he was 'very disturbed and angry about this Naval debate. . . .' 'The King wants to find out *who* it is who is to blame for letting Germany get ahead of us. Whether it is the Naval Intelligence who didn't know the facts, or the Cabinet, or whether it's the Cabinet who all along knew the facts and ignored them.'[1]

Fisher replied to the royal rebuke somewhat inconsistently, first accusing the Germans of lying about the number of their ships, then declaring that he had sent a memorandum to the First Lord of the Admiralty some time ago stating his anxiety, and lastly, in a pacific vein, assuring King Edward that he was now pressing for eight dreadnoughts, rather than six. The King exerted influence of his own, and the eight were built.

The year brought still another problem, this time on the home front. The bitter quarrel between the Lords and Commons reached a climax in November when the peers rejected the Finance Bill. This virtually brought the government of the country to a standstill.

Repeatedly the King had urged the Upper House to act with moderation, but Lord Lansdowne, the Conservative leader in the House of Lords and ex-Secretary

[1] *King Edward VII:* Sir Sidney Lee.

for Foreign Affairs, had the bit between his teeth and refused to listen to reason. He insisted that the Lords were perfectly within their constitutional rights in forcing the Government to secure a mandate from the people before passing a measure of which they disapproved. And on this point he was supported by such eminent authorities as Professor Dicey and Sir William Anson.

The opposition, of course, hotly disputed the contention, describing the move as the most flagrant effort to subvert the parliamentary system since the revolution of 1688. However, the Government had no alternative but to hold an election, which was fought on the slogan 'The Lords versus the People'. The Liberals were returned to power, and the Budget quickly passed through both chambers. Nevertheless the rancour remained. The Government was determined to curtail the power of the Lords once and for all, and there was even talk of abolishing the Upper House and creating a new second chamber.

Throughout the controversy the King had expressed the hope that the differences of opinion would be settled first without dragging the Crown into the dispute, and second without drastically altering the character of the House of Lords. He sent for Lord Crewe, the Liberal leader, and outlined an idea which he said was entirely his own. What if the leaders of the two parties in the Lords agreed to select fifty followers each, who alone would have the power to vote? This, he felt, would safeguard the Government, yet at the same time preserve the usefulness of the House without disfiguring it too badly. Lord Crewe wrote that he was impressed by His Majesty's 'shrewd appreciation of the difficulties surrounding the creation of a Second Chamber', but pointed out that party leaders were certain to select only those followers who could be relied upon to toe the party line, and he feared the plan would deprive the Upper House of the talents of independent-minded men. Here the matter rested. In March the King went to Biarritz for a seven weeks' stay. The decision would be taken soon after his return.

THE struggle for power, both at home and abroad, derived its strength from the same inspiration. It was an onslaught against the old, established order. In Europe a young, untried Germany was challenging the century-old supremacy of Britain; at home, the lower and the middle classes were challenging the domination of the aristocracy.

The feeling of change was apparent everywhere. The invention of the internal-combustion machine had brought revolutionary ideas in its wake. Soon they would affect the factories, the land, the armed forces. Already they had made an impact on the social world. The drawing-room scene of 1909 had a very different look from the Victorian setting King Edward had inherited from his mother. The motor car was establishing 'the week-end' as a national institution. The carriages in Hyde Park were thinning out and the Sunday church parade threatened to become a thing of the past. Women were increasingly rebellious. They were not only still loud in their demands for suffrage but asserting their independence in many other fields. They were taking up sport, talking about jobs, and, in the smart set, discussing their love affairs with a shameful lack of discretion. A current joke told how a well-known London club had pinned the following announcement on its notice board: Members are requested not to bring their mistresses into the dining-room unless, of course, they are the wives of other members.

No matter what changes were threatening, the King still found life agreeable. He loved Biarritz with its wild coastline and its charming red and white villas. Every morning he liked to stroll along the promenade in front of the hotel and watch the grey, noisy sea beating up against the rocks. If on these walks his mind ranged over the nine years of his reign he could only have felt satisfaction. A King automatically has a great position, but Edward VII had established a great reputation. In the popular opinion he towered above all the other statesmen and rulers in Europe. He was credited with wisdom, knowledge and adroitness. By his persuasive personality and his brilliant grasp of diplomacy, people said that he had pulled off the two greatest *coups* of the decade. In 1900 France and Russia were Britain's two most bitter enemies; in 1910 France and Russia were bound to Britain by ties of friendship which held fast when the test came. Edward VII was regarded by the public as the architect of the new European alignment.

The King's prestige must have given him satisfaction, yet he was always modest about his attainments. During the last few years he had done more work at his desk than at any other time in his life. When he returned to London at the end of April he immediately took up the threads of the royal routine. He spent the mornings reading state papers, and the afternoons receiving members of his Cabinet.

The Queen was cruising in the Mediterranean, and on Friday, April 30, he went to Sandringham accompanied only by old Sir Dighton Probyn. He was not feeling well but on Sunday, despite the cold and rain, spent a long time in the garden supervising planting operations.

The next day he returned to Buckingham Palace, and that night dined with Mrs. Keppel at her house in Grosvenor Street (which now belongs to Jacqmar, a ladies' dress shop). She thought he looked ill and feverish and induced him to go home early. The next morning his breathing was difficult and his doctors diagnosed a severe attack of bronchitis.

For four days the King exhibited a strange, almost fanatical effort to carry on with his daily life. Each morning he insisted on dressing, on reading the official papers and receiving visitors whom he regarded as important. He saw Lord Roberts and Mr. Whitelaw Reid; he saw the Premier of Western Australia, the Commander-in-Chief in the Mediterranean, the Governor-General of New Zealand, and the Agent-General of Queensland.

On May 5 the Queen arrived back in London. The doctors were now seriously worried and all the Royal Family had gathered at Buckingham Palace. That evening a bulletin announced that the King's condition 'causes some anxiety'.

King Edward died the next day, on Friday, May 6. That morning, however, he had persisted in rising and dressing as usual. His doctors tried to dissuade him from seeing Sir Ernest Cassel with whom he had an appointment, but he flatly insisted on keeping the engagement. And ill though he was, when his friend came in to the room, he rose to greet him. They talked of trivial matters for only a few minutes and the King admitted that he felt 'miserably ill'.

In the afternoon he fainted twice but he still refused to go to bed. His horse, Witch of the Air, won the 4.15 race at Kempton Park. When he was told he smiled vaguely but his waning energies were concerned only with clinging to life. 'I shall not give in . . . I shall go on,' he kept murmuring.

It was not until evening that he consented to be undressed and laid in his bed. 'I shall go on . . .' he repeated, and then fell into a coma. His family knew that the end was not far off. At this point Queen Alexandra, who had never completely possessed him, but always deeply loved him, showed the rare nobility of her nature. She sent for Alice Keppel and led her to the bedside. Fifteen minutes before midnight Edward VII died.

The nation was shocked by the news, for the public had been given no intimation that the King was seriously ill. A wave of grief, inspired by a feeling of real loss, gripped the country, and reflected itself in the almost hysterical obituary notices which appeared in the newspapers. By many of them Edward VII was described as the greatest king England had ever had. In the House of Commons the Prime Minister referred to 'his powerful influence' in external affairs, and in the House of Lords, the Liberal leader Lord Crewe dwelt upon 'his potent influence in international politics'. From every corner of the world the highest praise flowed in. On May 9 *The Times* acknowledged these moving tributes from abroad with a leader entitled 'The Sorrow of the World'. 'The intensity of the sympathy has astounded us. . . . Never in our long history . . . has any sorrow of ours been more deeply and more generally felt than the death of King Edward. . . . All bear witness to the greatness of his Kingly qualities, to the wisdom of his statesmanship, to the lovableness of his personal character, and to his unwearying care for the welfare and the interests of his people. . . .'

THIS glowing light was not allowed to shine on the King's memory for long. Two years after his death a competent Elizabethan historian, Sir Sidney Lee, published a 'life' of King Edward in the *Dictionary of National Biography*, of which he was editor. This long, scholarly, laborious appraisal was studded with acid comments. The author observed that the King was 'no reader of books. He could not keep his mind upon them'; that 'he lacked the intellectual equipment of a thinker, and showed on occasion an unwillingness to exert his mental power'; that 'he did not sustain a conversation with much power and brilliance'; and 'he had no personal control of diplomacy'; that 'no originating faculty can be assigned to him'; that he possessed 'no conception of any readjustment of the balance of European power'; and even on the subject of the Entente that 'no direct responsibility for its initiation or conclusion belonged to him'.

The controversy raised by this relentless assessment evoked front-page newspaper comment all over the world. First there was the furious resentment of the King's friends, then the anger of the people who believed they had been the victims of a gigantic bluff. 'Now we know,' cried the Labour leader, Keir Hardie, 'that whilst he was supposed to be labouring abroad for the country's good he was simply enjoying himself as a very amiable, pleasure-loving man of the world, who was bored with politics and had not the capacity to understand foreign relationships.' 'A British pen was necessary,' wrote M. Judet in the *Éclair*, 'to dare to reveal under the mask by which the world has been duped, such a mediocrity and faculties so superficial . . . There is rancour, and some retrospective hatred in the implacable Sir Sidney Lee's study of the *grande incapacité méconnue*.'[1] 'The astonishing thing is,' wrote the *New York Times*, 'that there has not been a great outburst of popular indignation against a Memoir which is destructive of a cherished popular trust. . . .'[2]

The British press, which two years before had poured its adulation on the dead King's achievements, seemed completely unnerved. Sir Sidney Lee was a man of

[1] June 7, 1912. [2] June 1912.

standing; he was an objective seeker of truth, and he had, he claimed, drawn his information from reliable private sources. The *Evening Standard* commented on the 'cruel light' he had thrown on the King, but did not challenge its authenticity. And the *Manchester Guardian* explained: 'Those who were privately intimate with the King are very angry that his abilities and command of the political situation should, as they consider, be unjustly minimised. It must be said, however, that they are totally unable to disprove Sir Sidney's facts.'[1]

No one could deny Lee's implication that the King was a pleasure-loving man who all his life demanded the stimulus of pretty women; nor Lee's contention that he was a man of limited intellect with an aversion for detail and an incapacity to master subjects which bored him. These facts were correct, but the conclusions he drew from them were wholly false. Himself an intellectual, he laboured under the naïve impression that the power to influence depended on the power of application. Lee was born of Jewish parents and had changed his name from Solomon to Sidney. He had never moved in the fashionable, oligarchic circles which made history over the tea-tables, and he failed completely to understand the King's approach.

Queen Victoria had discharged her royal duties by the pen. She conceived her obligations to centre almost exclusively on the perusal of state papers, followed by impulsive comment and advice. This proved useful if only for the purpose of keeping Her Majesty's ministers on their toes. Nevertheless it was a limited conception of the role of constitutional monarch. King Edward had no use for the pen and accidentally stumbled on far more potent weapons. He proved that kingship is more effective when it exerts its personality than when it exerts its brain.

[1] June 12, 1912.

Edward VII began his reign with a larger number of personal friends than any monarch who has ever sat on the British throne. His love of people and his enjoyment of Society had taught him wisdom. As the repository of countless private confidences, there was little he did not know concerning the frailties of human behaviour. He was aware of the perpetual clash of vanity, jealousy and ambition with the nobler qualities of man's nature. When he became King of England he was equipped with the rarest of all qualities for a Sovereign to possess: a deep understanding of his fellow beings. 'He knew better than anyone else in England or abroad the character of individuals, the mind of rulers, the feelings of the governed,' asserted M. Poincaré, the President of France. 'He knew the strong and weak points, the ostensible and the real character of every man and of every thing.'[1]

From this one quality of understanding flowed the tact, the persuasiveness and the brilliant diplomacy for which he was famous. He could assess men's motives unerringly; he knew exactly how to smooth ruffled feelings, how to pacify, to reassure, to captivate hostile critics, to give real pleasure. He never read his speeches, nor even had notes, yet he was not guilty of a single diplomatic breach.

For thirty-five years before he reached the throne he had talked about an Entente with France, and for fifteen years he had pressed for a *rapprochement* with Russia. These desires were not part of a well-formed plan. No doubt they were largely emotional, yet the fact that his ministers reached the same conclusions by the path of reason the year after his reign began is some indication of how true his instinct was.

The Foreign Office made full use of the King's talents.

[1] Speech delivered by M. Poincaré and reported in *The Times*, April 15, 1912.

In later years it was easy for the Marquess of Lansdowne to grumble that he, and not the King, deserved the credit for the Entente; and it was easy for Sir Edward Grey, who had solicited the King's help and advice so often, to describe as a 'legend' that 'British foreign policy was due to his initiative, instigation and control'. It had been gratifying, but also probably irritating, that while the King's ministers sat at their desks trying to work out the right methods of approach, the King's personality effortlessly removed the stumbling blocks. Everyone admitted that his appeal to the heart of France in 1903 had cleared the way for the negotiations for the Entente to proceed. Everyone admitted that his trip to Reval in 1908 had set the seal of friendship on the new Anglo-Russian convention, and at the time was spoken of as a 'diplomatic victory'.

In helping the Admiralty to increase its defences he had been no less successful. Even Sidney Lee was forced to admit that Admiral Fisher would not have been able to redesign and modernise the Navy if it had not been for the King's backing.

Sir Sidney had compiled his biographical sketch from material gathered conversationally. Because of the indignation it aroused he was invited to study the official papers in the Windsor archives. After reading them he admitted he had not done the King full justice, and on the strength of this was pressed to write the official life.

The task took him over ten years. The book is a mine of detail and information, but the King remains lifeless. In building up the personality and character of the Sovereign so many facts are stated, but ignored or under-developed, that one cannot escape the impression that Sidney Lee was more concerned in preventing his original portrait from appearing a travesty than in making free use of his material. The result is a curiously contradictory and lethargic work.

It has never been possible to measure influence in concrete terms. One can speculate whether or not the agreements with France and Russia would have been reached if Edward VII had not been King, but one can never know the answer. Nevertheless, the facts are these. There was scarcely a diplomatic move between the years 1901 and 1910 which did not receive his active help; and with the exception of the attempt to reach an understanding with Germany in 1901, of which King Edward was openly sceptical, British diplomacy did not meet with a single major failure in building up its new network of foreign agreements. In 1906, when there was a premature effort to persuade the King to visit Russia, Sir Charles Hardinge, the head of the Foreign Office, advised against it saying the time was not ripe, and observed that if the Sovereign met with failure it would be 'his *first* one'.

Edward VII loved being a King. Perhaps it was galling to a man of Sidney Lee's background that he managed to combine pleasure and duty so easily; that he could satisfy his desires to the full, and at the same time perform invaluable services for his country.

Edward VII sat on the throne for only nine years, yet the stamp of his personality transformed his short reign into an Era. The Edwardians had many faults. They may have been improvident and superficial and even vulgar. Yet four years after the King's death, when civilisation was plunged into darkness, it was the indomitable spirit of Edwardian England that moved forward to save Europe from tyranny.

The island Empire did not fight alone. The friends that Edward VII had gathered stood firm, and the ships that Edward VII had fathered kept the sea lanes open until the new world could come to the aid of the old.

INDEX

Note: 'Prince of Wales' is used here only with reference to Edward VII before his accession. 'William II' is Wilhelm, Kaiser of Germany. Authorities and sources are indexed by titles only.